UXB
MALTA

UXB MALTA

ROYAL ENGINEERS
BOMB DISPOSAL 1940–44

S.A.M. HUDSON

First published 2010
Reprinted 2021

This edition published in 2012 by Spellmount, an imprint of
The History Press
97 St George's Place
Cheltenham,
Gloucestershire, GL50 3QB
www.thehistorypress.co.uk

British Library Cataloguing in Publication Data.
A catalogue record for this book is available from the British Library.

ISBN 978 0 7524 6619 4

Typesetting and origination by The History Press
Printed in Great Britain by TJ Books Limited, Padstow, Cornwall

CONTENTS

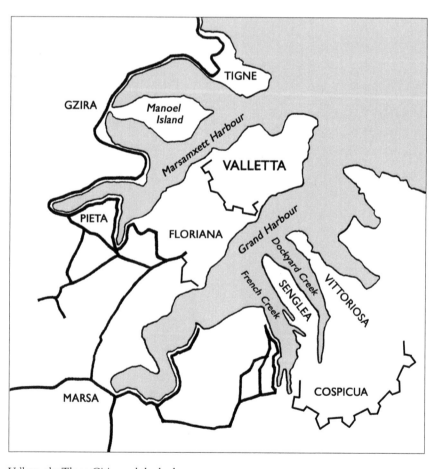

Valletta, the Three Cities and the harbours.

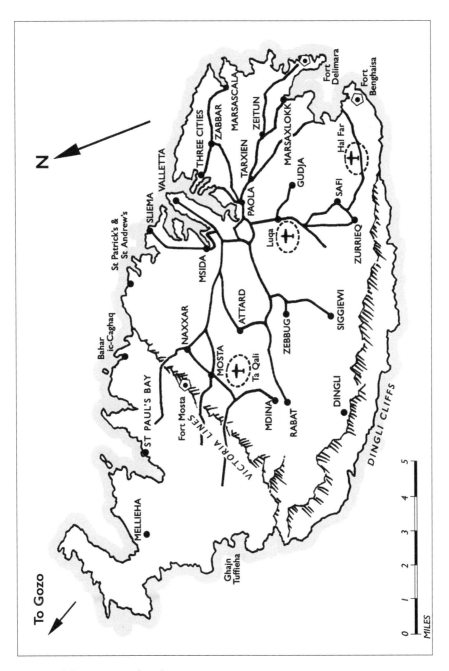

Malta, with key maintained roads, 1943.

FOREWORD

In September 2005 I visited Malta in the company of former RE Bomb Disposal officer Lieutenant George D. Carroll. Like many visitors to the Island, we went to the Rotunda at Mosta to see an exhibition commemorating the events of 9 April 1942, when a Luftwaffe bomb penetrated the great dome of the church during Mass, but did not explode. George Carroll looked up at a photograph on display and said 'That's Edward Talbot!' Seeing our interest, the gift seller held out a postcard of the same picture, which he said showed the men who removed the unexploded bomb from the Church in 1942. George turned to me. 'That's impossible,' he said. 'Edward was dead.'

During our stay on the Island, George was interviewed by a local historical organisation and recounted many stories about his wartime service in Malta. However, at the age of 87, his memory was incomplete – a phenomenon I have since learned was not uncommon among those who experienced the height of the blitz on Malta in the first months of 1942. Back in the UK, I was surprised to receive an email from the interviewer casting doubt on George Carroll's service in Malta, because his name did not appear on any 'list'. I was curious; what were these 'lists'? And how could they not include someone who had served in such a key role for over a year?

Sifting through the many books written about Malta and the Second World War, it seemed that little was known about the role played by army bomb disposal in the defence of the Island. This was surprising, given what I knew of Lieutenant Carroll's experiences, and considering the extent of the bombing endured by Malta during the conflict. When war was declared, the British outpost of Malta was on the front line of a battle to control convoy routes through the Mediterranean supplying forces fighting in North Africa. Malta stood alone, with her enemies just 60 miles to the north. The nearest Allied territory was almost 1,000 miles away. As the Axis powers embarked on a determined campaign to eliminate Malta as a vital Allied stronghold, the Island faced the second major siege in its history. In 1565 an Ottoman Turk enemy was defeated by the Island's natural and man-made defences, combined with the resilience of its people. In the twentieth century, Malta would bear the brunt of a new and devastating type of war: *blitzkrieg*. Even after the shock at German bombing during the Spanish Civil War, there was little realisation at the start of the Second World War of the scale of terror soon to be unleashed on civilian populations.

Malta is just 17 miles (27km) long and 9 miles (14.5km) wide – an area similar in size to Greater London. In 1940 most of the population was concentrated within a six-mile radius of its Grand Harbour – and close to key enemy bombing targets: the airfields, dockyard and submarine base. During March and April 1942 alone, the tonnage of bombs dropped on the Island was double the total for the whole of the worst year of the Blitz on London. Inevitably among the thousands of tons of bombs which fell, many failed to detonate. Unexploded bombs (UXBs) lay in the narrow streets, lanes and fields, a continuing menace to life and property long after the all-clear had sounded. Finding an unexploded bomb, the Island's people turned to the Royal Engineers (RE) Bomb Disposal officer. Every bomb which fell on Malta and Gozo and did not explode was his responsibility, unless it lay on an airfield or within the Royal Navy dockyard.

The RE Bomb Disposal officer's job was to respond to a report of a UXB and decide how it would be dealt with, at minimum risk to military operations, the civilian population, his own life and the lives of his men. Confronting danger at every incident, he had to be courageous, self-disciplined, technically adept and methodical. It was said that no-one volunteered for the job; thrill-seekers, and anyone who would take an unnecessary risk, would be a liability. At the site of a UXB, he had absolute authority over everyone, from ordinary civilians to the highest ranking officer – and had to be prepared to use it. The NCOs and sappers of RE Bomb Disposal also worked under constant threat of explosion. Strict conformity to army regulations was not always the best response to their situation. They needed to use their initiative – and act on it.

On the Home Front, an area such as London had six RE Bomb Disposal (BD) companies, each consisting of up to twelve BD sections. In 1940, Malta was allocated just one RE Bomb Disposal officer and section to handle all UXBs across the archipelago, outside of RAF and Royal Navy premises. And with no more senior officer in direct charge of their work, the Island's bomb disposal officers worked alone, managing their minimal resources to meet ever-increasing demands.

Based on personal memoirs and primary source documents, this book tells the story of what the officers and sappers of RE Bomb Disposal in Malta achieved, and what they overcame to achieve it.

S.A.M. Hudson

NOTE

Details of unexploded bombs originate from actual entries in the weekly bomb disposal reports of the Fortress Engineers, Malta, 1940–1944. Apart from actual accounts from former members of RE Bomb Disposal as specified, the author's descriptions of the methods used in dealing with individual bombs are derived from known circumstances, coupled with information from the 1941/2 RE Bomb Disposal Manual and published histories from other former Second World War bomb disposal personnel. However, these descriptions should be treated as reasonable conjecture, since no two UXBs were ever exactly the same.

ACKNOWLEDGEMENTS

Mrs Mary Ashall and Patrick Ashall
David Blackwell and Diana Barbour
George D. Carroll
Henry Lavington and Peter Lavington
Cyril T. Meager and Tom Meager
Maurice Turner

Frederick Galea, Hon. Secretary, National War Museum Association, Malta
John Mizzi, Editor, *Malta at War* magazine
Margaret Magnuson, former Librarian, Royal Engineers Library
Joseph Camilleri, Mosta
Antony Spiteri, Mosta
John Firman
Jane Elder
Chris How, Original Artists
Dan Willis

My thoughts were a little incoherent. Suppose this fuze turned out to be a modified pattern? Suppose it contained a booby-trap? All sorts of possible reasons for disaster chased through my mind. But in fact there was nothing to do but follow the directions I had learnt …

I now had twenty-five minutes to wait for the condensers to discharge. For that interval I could leave the bomb and the shaft. There was really no reason for staying; indeed, according to the instruction book, I ought to wait elsewhere. But I was trembling and if I rejoined the others they'd notice it …

Suppose the bomb should go off while I was here on the opposite side of the shaft? I might be maimed or blinded. It was ridiculous of course. If the 50kg SC had detonated in that confined space there would have been little left of me and I should have known little about it. But the thought persisted, so I went and squatted close to my impassive, cylindrical companion.

Eventually my watch showed that the time was up and I removed the discharger from the fuze. Then, with a spanner, I tried to turn the locking-ring that held the fuze-head. It was tight and would not stir. I stood up and looked down at the bomb; my hands were wet and I felt very scared. After a moment I bent down again, poised myself for the effort, and put everything into it. The ring slackened, and after that turned easily. When it was unscrewed I lifted it away and then removed the locating-ring. Nothing happened. I had half expected something new and devilish would come into operation at this stage, but everything was still going exactly to plan.

I climbed up the shaft and called the Sergeant as casually as I could, telling him to bring the fuze-extractor … I went back down the shaft and fixed the extractor to the bomb, screwing its business end into the threads lately occupied by the locking-ring … I climbed out and joined him and we both took cover behind a convenient wall … he heaved at the cord … soon we knew that the fuze must be out of the bomb.

Down I went again, removed the extractor, and unscrewed the gaine from the electrical fuze. The job was done.

A.B. Hartley

CHAPTER 1

MALTA'S FIRST UXB

The S.M. [Sergeant Major] said, 'I am looking for three volunteers for a dangerous job. What about it you three?' Well naturally we asked him what the dangerous job was and he replied, 'Digging out an unexploded bomb.' At that, I began to feel a little shaky, but as my two mates volunteered I just couldn't back out.

Sapper R. Walter [1,2]

At 6.30am on Tuesday 11 June 1940 the citizens of Malta were roused from their early morning routine by the wail of sirens, followed by the crash of exploding bombs. The Italians had declared war on the Allies just a few hours earlier. Overnight, Malta's once friendly neighbours became determined enemies. Six more air attacks quickly followed. One heavy raid battered the civilian district of Gzira leaving six dead and over 40 injured. As the final all-clear sounded, the stunned community could only count its losses and try to come to terms with a sudden and violent introduction to war. For the occupants of Rudolph Street the terror was not yet over. The police were going from door to door, telling everyone to leave their homes and businesses and not to return until further notice. Rumours quickly spread that a hole in the road contained an unexploded bomb. Malta had its first 'UXB'.

Next morning, Sapper Walter of the Royal Engineers had just started work making gas curtains for offices in the barracks when the sergeant major nabbed him for the 'dangerous job'. Sapper Walter boarded a 30cwt lorry and sat with his two mates, Sappers McDonald and Scott, waiting to be taken to the site of the unexploded bomb. The other sappers did not envy them for the job they were about to do. According to Walter, 'The sergeant in charge [Sergeant King] was receiving his final instructions and we were receiving such remarks as, "What sort of flowers do you like" from some of the lads.'

The small team arrived in Gzira to be greeted by a young RAOC officer, Lieutenant Eastman. His welcoming remarks were not reassuring:

'I don't know what's down there' pointing to a hole in the middle of the road which was about 1 foot in radius. It may only be an incendiary bomb, or it may be a high explosive bomb. In the first case we needn't worry, but if it's high explosive, it's very dangerous, and that's the one we have to cater for.' While this was going on, the police were evacuating everybody within 300yds of the bomb and posting constables to see that no person entered this danger area because it was a thickly populated part of the town …

By eleven thirty we had started and we uncovered the top of the road making a hole of about 5 feet wide and about twelve foot long. Then the officer left us and before he went he said 'After you get three feet down, don't use a pick and put the canvas covers on the spades …' At mid-day Sgt King was relieved by another RE volunteer, Corporal (Cpl) Brewer.

'… we were down three feet and we were throwing out the dirt and rocks on the pavements each side of the road. It was very heavy going because it was in the terrific heat of June and we were working in just shorts and singlets. One of the constables came down and told us that dinner was ready so we packed up and went for dinner. The officer told Cpl Brewer that we were not to pay for the dinner and if we wanted any beer we were not to pay for that either … when we resumed work we were feeling pretty happy. That's when nervousness left me.

At 5pm we came across the bomb after cutting through a sewer pipe which the bomb had cracked on its way down. As soon as we had spotted it the officer came to investigate and after a ten minute inspection told us that we had to be very careful as it was … a high explosive weighing

250lbs and after another two hours very careful work we had the bomb completely uncovered, but light was failing so we packed up and called it a day at 7.30pm. But before we left the officer told us to report at the same spot at 8am the next morning and told us to ride back [to our barracks] in his car …

… we were greeted by the S.M.'s smiling face. He told us to go to the mess-room where a hot supper was waiting for us. Naturally we didn't need a second telling so we dashed away to our meal since we'd had nothing to eat since dinner. We sat down in our dirt-stained clothes that were stinking of the sewer we had broken, our faces and hands were filthy, but washing was out of our minds until we had eaten… After supper we went for a wash and while we were washing our respective mates made our beds down and seated themselves on it waiting for us to come in and give them a detailed account of the day's happenings … 'Lights Out' blew, when I got into bed I needed no rocking. I was asleep as soon as my head touched the pillow.

The team had an early start next morning, reporting for duty on site at 7.30am – but there was no sign of Lieutenant Eastman:

… he told us why he was late. Evidently he had been to a conference held by Chief Officers, on how to explode the bomb with the minimum amount of damage to the houses in the vicinity of the bomb. He had also been to the Magazine to draw the Gun-cotton and instruments for exploding it. After that we got to work. One man down the hole at a time and we relieved each other. The first job was baling out the uric acid or waste which had leaked out of the sewer pipe, this was a dirty job, we were working in it up to the knees and the bomb was out of sight, so we had to be extremely careful.

As twelve o'clock struck we had cleared the hole and blocked up the sewer pipe, and the bomb was almost ready to be blown. The officer went to the police station and asked the 'Rediffusion' radio people to announce that the bomb would be blown up between two o'clock and four o'clock … we went back and built a sandbag wall around the hole, to prevent the blast causing too much damage. While we were doing this the officer was laying the charge on the bomb which was three slabs of gun-cotton, a primer, and a number 13 electrical detonator. Our Cpl was running out the electrical wiring to an exploder 300 yds away.

At quarter past three everything was set for blowing her up and the police were given orders to go round and make sure no one was in the danger zone. This done, and the plunger went down on the exploder, but there was only the report of the gun-cotton. The bomb hadn't gone off. 'Well,' said the officer, 'I'm afraid you fellows will have to dig for it again.' When we saw the hole it had all caved in so we got to work straight away. It was fairly easy digging because the earth was loose ... [then] Cpl Brewer found a fairly large portion of the bomb. The officer then informed the police to tell the people that they could return to their houses as the bomb had been rendered safe.

From that time onwards we had the best time of our lives. It was about 4.30pm when people came streaming back to their houses from all directions waving Union Jacks and cheering like the devil. We were still working in the hole recovering the rest of the bomb when a crowd of people came down the road and lifted the whole lot of us on their shoulders and carried us to the nearest pub where we never paid for a drink ...

... The officer said that they had the complete bomb in pieces and our job was finished ... We eventually got into bed at 12pm after what we called a perfect day. And so ended my first experience of digging a bomb out ...

Lieutenant W.M. Eastman had tackled his first unexploded bomb in Malta. Only a month before, the Royal Army Ordnance Corps (RAOC) had been given responsibility for all 'unexploded projectiles' outside of Admiralty and RAF premises. Eastman shared the work with Captain R.L. Jephson Jones and the two RAOC officers were assisted by a team of non-commissioned officers (NCOs) and sappers recruited from 24 Fortress Company, Royal Engineers.

Like Sapper Walter, Cyril Thomas (Tom) Meager had been going about his normal duties as a sapper in 24 Fortress Company RE when the first Italian bombs struck Malta. Recently married to a young Maltese girl, Maria Dolores, Meager was manning a Lewis gun on the harbour bastions – until one morning, when he took his place as usual on the parade ground. He was about to break one of the Army's unwritten rules:

Never volunteer for anything, they used to say in the army. I went on Parade one morning and they said 'We need volunteers to deal with an unexploded bomb. Nobody has to volunteer. So if you don't want to volunteer just fall out.' And they all went and left me standing there. He said, 'Are you sure?' and I said 'Yes, I'll have a go at anything.'[3]

Tom Meager was sent out to Luqa:

The first bomb we went on was an Italian 500 pounder and it landed in the surface reservoir by the airfield. There was about a foot of mud on the bottom of the reservoir and the bomb must have skidded in because it ended up in one corner and didn't go off.

We waded through the mud to the bomb. At this stage we knew absolutely nothing about bomb fuzes, so we were completely ignorant of what could happen if we dealt with a bomb at all. Not knowing anything, we just went over, unscrewed the fuze and took it out, and that was it. Nothing happened, because I'm still here. It wasn't until afterwards when we got more information about these things that we realised how close we had come to being blown up.

Malta had its first Army bomb disposal team of the war. Working alongside Tom Meager were the RE volunteers involved in that first UXB in Sliema – Cpl Cecil Arthur Brewer, Sappers William Douglas Scott, Duncan MacDonald and Robert Henry Walter – as well as Lance-Sergeant Reginald Charles Parker.

Captain Jephson Jones and Lieutenant Eastman and their RE team tackled some 275 unexploded bombs and shells in five months. With no specialist equipment available to them, and little access to detailed intelligence regarding the disposal of enemy bombs, they often had to improvise to get the job done. In recognition of their achievements both officers were awarded the George Cross, for 'most conspicuous gallantry in carrying out very hazardous work'. The recommendation for the award for Lieutenant Eastman read:

On various dates, Lieutenant Eastman, with Captain R.L.J. Jones, R.A.O.C. worked under dangerous and trying conditions and performed acts of considerable gallantry in dealing with large numbers of various unexploded bombs, some of which were in a highly dangerous state and of the German delay type.

On one occasion, these officers showed particular gallantry in dealing with an 1100lb (500kg) German bomb. Two attempts were made to explode this bomb but it failed to detonate; at the third attempt when it was in a most dangerous state, they succeeded in detonating it.

On a second occasion, these officers, assisted by a Master Rigger of H.M. Dockyard, succeeded in removing a 400lb high explosive Italian unexploded bomb which had been under water for a week in a 20ft deep well inside a house. This bomb, fuzed at both ends, was in a dangerous state. It had to be raised to the ground floor by means of a gin, tackle, sling and ropes. This operation was doubly dangerous, as: (a) There was a possibility of the sling slipping while the bomb was being hauled up and (b) The bomb was two and a half ft. long, the mouth of the well three ft. one inch wide, and for safety the bomb had to be kept horizontal, if possible, and pulled up thus. Lieutenant Eastman assisted by the Master Rigger, guided the bomb from the floor of the well, and Captain Jones went to the top to guide it through the opening. They succeeded in getting the bomb out although there was only a six inch clearance as it came through the mouth of the well.[4]

Theirs were the first of many such experiences in the work of bomb disposal in Malta during the next four years. But in November 1940 the two officers saw off their last UXB. Now very much in the front line of the war in the Mediterranean, Malta was clearly in need of military reinforcements. The Island was about to have its own Royal Engineers bomb disposal section.

At the end of August 1940, as the Luftwaffe were amassing huge forces in preparation for an all-out blitz on London, the War Office confirmed new arrangements for managing unexploded bombs. The Royal Navy would carry out bomb disposal on all ships, below the high water mark, on harbours, docks and other main admiralty property, and make safe all parachute mines, wherever they fell. The Royal Air Force retained responsibility for bomb disposal on all Air Ministry property including RAF stations. Bomb disposal over all areas outside of the above (i.e. the rest of the country) fell to the Army, who could also be called on by the Navy and RAF for bomb disposal services as required. The regiment chosen to take on the Army's role in bomb disposal was the Royal Engineers. Their technical expertise and experience of quarrying, tunnelling and construction were useful skills for uncovering and tackling unexploded bombs.

By the end of September 1940, Malta's first Royal Engineers bomb disposal officer was on his way to the Mediterranean. Ellis Edward Arthur Chetwynd Talbot was born in 1920 and brought up in Shropshire. Educated at Harrow School, in 1938 he went up to Trinity Hall, Cambridge, to study engineering. When war against Germany was declared, Talbot volunteered for the Royal Engineers; he was appointed 2nd Lieutenant in October 1939. The following August, aged 20, Lieutenant Talbot was posted to Swansea to lead No. 103 Bomb Disposal Section, one of eight sections covering the whole of Wales, with their BD Company HQ in Cardiff. He would be busy, with over 70 UXBs in the following five weeks. South Wales, with its docks, coalmines and steel works, was a priority target for enemy bombing.

At 3.15am on Sunday 25 August, Talbot was roused by an urgent telephone call: traces of an unexploded bomb had been spotted by a railway track near Loughor.[5] After ten hours of digging, the bomb was finally uncovered: it had a new and unknown type of fuze. To the young bomb disposal officer, this meant one thing: there was a real possibility it was a booby-trap. He telephoned his headquarters who decided that special equipment was needed. It would be brought by train from London – but not until next morning. Talbot was concerned about the delay; if the bomb exploded, it could destroy a vital railway line. He decided he must get it away. Well aware of the risk of moving a bomb with an unknown fuze, he picked it up and carried it away on his shoulder – a fact which was noted by his superior officers when they arrived next morning. Lieutenant Talbot's action earned him the Empire Gallantry Medal (converted to a George Cross on its instigation later in 1940). But before the announcement of the award reached No. 103 BD Section, Talbot had left Swansea. On 16 September he returned to Cardiff: he had orders to embark for Malta.

Talbot's ship approached Malta on a stormy November afternoon. As she reached the shelter of Grand Harbour the sky cleared to a golden autumn sunset, revealing crowds of children who lined the ancient fortifications, waving to the new arrivals. He reported for duty on 10 November 1940 to take charge of all Army bomb disposal work for Malta and Gozo. He was to join the Fortress Engineers, now comprising 24 Fortress Company RE and Nos. 1 and 2 Works Companies, Malta Territorial Force. Their headquarters were at Lintorn Barracks, a handsome complex of colonnaded buildings standing high above the inner reaches of Marsamxett Harbour, at the mouth of Msida Creek. Located just outside Valletta, and between the dockyard on one side and the submarine base and ordnance depot on the other, the barracks lay at the heart of a key target area for enemy attacks.

Lieutenant Talbot discovered that this posting would be very different from his former set-up in Wales, where he had been one of eight BD officers each leading a section. In Malta he was on his own, in sole charge of Army bomb disposal for the entire archipelago. He did not come under any bomb disposal company but reported directly to the commanding officer (CO) of the Fortress Engineers. And whereas in the UK reports of unexploded bombs went to a bomb disposal company headquarters (HQ), to be issued out to each BD section, here all reports would come directly to him, as bomb disposal officer. He would decide the order of importance of all UXBs, apart from those designated 'Priority' by a senior military or civil defence official. It was a much greater level of authority for the young 2nd Lieutenant than he was used to back home.

His first task in Malta was to set up and train his own squad, No. 1 Bomb Disposal Section, RE, to be formed from members of 24 Fortress Company. He was allocated about twenty men: fewer than the 24 intended by the War Office for a BD section overseas. In Malta, provision for RE Bomb Disposal was limited by the resources available on the Island, at a time of many competing priorities.[6] The new bomb disposal officer was pleased to find a core of men already experienced in bomb disposal. Early volunteers L/Sgt King, L/Sgt Parker, Cpl Brewer, Sappers Meager, Scott, MacDonald and Walter who had worked with the RAOC were willing to continue into the new bomb disposal section. They were joined by others including Sergeant Thomas Piggott, Lance-Corporal Rowland Hilliar and Sappers Joseph Birchenall, Thomas Hammond, James Leonard, Lockyer, Daniel McCarthy, Laurence Miller, C.E. 'Inky' Reeves and Henry Reeves.[7]

A call went out for more volunteers to make up the full complement for the section. Stories such as Sapper Walter's of the generous hospitality shown by local communities might have encouraged some to join. But Sapper Harry Turner also heard that those who volunteered would be let off certain parade ground duties. That idea appealed to 20-year-old Harry, who had been serving in Malta since August 1939, so he put his name down. As a trained carpenter, Harry Turner had something to offer. Each bomb disposal section needed 'tradesmen' with skills relevant to the excavation and removal of bombs, such as carpenter/joiner, driver, mechanic, electrician, fitter, mason and timberman, plus a number of general workers ('pioneers'), and a cook. But in BD sections overseas, the tradesmen had to acquire an extra skill: the War Office had decided they would be trained in bomb disposal. Their training could partly compensate for the shortage of manpower in overseas theatres of war such as Malta. Trained sappers could clear small incendiary and anti-personnel bombs, as well as Allied shells. NCOs could tackle UXBs up to 50kg with straightforward fuzes, when required. The bomb disposal officer himself would take on all UXBs marked 'Priority' and normally all high explosive (HE) bombs weighing over 50kg, as well as any smaller bombs with complex or challenging fuzes.

By the end of November 1940, No.1 Bomb Disposal Section was ready for action. The Lieutenant Governor issued a top-secret message to commanding officers of all military forces in Malta, and to the police and ARP. From 0600hrs on 1 December 1940, the bomb disposal officer would take over from the RAOC responsibility for the disposal of all unexploded bombs on land in Malta and Gozo, other than that belonging to the Royal Navy or RAF. The announcement set out the procedures for unexploded bombs. In civilian areas, police constables and ARP wardens were accountable for the reporting, locating and guarding of UXBs, supported by a voluntary special constabulary. The co-operation of these civil defence organisations was crucial to the work of the bomb disposal officer, providing an essential network of communications and support across the Archipelago. But unlike on the Home Front a high percentage of UXB reports in Malta came direct from the many military units on the Island, via their own company HQ.

From now on all UXBs outside of Royal Navy or RAF premises must be reported to the bomb disposal officer, via Fortress Headquarters G Branch at Lintorn Barracks. All UXB reports should include full details of the bomb(s) including exact location, approximate time of falling, quantity and whether in the open or buried in the ground. Any unexploded bomb in a critical location, such as an area vital to the war effort, could be given 'Priority' status by a senior civil defence or military officer. Each UXB report was noted and given a number. Once in receipt of a report, the bomb disposal officer made a reconnaissance visit. Based on the type, location and position of the bomb, he defined a safety zone which was cleared by the police and guarded until the bomb was disposed of.

The BD officer then decided the action to be taken. Any UXB designated 'Priority' would be made safe straight away. The lives of the bomb disposal officer and his men might even be put at risk in its disposal – although only if absolutely essential. Bombs in less vital locations could be left for an interval of 96 hours, to allow for the maximum time within which a clockwork-controlled fuze might function.[8] After that time, the bomb disposal section attended and the bomb was dealt with. If circumstances allowed – i.e. where little damage would be caused, such as in open countryside – the bomb could be exploded 'in situ'. Otherwise it would be defuzed or by some other method rendered harmless, then removed and disposed of appropriately.

Things got off to a steady start for the new bomb disposal section. Since September 1940, the rate of air attacks on Malta had declined to one per day; they reduced still further at the end of October. By mid-December, Lieutenant Talbot and his men had seen to three Italian HE bombs, four incendiaries and one British anti-aircraft shell. Then the weather turned exceptionally cold – there was even snow on the hilltop town of Rabat – and the *Regia Aeronautica* kindly refrained from taking to the air for a whole week over Christmas. At the end of the month, Talbot reported in to the Adjutant's office at Lintorn Barracks. It was time to produce his first Bomb Disposal Report for Malta. From now on, every UXB report dealt with was typed in numerical order on a Weekly Bomb Disposal Report, giving the date the bomb was reported, its location, whether it was on the surface – or how far underground – the nationality and type of bomb, and the date and details of action taken by the bomb disposal section. The report was signed by the bomb disposal officer and the CO of the Fortress Engineers, and attached as an appendix to the official War Diary, a formality required by every military company.

After Christmas, RE Bomb Disposal work resumed at an easy pace, with only a few call-outs, most involving unexploded Ack-Ack shells.[9] Those which held up the life and business of the community had to be treated the same as any unexploded bomb; the rest could be cordoned off and disposed of in due course. Talbot had begun to establish his routine, unaware that everything was about to change. Allied ships and aircraft from the Island were successfully disrupting Axis convoys running supplies through the Mediterranean. In mid-November, the Allies' new state of the art aircraft carrier HMS *Illustrious* had attacked the Italian navy base at Taranto. Deciding that the Italian Air Force efforts were inadequate to neutralise the threat from Malta, German high command decided to deploy their own forces on the attack. The Luftwaffe moved into Sicily.

Notes

1 Walter, Sapper Robert 1940. Personal account by Sapper Robert Walter No 1873669, Royal Engineers, Malta. Royal Engineers Library
2 Sapper: a regular soldier in the Royal Engineers
3 Cyril Thomas Meager, 2008
4 Recommendation for award for conspicuous gallantry, Lieutenant W.M. Eastman
5 Lacey, J. *Diary of Jim Lacey*. Available: http://www2.army.mod.uk/ royalengineers/assocations/reabd/diaries/jimlacey.
6 By the middle of 1941, the regulation establishment of a section overseas was one officer and 24 OR: one sergeant, one lance-sergeant, three corporals and three lance-corporals including one driver, six other drivers and nine sappers. According to Lieutenant Carroll, when he took over responsibility for bomb disposal in April 1941, the establishment of his section 'grew to about 20 men'.
7 Sources of names: Historical account of 24 Fortress Company, Royal Engineers in Malta. Royal Engineers Library; Hogben, Maj. A 1987. *Designed to Kill*. Wellingborough: Stephens.
8 The standard time was 96 hours, made up of the 80 hours maximum delay of a clockwork setting, plus a margin of 20 per cent.
9 Anti-aircraft shells fired by Malta's defensive forces

CHAPTER 2

ILLUSTRIOUS BLITZ

Bomb disposal comprises the disposal of unexploded projectiles of various kinds, e.g., high explosive bombs of various sizes, incendiary bombs, A.A. shell, aeroplane cannon shell, parachute mines of the magnetic and non-magnetic type, gas bombs and any other form of missile dropped from enemy aircraft. *Manual of Bomb Disposal*

St Anthony Street was an anti-climax. The BD squad arrived expecting to find an unexploded mine: it turned out to be a discarded petrol tank. Still, with only one job remaining – an Ack-Ack fuze to collect from Valletta – they could look forward to an early end to the working day. Cheered by the prospect, they loaded the tank onto their lorry and headed out of Vittoriosa. Even the weather was looking up: the murky morning cloud was clearing to a bright afternoon sunshine.

Suddenly a formation of Stuka dive-bombers screamed across the sky over Grand Harbour. Wave after wave of Luftwaffe aircraft followed in their wake – more than 70 of them, raining bombs on the dockyard and surrounding areas. The target was HMS *Illustrious*. Battered by enemy attacks as she struggled to protect Allied convoys in the Mediterranean, the massive aircraft carrier had limped into Grand Harbour six days before. In the shelter of French Creek, and protected from further raids by bad weather, rescue work and repairs of the ship were progressing well. Now the Luftwaffe had their target clearly in sight.

The Germans had launched their first concentrated and ferocious attack of the war in the Mediterranean. Barely able to prepare for the onslaught, Malta's few defending Hurricane and Fulmar aircraft took to the air to try and repel the raiders. Bofors guns boomed out constant rounds which echoed and re-echoed across the harbour. The valiant response succeeded in preventing all but one bomb from falling on *Illustrious* but could not protect the surrounding 'Three Cities' of Senglea, Vittoriosa and Cospicua[1] from heavy bombing. Valletta, too, was badly hit.

Malta's oldest urban communities, established and fortified in the sixteenth century by the Knights of Malta, were reduced to rubble. Some 200 houses were destroyed and another 500 damaged. The effect on the population was devastating. The majority had fled their homes to take refuge inland during the early raids of June 1940. But when enemy activity quietened down in the autumn, many evacuees drifted back home to rejoin dockyard workers who had stayed behind. Now these civilians were in the eye of the storm and large numbers fell victim to the Luftwaffe raids. Most lost their homes and everything they owned; hundreds were trapped under collapsed buildings and many were killed.

As the clouds of dust drifted away, Lieutenant Talbot and his men could only stand alongside the islanders in stunned silence, staring at the scene of devastation which had replaced the ancient and beautiful surroundings of Grand Harbour. The squad could scarcely imagine the huge challenge ahead of them; but for now their help was needed for other more pressing work. All but the most essential bomb disposal activities were put on hold. Every available man from 24 Fortress Company was called to Senglea and Vittoriosa to join their Army comrades in helping the civil authorities. Combined teams worked in shifts day and night, clawing at the wreckage to rescue survivors.

As soon as they could be spared, No. 1 Bomb Disposal Section was back in business. As workmen scrabbled among the collapsed buildings, traces of unexploded bombs were coming to light, bringing recovery work to a halt. It was time to move in and start clearing them. The ancient thoroughfares of the Three Cities were little more than alleys a few feet wide, with tall stone houses on either side; now they were blocked with heaps of stone and rubble. The section could barely find a way through the streets. Scrambling over the debris on foot to reach the site of one UXB, L/Sgt Parker and his squad of sappers arrived at their destination to be confronted by yet another building crumbling into ruins.

> … we were of the opinion that a bomb had gone off … because of the amount of damage that faced us. What we later were told had been a nunnery had collapsed into a mountain of stone and rubble. Fortunately it had been evacuated prior to the raids. This nunnery was in a [steep and] narrow street of steps. It had been several storeys high and was originally attached to similar buildings on either side. The adjacent buildings were now also in a very shaky state. It was obvious that we either had something very large in the form of a bomb, or that something large had crashed into it …
>
> In this early stage we were hampered by herds of wild cats. These were the poor animals left behind by the inhabitants. They were herded together in fear and were starving. They stubbornly barred our way and were very vicious and in the end we had to shoot some of them.[2]

The sappers had a mammoth task on their hands – removing the remains of the collapsed upper floors of the building layer by layer to find the bomb.

> We started to dig into the mountain of rubble and stones. This proved difficult as we had no mechanical equipment. The location up the street of steps would have denied us the use of any heavy equipment even if we had it. After several days we had still found no evidence of a bomb having exploded (evidence had to be found consisting of blast marks or splinters from a bomb before we could abandon a reported UXB). The excavation had reached the state of a funnel-shaped hole with steep sides down which occasional large building stones would crash. We had suffered minor bruises and cuts from such falls and I became worried that we might get more serious injuries as we worked …
>
> After a few more days and the removal of tons of stone and rubble we found pieces of cast light alloy, some wire, and what seemed like pieces of electrical equipment. Our thoughts again returned to the possibility of an aircraft crash, or part of one. When seeking buried bombs the first thing to come to light is the tail or part of it that has been torn from the bomb. This would be of sheet metal, not the cast alloy painted sky blue that we had found …

L/Sgt Parker was concerned. This was nothing like any bomb he had worked on before. Before going any further he must consult his bomb disposal officer. Lieutenant Talbot came to inspect the site but could offer no easy solution. They would have to keep at it – but as the bomb was as yet unidentified he reminded them to proceed with the utmost caution. There was still a long way to go.

> ... at last we got to the ground floor level in our enlarged funnel-shaped excavation finding more of the light alloy blue painted pieces. In the floor was a distinct hole with sky blue paint marks around its edge. At this stage we discovered that we had cellars, and that the ground floor was in a dangerous state, broken through in some places and liable to collapse under the mountain of rubble on top of it.
>
> Looking into the hole with the aid of a torch, we could just see a cylindrical shape painted sky blue partly covered with rubble from a break in the floor. We again cleared the area, enlarged the hole which fortunately was not over the bomb and got into the cellars. We cleared the rubble from the bomb and found it to be the largest we had seen to date, and of a shape that we had not before encountered. As the bomb lay we could not see any fuzes ...
>
> We next reviewed our situation and cleared the area further, including the propping up of the ground floor with timber to prevent further falls, and to allow us to work in the cellars in some degree of safety.

It was time for Parker to report his findings to Lieutenant Talbot, who would examine the bomb and decide what must be done.

> ... [he] informed us that it was an armoured piercing type designed to penetrate the armoured decks of capital ships. Our first problem was to render the brute safe by removing the fuze. We attempted this in the cellars after rolling it over to reveal the fuze. We found that the fuze was not of the delayed action type or anti handling or [anti] withdrawal variety. (It was obviously intended to go off).
>
> ... efforts to remove the fuze were abortive, the retaining screw ring was so battered as the bomb crashed through the building that we could not move it. We had no wish to use excessive force in the still shaky

cellars. I … suggested that we blew the thing up where it stood. There would be little extra damage in the currently very damaged area. To move the bomb fuzed would be dangerous, apart from getting it out of the tricky location of the cellars, the crumbling funnel-shaped excavation and the street of steps to get it away. There was the problem of moving it out of the densely built up area of the 'Three Cities'…

Exploding the bomb was ruled out: a bomb of this size would cause devastation over too wide an area. Conscious of the efforts already made by Lance-Sergeant Parker and his squad, Talbot urged them on to even greater endeavour. Somehow they would have to get the bomb out.

> We were told to recover it fuzed or not. But take every precaution possible. To get this unusual shape (slim, egg-shaped with pointed nose) weighing … over a ton out of the cellars, up the crumbling funnel shape, and out on to the street of steps, still with the fuze in it was a worrying problem. By means of blocks and tackles, the rigging of steel girders across the excavation to adjacent shaky buildings, and using brute force where all else failed, we managed at last to get the 'beast' on to the street of steps …

It had been an immense undertaking which would not go unrecognised. L/Sgt Parker was awarded the George Medal.[3] Lieutenant Talbot was specially commended, as were Sappers James Lee Leonard, Lawrence Miller and Daniel McCarthy.[4]

The first major blitz on Malta continued for several days. Attacks spread to the airfields at Luqa and Hal Far; for a time Luqa was completely out of action. The Luftwaffe then extended their raids to military targets beyond Grand Harbour and the airfields. On Saturday 8 February 1941, a call came to Lintorn Barracks from Fort Mosta. There was evidence of four UXBs in the ground nearby. It was the site of major underground stores of ammunition, including precious Ack-Ack shells. Not only could a major explosion have devastating consequences for the surrounding area, it could destroy supplies essential to Malta's defences. Lieutenant Talbot set off at speed, ordering a squad to follow him. Fort Mosta was five miles from Floriana, high on a promontory of the Victoria Lines, the ridge traversing the centre of the Island. Its massive curtain walls were an impressive site, offering a commanding view over the fertile plains of the Pwales valley to the north.

A guide was at the guard house ready to direct the bomb disposal officer to the UXBs. Talbot estimated all four bombs were fairly large. He knew the terrain was softer in this part of the Island than in the south: there was no way of knowing how far underground they might be. They were near the outer perimeter of the fort – but two of them were close enough to the access road to disrupt the distribution of ammunition supplies. These bombs must be rendered harmless as soon as possible. Lieutenant Talbot issued orders for work to begin sinking two shafts to try and locate the bombs, then handed over to an NCO to supervise the digging.

Talbot had plenty to occupy him elsewhere, with several reported UXBs in other parts of the Island. He had just returned from an incendiary bomb at Qrendi when a call came from his sergeant in charge at Fort Mosta: both bombs had been found at depths of five and six feet. They were a 200kg AP and a 300kg AP – armour-piercing bombs – well chosen for the job of penetrating heavy fortifications. Talbot now had to decide what to do with them. The bombs were as yet only partly exposed – just enough to identify their fuzes. Both were the type designed to explode on impact but their fuzes had failed in some way. It would be possible to dig the bombs out completely, but this would be more time-consuming – and time was short. He would much prefer to explode them where they lay – but what about the fort? An explosion on the surface was out of the question but the bombs were several feet underground – it might just be feasible. Talbot surveyed the area, calculating the distance of the bombs from the ammunition stores. Taking into account their size, and their estimated blast effect in relation to their position, he came to his decision: he would blow them up. First he reported his plans to the CO of Fort Mosta, who would make sure the area was cleared of all personnel. Then the shafts were surrounded by sandbags to provide extra protection. He descended the ladder alone into each shaft to attach the explosive charges to the bombs. With everything in place, he retired to a sheltered 'safe point', gave a final warning signal and detonated the two bombs. The explosion boomed out across the valley below as debris shot into the air, rattling down in a hailstorm of rock and stones. Success.

The NCOs could now concentrate on the remaining two shafts. They were already several feet deep, with no sign of the bombs. It took another day of hard slog to reach them: one 200kg bomb had been unearthed at 14 feet, followed soon after by the second, 16 feet underground. After two more controlled explosions, the bomb disposal officer informed the CO that the fort could return to normal operations.

Thankfully after the '*Illustrious* blitz', enemy attacks became less frequent and intense. The bomb disposal section gradually eased back into the routine of clearing British shells from locations across the Island, from the remote Fiddien Bridge in the north-west to the headland at Delimara Point in the south-east. Only occasional nuisance raids courtesy of the Italian Air Force disrupted the relative calm. Malta's inhabitants could retire to their beds each evening anticipating a reasonable night's sleep.

In the early hours of one Saturday morning, the occupants of Balbi Street, in the dockyard district of Marsa, were woken by a terrifying crash. Bracing themselves for an explosion, they were left with an eerie silence. One intrepid resident ventured out to take a look. Peering through the gloom, he thought he could see an object lying at the edge of the roadway. Stepping forward to take a closer look, he recognised the unmistakable shape of an unexploded bomb. The sound of footsteps behind him made him jump. Turning to see who was coming, to his relief he recognised his local air raid warden. The warden was one of 600 who in 1939 responded to the call to volunteer for Malta's Air Raid Precautions (ARP) organisation. He was proud of his work, helping the police and his local community through the bombing raids of the past six months. He identified and recorded the position of every bomb that fell in his area, exploded or not. Now he had a UXB on his patch, and it could be one of those 'delayed-action' types which might explode at any moment. The whole street could be at stake.

The warden took command of the situation, telling the nervous resident to stay well away and to warn any others approaching to do the same. He scoured the area for any suitable debris to construct a makeshift barrier to fence off the bomb. He looked up to see the local police constable heading towards him: he too had heard about the crash and come to investigate. Seeing the UXB in the street, the constable was worried about the safety of civilians. He decided prompt action was needed. Leaving the warden to stand guard over the bomb, he went off to the police station. Within minutes he was back; the senior officer on duty had ordered the evacuation of Balbi Street. Temporary shelter was hastily arranged in a local hall. Between them, the two men knocked at every house to rouse the occupants and tell them to leave immediately. It was an unwelcome task – many had only just settled down after the 'all-clear'. When the last of the unhappy residents had left the street, only a solitary guard remained, dutifully keeping watch over the unexploded bomb. The ARP warden noted down the exact time and place the bomb had fallen, along with a description, for the official UXB report. The details were telephoned through to the emergency number for Army bomb disposal, with an explanation of the action already taken. But as the residents had already been evacuated, Fortress Engineers HQ decided not to rouse the bomb disposal officer until morning.

Lieutenant Talbot arrived in Balbi Street early next day, guided to the spot by a boy scout provided by the police station. He saw that the bomb was an Italian incendiary weighing in at 43lbs. It was designed to ignite on impact, and violently blow out showers of sparks over a radius of about ten yards. Its Thermite filling would burn for ten minutes with a searing white heat. If the bomb had functioned, it could have threatened nearby houses. This one was probably intended for the nearby dockyard ammunition stores or fuel tanks, where it could have caused major destruction. But it had not ignited, and Talbot knew it was relatively harmless. It was a simple matter to unscrew part of the bomb's base and take out the fuze. That done, he walked over to the ARP warden, keen to reassure him that this type of unexploded bomb was unlikely to go off unexpectedly: residents could now return to their homes. Talbot went on his way: there was another 43lb incendiary at nearby Church Wharf.

Back at Marsa ARP Centre, however, the authorities were not entirely satisfied with the chain of events – and they decided to express their views in a letter to the Lieutenant Governor. They complained that the evacuation of houses, with all its inconvenience and alarm to residents – and the difficulty of finding accommodation for them in the middle of the night – was after all unnecessary. Surely it could all have been avoided if the bomb disposal officer had attended as soon as they called on Saturday night? The chief officers of Malta's various military and civil defence authorities considered the letter carefully, acknowledging the difficulties experienced in Marsa. They looked at possible solutions: perhaps others, such as selected

ARP and police personnel, should be trained to recognise unexploded bombs. Eventually they came to their conclusion: the bomb disposal officer was the only person with suitable knowledge to decide on the need to evacuate buildings surrounding a UXB. They issued a notice confirming that the final decision to evacuate would still be taken by the police, based on the requirements of the bomb disposal officer.

The events in Marsa added to a concern which had been growing since the *Illustrious* blitz: when Malta's sole Army bomb disposal officer was unavailable, the Island's civil defences were vulnerable.

Notes

1 Senglea is now known as Isla, Vittoriosa as Birgu, and Cospicua as Bormla.

2 Extracted from Major R.C.M. Parker GM. (1980). *Account of defuzing of a radio-controlled bomb recovered from Vittoriosa or Cospicua in January 1941*. National War Museum Association, Malta. However, it may be that Major Parker's story recalls his experiences with more than one UXB. Two bombs dealt with by No.1 Bomb Disposal Section in early 1941 fit his description:

Serial No	Location	Date reported	Nationality	Type	Depth	Remarks
25	Polverista Gate	19/1	German	*1000kg GP	5´	*Weight uncertain. Defuzed & removed. 23/1
44	18 Steeple St, Cospicua	27/1	German	1000kg AP	2´	Moved fuzed to San Pietru. Demolished. 18/2

According to the records of 24 Fortress Company, RE, the awards/commendations to Lieutenant Talbot, L/Sgt Parker and his squad were made on 21 January 1941 'for highly dangerous work in connection with a 2000lb bomb at Bittoriosa', more consistent with the UXB at Polverista Gate. His description of the surroundings locates the bomb at 18 Steeple Street (triq il-Kampnar), Cospicua. In the full memoir, Major Parker describes dealing with an entirely unknown bomb. He attributes the characteristics of the bomb to a P.C. 1400FX radio-controlled armour-piercing bomb – a type not believed to have been used until 1943. If it was an unknown bomb, the UXB would not have been demolished but would have been kept as an example for examination – and a detailed report forwarded to the War Office. The physical description of the bomb carcass in Major Parker's account could indicate a German 'G' mine (BM 1000), which carried photo-electric cells.

It is also consistent with either a 1,400kg 'Fritz' anti-armour or a 1000kg PC 'Esau' anti-armour bomb, both of which were sky blue with an aluminium tail. The Esau best fits the 'slim egg shape with pointed nose'. Records suggest that no bombs or mines of these types had previously been encountered in Malta. The 'wire, and what seemed like pieces of electrical equipment', are also consistent with the PC 500RS rocket-controlled bomb, the first of its kind encountered during the Second World War, dealt with by RE Bomb Disposal in Malta a year later, in January 1942. Major Parker was still serving in bomb disposal at the time and is believed to have been involved in its recovery.

3 The George Medal is the second highest gallantry medal to the George Cross. Although it is normally awarded to civilians, military personnel are eligible for the George Medal if their act does not qualify for a military gallantry award.

4 (Date/author unknown). Historical account of *24 Fortress Company, Royal Engineers in Malta*. Royal Engineers Library.

CHAPTER 3

A VEILED THREAT

We had *The Times* in the Officers' Mess: it had a back page, half of which was photographs. There was a big picture of the *Illustrious* being bombed in Malta harbour. We all looked at it and said we didn't fancy going there. Shortly after this, I went into headquarters and the Adjutant said, 'What are you doing here? You should have been on leave two days ago – you're going to Malta.' Lt G.D. Carroll[1]

The second 'siege of Malta' had begun. Lieutenant Talbot and No.1 Bomb Disposal Section were working flat out to cope with unexploded bombs from the '*Illustrious* blitz'. Sixteen were reported on 19 January alone. Recognising the risk to the population of having only one Army bomb disposal officer, Acting Governor and Commander in Chief Lieutenant-General Dobbie applied to the War Office for more manpower. On 20 February he received a telegram.

Lt G.D. Carroll and Sgt Holland (102309) who are trained and experienced in bomb disposal have sailed long sea route. Date of arrival not (repeat not) known. It is intended that they should strengthen your Bomb Disposal organisation. Lt Carroll is in possession of all latest information in respect of BD up to time of embarkation.[2]

From his experience of German bombing on the Home Front, Lieutenant Talbot knew that he was now facing a much tougher enemy than the Italian *Regia Aeronautica*. The Luftwaffe dropped bombs weighing anything from 50kg–1800kg. The GP (general-purpose) or SC (*spreng cylindrisch*) bomb was the most common, particularly in Malta. With its thin walls, the bomb was designed to fragment easily, scattering lethal shrapnel over a wide area. The thick-walled AP (armour-piercing) or SD (*spreng dickenwand*) bomb was used for deep penetration into a target before detonation – such as through the deck of an armoured ship, or the solid walls of buildings like power plants and factories. Its explosion produced heavy steel splinters which could undermine solid structures. The thick-walled bomb was chosen for attacks on Malta's airfields – to cut through the rocky ground and break up runways, as well as the Island's stone buildings.

But it was the German bomb fuzes which presented the greatest challenge – especially to the bomb disposal officer. Unexploded Italian bombs dropped on Malta in 1940 all had mechanical fuzes which were relatively straightforward. The Germans fitted their high explosive bombs with Rheinmetall electric fuzes – a much more complex system according to Lieutenant Carroll.

> The fuzes were supplied with an electrical charge into a condenser …
> At the bottom of the fuze there was a 'gaine' containing a very sensitive explosive. That explosive went off in the middle of a picric pellet containing another less sensitive explosive. There were three or four picric pellets in the tube and they in turn set off the TNT. The fuze was armed as the bomb left the aeroplane.[3]

There were three main types of German electric fuze: impact or short delay, delayed-action (also known as long-delay), and anti-handling. A German impact fuze was detonated by the impact of the bomb on target. One which had not operated was unlikely to do so unless subjected to violent movement, but the bomb was still a hazard until the fuze had been rendered harmless and removed.

By 1940 Allied bomb disposal officers had the skills and equipment to deal with impact fuzes. Realising that their bombs were being successfully neutralised, the Germans began developing more sophisticated types of fuze, some designed specifically to kill the bomb disposal officers trying to immunise them. They introduced the Type 17 delayed-action (DA) fuze, controlled by a clock which could be set to activate at any time up to 80 hours after it fell. From then on, no bomb which had failed to explode on impact could be considered harmless. On the Home Front, one in every seven German unexploded bombs contained such a fuze. Even more lethal were the 'booby-trap' fuzes designed to operate as the bomb was worked on.

Now the Luftwaffe were leading the bombing campaign against Malta every unexploded bomb presented a threat of explosion – at any moment. It was no longer enough for the bomb disposal officer to know what type of bomb he was facing. Until he could see and identify the fuze, it was impossible to know whether the bomb held a functioning clockwork fuze and was still liable to explode. At least the fuzes on German bombs were normally stamped with a number, so that their own bomber crew knew how to arm each bomb – once he saw the head of the fuze, the Allied bomb disposal officer knew what he was dealing with. However, if a bomb was below ground, it would be some time before the head of the fuze was visible. The officer – as well as the NCO and sappers digging for a UXB – had to press on knowing that the bomb might explode at any moment.

With extra strength in numbers, the Luftwaffe was intensifying its efforts to destroy Malta's airfields and prevent the launch of defensive sorties. The RAF was in trouble. Large numbers of unexploded bombs were holding up operations – and they did not have the manpower to cope with them. They called on the Army bomb disposal section for help.[4] Ten large unexploded bombs were strewn across Hal Far, the coastal airfield at the southernmost point of the Island. Several were within the complex of headquarters and accommodation buildings. One 250kg GP was perilously close to a petrol store and a hangar. It took Lieutenant Talbot and his men four days to clear them all.

The full force of the enemy's intentions was felt on the afternoon of 26 February when a pack of dive-bombers, escorted by fighters, carried out one of the fiercest raids of the war so far. This time the target was Luqa: by the time the all-clear sounded, sixteen UXBs were spread across the runways and the airfield was out of action. With a second call from the RAF, Talbot mobilised his BD section. Just two miles south of Grand Harbour, Luqa airfield was laid out on a plateau, with open views across to Valletta.

Talbot toured the site of each UXB in turn, deciding his plan of action. Then he issued his orders and the sappers unloaded their equipment to start work on the buried bombs. Two were near the Control Tower and four more on the south west runway. All of them were 50kg GP and could be defuzed by the NCO in charge.

Lieutenant Talbot had two larger UXBs to attend to. His first priority was a 500kg armour-piercing bomb lying on the runway, preventing aircraft from taking off. The fuze should be reasonably accessible – or so he hoped. Approaching the bomb to take a look, he hit a snag: the fuze head was completely covered by a cap. Talbot had come across these 'extension' caps before: nearly every heavy-cased 500kg and 1000kg bomb he had seen in the past month had one. But up to now they had been in places where they could be destroyed, or left alone until any possible clockwork mechanism had run its course. This bomb was lying in the path of aircraft essential to the Island's role in the Mediterranean conflict. Talbot had no option but to defuze the bomb, and promptly. But first he had to get the extension cap off. His safety depended on two things: one was under his control – by placing his ear to the bomb he might be able to detect the ticking of a clock.[5] The other relied on chance – that if there was a clockwork mechanism, it might have been rendered useless by the impact of the bomb on the rocky ground.

Steadily, he unscrewed the rings holding the extension cap in place. The cap was free. Pausing for a moment, and keeping a firm grip to make sure the cap didn't fall, he gradually eased it away to expose the fuze: it was stamped with the number 15. The fuze was a 'Series 5' – designed to explode on impact.[6] What a relief; this one was unlikely to go off if carefully handled. A No. 15 fuze could be rendered harmless by discharging its condensers. Taking out his Plug Fuze Discharger[7], he located its two pins onto the head of the fuze and depressed its two plungers for ten seconds, then released them for ten seconds. The process was repeated eight times to ensure the fuze fully discharged. Now to take out the fuze; this was a necessary precaution even with an impact fuze, as his discharger might not have worked for some reason. He unscrewed a retaining ring and a locking ring from the bomb casing. Then, taking firm hold of the head of the fuze with the tips of his fingers, he gently withdrew it from the bomb. Before going any further, he must unscrew and remove the gaine and picric pellets from the fuze; only then could it be considered harmless. The main TNT explosive would not explode without the action of a detonator. The bomb was ready to be hoisted onto the bomb disposal lorry and taken away.

There was still the matter of a second bomb on the runway. Buried under three feet of soil and stone, it took some time to uncover – another 500kg, and another extension cap. There was no question of assuming that this was another Series 5 fuze – the Luftwaffe had every reason to deliver the unexpected. Once again, Talbot went through the delicate process of removing the cap before he could confirm it was an impact fuze and neutralise the bomb as before.

He decided that all the remaining reported UXBs at Luqa were far enough from buildings, roads or runways to be cordoned off. Any which did not explode within 96 hours would be tackled as soon as possible after that. There were other more urgent UXBs, including two reported from Tigne, a headland fort built to defend the outer reaches of Marxamsett Harbour from the north and now a headquarters of the Royal Artillery. The Gunners had reported two unexploded bombs at the base of the cliffs near their barracks. One of them was a massive 1,000kg armour-piercing bomb – a type known as 'Esau'.

Following directions from the guard house at Tigne, Talbot made his way across to the perimeter of the fort, overlooking the open sea. There was the bomb, in two feet of water at the foot of the shallow rocky cliffs. Clambering down to take a closer look, he could just make out the fuze pocket below the water line. He would rather not try and defuze the bomb in these conditions. Removing the carcass – five feet long and twenty inches in diameter – would be a difficult and dangerous task. But lying where it was filled with TNT, it could be driven violently onto the rocks by the waves, or hit and exploded by a stray shell in a future enemy attack. The blast could kill anyone manning the nearby guns. A controlled explosion was the best solution, while the area was still cleared of personnel. He surveyed the area; it was viable at this distance from the main fort – and the water would absorb some of the blast.

Attaching the explosives would not be easy. Although the weather was kind, and only gentle waves lapped the bomb, it needed to be stabilised for him to work on. Lieutenant Talbot called to his sergeant to organise ropes, to tether the bomb and hold it in position while he fixed his charges. While this was being done, he went across to the second bomb which lay on the rocks nearby. It was a straightforward 50kg but Talbot decided it was better to blow both bombs together. He reported his intentions to the CO of Fort Tigne, who gave orders for the alert to be sounded within the barracks. All other bomb disposal personnel were ordered to shelter behind a building a suitable distance away. Gathering his equipment, Talbot carefully made his way down to the foot of the cliffs to attach the explosives. It was a difficult business, but at last he was satisfied. Playing out his fuze wire as he went, he made his way over the rocks, up onto level ground and over to join his men. Checking all was in order, he sounded the alarm and blew the bombs. The huge explosion threw water and fragments of rock and steel high into the air.

Back at Luqa, there were bombs still outstanding from the recent raids. While the sappers got rid of four more 50kg GP from Schinas Reservoir to the north of the airfield, Talbot went off to find three 500kg AP near the south west runway. The one in the open had to be tackled first. The fuze had an extension cap but was badly distorted, probably due to landing on the rocks at the edge of the runway. He would have to be careful: if the bomb had a clockwork fuze, there was always the possibility that its mechanism had jammed on impact. If so, any violent movement could cause it to re-start.

He tried to dislodge the cap. It would not budge. He leaned down and listened to the bomb – no ticking. He had another go – no luck. After several attempts, he accepted defeat. It was thoroughly jammed. It was impossible to get at the fuze; he could not establish whether it was an impact fuze, or a clockwork fuze with minutes or seconds to run. He did not know whether the fuze was still liable to operate. And he could not defuze the bomb.

The standard action for a jammed cap was to blow the bomb in situ – but that was impossible so close to the runway. Still, the airfield must be brought back into full use somehow. Lieutenant Talbot decided there was no alternative but to remove the bomb, with its fuze still intact. He did not want to move it far. Fortunately, there was a quarry at the south eastern end of the airfield which was used by the RAF to dump its own defuzed UXBs and destroyed aircraft. This was a dangerous operation if not handled with care: dropping the bomb could activate the fuze and cause a massive explosion. At the same time, to avoid unnecessary loss of life, the minimum number of men were allocated to the task.

To start with, the sappers gently looped ropes around the cylindrical bomb-casing. It was important to get them in a secure position so that the bomb would not slip out as it was manoeuvred. The lorry was reversed into place and a wooden ramp set up from the tailgate to the ground. All the knots were double checked before the sergeant gave the order to take up the slack on the rope. Slowly but surely, the sappers hoisted the bomb up the ramp and onto a pile of sandbags to hold it steady. Now for the journey to the quarry. In case of accident, only the driver would be on board the lorry. The volunteer was ready; he climbed in and started the engine, driving forward as smoothly as he could over the uneven ground. Approaching the quarry, he turned the vehicle and reversed to a position as close as possible to the edge. A handful of sappers joined him again, to replace the ramp, ease the bomb from its sandbags and lower it to a suitable ledge inside the quarry. Talbot gave the order for the lorry to be driven away to a safe distance, taking everyone else with it. He clambered down to the bomb and attached a charge before retreating to the lorry, from where he exploded the bomb. There were three more bombs with jammed fuzes at Luqa that day. Each time, the same painstaking process was followed before they could be exploded and Talbot could declare the day's work finished.

24 hours later, on the evening of Wednesday 5 March 1941, the skies were filled with the steady drone of over 100 aircraft, as Dorniers, Junkers and Messerschmitts launched another heavy attack. This time it was the turn of Hal Far. Many buildings were hit, including aircraft hangars, and the airfield was put out of action. As the airfield's commander surveyed the destruction, he realised there was more bomb disposal work to be done than RAF Warrant Officer Bishop could cover alone.[8] The RE Bomb Disposal section were on their way early next morning. The airfield had to be operational as soon as possible.

Lieutenant Talbot took on nineteen of the unexploded bombs warranting immediate attention, all within reach of the runway. While he concentrated on those on the surface, his sappers began hacking away at the ground for the remaining eleven. Fortunately the hard limestone had prevented the bombs from penetrating too far. By early afternoon one 500kg AP and ten 500kg SAP bombs were exposed – all of them with extension caps. In several cases the cap was jammed in position and the bomb had to be carted from the runway still fuzed. This time, the location of Hal Far on the coast offered an alternative solution to exploding the bombs. Each one was driven steadily to the nearby cliffs, to be rolled over the edge. Work continued late into the day, by which time another two 200kg GP and seven 50kg GP bombs had been defuzed and dropped into the sea. The exhausted bomb disposal section could pack up and return to barracks, to be rewarded with a weekend break from duties. They were back at Hal Far on Monday, and by the end of Tuesday they had cleared six more large HE bombs from the airfield and the nearby coast. The airmen showed their appreciation for the sappers' efforts with a most welcome gift, as recalled by Sapper Scott: 'we got a sack of spuds from the RAF'.[9]

Towards the end of March, the Luftwaffe again extended the range of their bombing campaign against Malta. With no let up on the airfields and military targets across the Island, they turned on the dockyard again. The section was called back to the Three Cities, and the task of getting bombs out from beneath collapsed buildings. An NCO and his team of sappers often worked for several days removing rubble to get at a single unexploded bomb.

After four months in Malta it was time for Lieutenant Talbot to take stock. Since No.1 Bomb Disposal Section had begun operations in December 1940, they had received 96 UXB reports. 10 tons of bombs had been dealt with – 40 high explosives, 9 incendiaries and 10 Ack-Ack shells. It was a considerable achievement for one bomb disposal section operating alone – and yet it was merely a taste of what was to come.

There was something more to celebrate. For their work clearing UXBs from the aerodromes at Hal Far and Luqa during February and March 1941, members of No.1 Bomb Disposal Section received a reward even more welcome than a sack of potatoes. There were official commendations for Sergeant Thomas Piggott, Lance-Sergeant George Henry King, Corporal Cecil Arthur Brewer, Lance-Corporal Rowland Hilliar, Sappers Joseph Birchenall, Thomas Hammond, Duncan MacDonald, Cyril Thomas Meager, Henry James Reeves and Robert Henry Walter.[10] The Royal Engineers Bomb Disposal Section in Malta was to be further recognised for its achievements. In May 1941, the *London Gazette* announced that awards for bomb disposal work in January 1941 were to be made, as follows:

> To be an Additional Member of the Military Division of the Said Most Excellent Order [of the British Empire]: Second-Lieutenant (Acting Lieutenant) Ellis Edward Chetwynd Talbot, G.C. (100411) Corps of Royal Engineers.

The award of the George Medal for conspicuous gallantry in carrying out hazardous work in a very brave manner, to the undermentioned: No 1871236 Lance-Sergeant Reginald Charles Mons Parker, Corps of Royal Engineers.

Awards of the British Empire Medal (Military Division) in recognition of gallant conduct in carrying out hazardous work in a very brave manner, to the undermentioned: No 1866450 Corporal Cecil Arthur Brewer, Corps of Royal Engineers. No 1871172 Sapper William Douglas Scott, Corps of Royal Engineers.[11]

After weeks of constant toil, the beginning of April brought a welcome respite. Raids were much less frequent and only three UXBs were reported during the first ten days of the month. For now Lieutenant Talbot and his men had time to reflect on a good job done – but not for long.

Notes

1 Lieutenant G.D. Carroll, 2005
2 Ed. (1941) *Situation Reports & Operational Messages Out.* WO 106, National Archives, London.
3 Lieutenant G.D. Carroll, 2005
4 Ministry of Information. (1944). *The Air Battle of Malta.* London: HMSO. It appears that at this point the Royal Air Force did not have a co-ordinated bomb disposal operation which could cover all of the airfields of Malta. Flight Sergeant D. Bishop, the NCO who had dealt with unexploded bombs at Luqa during 1940, had been promoted to warrant officer and assigned a full-time bomb disposal role at Hal Far.
5 Standard bomb disposal equipment included an electric stethoscope. However, indications are that one was not available to the RE Bomb Disposal officer in Malta until April 1941.
6 Series '5': fuzes stamped with a number ending in 5 were impact or short-delay. In Malta, the most commonly found fuzes in UXBs were numbers 55, 15 and 25.
7 In this case Lieutenant Talbot is described as using the Two-Pin or Crabtree discharger; it is believed both he and Lieutenant Carroll used this method for No.15 fuzes in Malta. However, both had served in the early days of RE bomb disposal, when impact fuzes were believed harmless after three days. They might then be removed without discharging, preferably by remote control but sometimes by hand. A later method of discharging fuzes was with the steam fuze discharger or the liquid fuze discharger which short-circuited and so discharged the condensers. It seems that neither was available to the RE Bomb Disposal section in Malta until 1942.

8 3 Ministry of Information. (1944). *The Air Battle of Malta.* London: HMSO.

9 (1983). *Correspondence from former Sapper W.D. Scott.* Camilleri, A. Collection of documents relating to UXB in Mosta Dome, 9 April 1942.

10 Date/author unknown. *Historical account of 24 Fortress Company, Royal Engineers in Malta.* Royal Engineers Library.

11 Ed. (1941). *London Gazette.* May 1941.

CHAPTER 4

NUMBERS UP

All unexploded bombs are dangerous. A 50kg (113lb) bomb was small but
as deadly as any other to a bomb disposal officer if it exploded.[1]

It was Good Friday, and Malta was preparing to mark its most important
religious festival, when enemy bombs struck the ancient and beautiful
walled city of Mdina, the Island's former capital. The islanders were stunned
at the Luftwaffe's action against their 'silent city'. Could it really be an accident – merely due to the proximity of the RAF airfield at Ta' Qali? The
bombing certainly affected the airfield, prompting a request for the help of
RE Bomb Disposal to excavate and remove a 500kg GP bomb. Luqa was
also attacked during Easter, giving the squad three more days of arduous
work unearthing five bombs – one from a depth of fourteen feet.

As April entered its third week, the Island was disturbed by several heavy
night raids. News soon broke to explain the attacks: a convoy was approaching.
Among its passengers were the reinforcements for bomb disposal. Lieutenant
Carroll's arrival had been delayed. Having embarked from Greenock on 31
January 1941, he sailed the 'long sea route' via South Africa and the Suez
Canal to Egypt, only to find that convoys to Malta were suspended while
British vessels responded to emergencies in the Mediterranean.

Born in 1918 and brought up on Tyneside, Lieutenant Carroll was at university studying for a second degree in engineering when he signed up in
1939. Having passed out next to top of his officer training (OCTU) cohort,

he was appointed 2nd Lieutenant in the Royal Engineers in May 1940. He was surprised to be told there were currently no vacancies in his chosen field. So for the time being Carroll served as an 'attached officer' – assigned temporary appointments with RE companies in need of his skills. One of his duties that summer was to lay explosives along the Sussex coast, ready for an expected invasion by German forces. The work complete, Carroll was posted to Longmoor in Hampshire as a drill instructing officer, where he was soon recommended for the rank of captain. Unfortunately, as he was an 'attached officer', his CO had no authority to promote him. Instead, Carroll was to have a permanent appointment – as a bomb disposal officer. He was posted to London to lead a section of 854 Quarrying (Q) Company RE, a Welsh unit recently redeployed to bomb disposal.[2]

It was September 1940 and the height of the Blitz, a period when 100–200 bombers attacked London on 57 consecutive nights, dropping 200 tons of bombs and 300 incendiaries per night. There was already a backlog of nearly 4,000 unexploded bombs. It was good preparation for Carroll's future service in Malta.

I'd had no training in bomb disposal when I arrived [in London]. Within a day I was given a report of an unexploded bomb and was sent to deal with it. I took with me four or five Welshmen and we found a hole. When bombs come down, they don't do so vertically but on what's called a parabola [a curved flight path, often causing them to change direction, sometimes upwards, after entering the ground]. In London the ground is clay through which they can travel well. It used to tear the tail off and the bomb would move into an upright position but you would not know where it had ended up.

I arrived at the bomb and was keen to demonstrate how well-equipped I was as an officer. I stood at the hole, trying to figure out which way the bomb had entered. I asked the Welshmen to help find the tail fin and one enthusiastically leapt into the hole and found it. This meant they could start digging and [then] I could deal with the bomb, as though I knew exactly what I was doing.[3]

It was only after a month of tackling unexploded bombs that Lieutenant Carroll received any formal training: a one-week course at the newly-established bomb disposal training centre at RAF Melksham in Wiltshire. Then it was straight back to London and the Blitz.

Of the 161 unexploded bombs handled by 854 Q Company between September 1940 and January 1941, one in particular would stay in Carroll's memory. On 6 November 1940, he was called out to a possible unexploded bomb at a house in Audley Road, Hendon. Confirming the probability of a UXB, he ordered his squad to begin an excavation. After endless probing and digging, by the end of January to Carroll's frustration they had still not located the bomb. Little did he know that they had begun to unearth what would go on record as the deepest UXB in London. It was finally located some 60 feet below ground level on 28 February 1941, by which time he was well on his way to Malta.

It was on 18 April 1941 that he finally embarked from Alexandria on board the fast transport ship *Breconshire*, accompanied by a small protective convoy on its voyage through the Mediterranean. On the morning of 21 April, *Breconshire* entered Marsaxlokk Harbour in the south of the Island, to deliver its load of fuel, ammunition and manpower. The ship's arrival, along with the entry of the rest of the convoy into Grand Harbour, inevitably attracted further enemy air attacks. Mercifully their targets were partly obscured by moist cloud cover. Known in Maltese as the '*xlokk*', the misty weather acted as a screen, allowing the ships to be unloaded free from disturbance.

The landscape of Malta was a pleasant sight for Lieutenant Carroll after the desert sands of North Africa. Dry stone walls of pale gold enclosed tiny fields of dark red soil, overlooked by occasional prickly pear, fig and carob trees. Spring flowers lined the narrow roadways with splashes of bright colour. Then, as their transport climbed a long steady incline towards Valletta, the new arrivals began to see the devastation already wreaked by the enemy on the Island – beyond even what Carroll had witnessed in London. At the sight of the ravaged skyline of the Three Cities they fell silent, as they began to contemplate what might be to come. Carroll made his way to Floriana, to report for duty at Lintorn Barracks. There he learned that he was to take over responsibility for all Army bomb disposal across Malta and Gozo, relieving Lieutenant Talbot.

Edward had been in Malta for five months as sole bomb disposal officer for the army, including the period of heavy bombing known as the

'*Illustrious* blitz'. With the level of bomb disposal work he had faced, it was realised he could be killed, or succumb to the stresses of the job, and in that case there would be no-one. So they decided to send out someone to relieve him and they picked me.[4]

Unfortunately, due to recent increases in Royal Engineers personnel, Lieutenant Carroll could not be accommodated with the Fortress Engineers in Lintorn Barracks; he was to be billeted in Valletta. His new home was a *pension* in South Street, run by a cheerful and fiercely pro-British Maltese man who took fatherly care of the young Royal Engineer officers in his charge. The street was a busy thoroughfare and the location of Admiralty and other British government buildings. Yet to Carroll's surprise flocks of goats were a regular sight outside his pension, providing milk on demand to households in the neighbourhood. Thankfully South Street was only a few minutes' walk from Lintorn Barracks, via the main gateway of the historic city.

Malta's new bomb disposal officer received a warm welcome to his lodgings. At five in the morning of 22 April he was woken by the first of six raids which were to mark his 23rd birthday. Bombs rained down on the bastions and central streets of Valletta, as the enemy tried to destroy the ships of the convoy moored in the Harbour. Another even heavier raid in the evening by some 40 aircraft spread UXBs across densely-populated areas. Night raids and heavy bombing of the streets around his new home were a regular feature of Carroll's first week on the Island. The sound of the air-raid warning became his morning wake-up call.

On Wednesday morning, 23 April, the bomb disposal section took a break from its activities to meet their new BD officer. Lieutenant Carroll was warmly welcomed by Lieutenant Talbot and the two hit it off straight away. As well as 'showing him the ropes', Talbot introduced his replacement to social events at the British Institute and the Union Club.

I was absolutely delighted by the man I found when I got to Malta – he was friendly, had a great sense of humour. We immediately became good friends, going swimming together, socialising and so on. He made me feel completely at home, including taking me down to the British Council tea dance, where he introduced me to a number of Maltese, especially young ladies![5]

Next morning the two officers embarked on a tour of the Island, to familiarise Lieutenant Carroll with the work. He was left in no doubt about the
challenge ahead. There were 30 UXB reports from the previous day's raids
on the convoy – it seemed the new bomb disposal officer had brought
plenty of work with him. Squads could be seen hard at work uncovering
UXBs in the Three Cities and at the string of forts along the north-east
coast, as well as on Manoel Island. Then after a tour of the airfields at Hal
Far, Luqa and Ta' Qali, the two officers climbed the hill to the historic town
of Rabat, where the sappers were clearing a large number of bombs from
the surrounding countryside. From Rabat, their road led across the Island
to the north coast and along a narrow lane with beautiful views of St Paul's
Bay. Their destination was the end of a narrow peninsula and the observation post at Qawra Tower. Four bombs were defuzed; the fifth was far
enough away to be left and was demolished the following Saturday.

They returned to Lintorn Barracks to find an urgent message from
Ricasoli, one of the two massive fortresses which defended the entrance to
Grand Harbour. The fort had suffered heavy attacks and traces of two unexploded bombs had been found – one on the parade ground and the other in
the south-east corner of the barracks: they were designated 'Priority'. The
two bomb disposal officers went immediately to the fort with a team of
sappers and it was late evening before the two 50kg bombs were uncovered
and defuzed.

Still, there was no time to rest for Lieutenant Carroll: every spare minute
was spent studying a 'Composite Summary of Bomb Disposal in Malta' for
the three months to 31 March 1941. From this routine quarterly report, he
discovered the range of UXBs he could expect, the average depth of bombs
which had penetrated the ground and, vitally, the types of fuze encountered so far by Lieutenant Talbot. A total of 89 unexploded HE bombs (not
including shells and incendiaries) had been dealt with by the bomb disposal
section since December. Two-thirds were on the airfields, most of which
were rendered harmless within 24 hours. Carroll learned that in Malta
reports direct from the military were much more common than on the
Home Front:

> We had a lot of troops here: they would witness the bombing and recog-
> nise an unexploded bomb from the silence in a series of bombs falling. We

had an observer, as did other places, on top of the [Lintorn] barracks or HQ – sometimes I went up to the observation post myself.[6]

Carroll could see there would be other differences in his new posting. So far all fuzes encountered in Malta by Lieutenant Talbot were the impact type, whereas in London he was used to finding delayed-action or anti-handling fuzes in a significant percentage of UXBs. Still he must be prepared for them to appear at any time. Then there were the problems with extension caps, fitted to almost all 500kg and 1,000kg bombs in Malta. Because the cap projected from the bomb, it was often distorted on impact, making it impossible to unscrew. And there was no specialist equipment available on the Island to loosen the jammed caps.

The War Office intended that a complete set of up to date bomb disposal equipment should be sent out to coincide with the arrival of Lieutenant Carroll. Although some items did arrive, the set was incomplete. But as neither he nor Talbot knew what to expect in the supplies, they had no reason to query the situation. It was not unfamiliar for Carroll – in his experience bomb disposal equipment in London was always in short supply – but there he could share with another section in his BD company. With no expectation of further deliveries, the section in Malta would have to make do with the limited tools they had – a constraint which would test their resourcefulness to the limit.

Lieutenant Carroll was ready to take over command of the section from Lieutenant Talbot, who was entitled to a break after six months in post. At the same time, some NCOs and sappers who had volunteered in June 1940 could also be allowed a respite.[7] Sapper Scott was one of those engaged in the work from the onset of hostilities. He understood the reasons for taking a break: 'We were often interchanged with personnel of 24 Company when we became bomb happy.'[8] Bomb disposal personnel were susceptible to the effects of constant raids and call-outs on their work, effects which might cause them to cut corners with their safety procedures. A single error could have fatal consequences. Many who joined the BD section on the arrival of Talbot in November 1940 continued to serve under Lt Carroll. They included Sappers Tom Meager, Harry Turner and his friend Daniel McCarthy. Corporal Brewer, who volunteered in June 1940, and Lance-Sergeant Parker also served in Carroll's BD section.

I had something like twenty men working for me; with a sergeant, corporals and a number of men who did the digging. The sappers and NCOs lived in the barracks – Lintorn Barracks, Floriana – where the Fortress Engineers were based. I had an office in the main barracks but later I was mainly based in the bastions where there was a … place where bombs could be taken for dealing with.[9]

New volunteers were recruited to make up the numbers. Before the handover could be completed, they had to be prepared for the work ahead of them. As well as training in bomb disposal techniques, the new recruits worked alongside more experienced hands until they knew enough to operate safely. The extra manpower was about to be badly needed, with plenty of hands-on experience to give the 'rookies' an intensive course in the practical side of the job. With recent reinforcements of personnel and aircraft, the RAF turned the tables on the enemy, attacking Axis convoys in the Mediterranean. The Luftwaffe retaliated by raining hundreds of 50kg bombs on the civilian areas surrounding the dockyards. An extract from a police report outlines just some of the escalating violence through one 24-hour period:

29th April:
Zabbar *(8.15pm)* 4 bombs dropped – 5 houses were totally demolished, 1 house and 2 farmhouses received blast damage. 2 women injured.
Cospicua *(8.15pm)* 1 bomb was registered – 1 house seriously damaged.
Zurrieq *(8.15pm)* 6 bombs were dropped – 10 houses seriously damaged, 7 houses received blast damage – 1 woman injured.
Zebbug *(8.8pm)* 18 bombs and a mine were dropped in the village. Many other bombs fell on the outskirts. 4 houses and a store were totally demolished. 53 houses seriously damaged. 53 received blast damage. Casualties: 5 men, 1 woman (killed).

30th April:
Cospicua *(1.25am)* 16 bombs were dropped – 8 houses totally demolished – 5 houses and 2 shops seriously damaged – 5 shops received blast damage.
Kalkara *(8.30pm)* 10 bombs were registered, many more fell in the sea – 10 houses seriously damaged.

Sliema *(8.30pm)* Many bombs and mines were dropped – 86 houses were demolished – 80 houses and a convent seriously damaged – 20 houses, including police station, received blast damage.

Valletta *(8.30pm)* Number of bombs dropped – many demolished premises – 27 houses, 47 shops, the Law Courts and St. James Hotel (destroyed).[10]

Following one single night raid, twenty unexploded bombs were reported – more than were handled in a fortnight following the *Illustrious* blitz. Through Friday 25 and Saturday 26 April 1941, the sappers worked in teams to clear eighteen unexploded 50kg GP bombs from among the ruins of the Three Cities, followed by another 44 in the last week of April.

Ten days after Lieutenant Carroll's arrival and following another sleepless night he left his pension in South Street, heading for Lintorn Barracks. Turning into Kingsway[11] he stopped in dismay. His route out through the City's Main Gate was completely blocked by debris. The fiercest night-time attack of the war to date, on the night of Wednesday 30 April, had brought heavy bombardment to the beautiful City of Valletta, already scarred by raids. The massive fortifications, strong enough to repel invaders over centuries, were proving no defence against Luftwaffe bombers. St John's Cathedral and the Law Courts were shattered, along with many other buildings across the city's commercial centre. Central Valletta had been brought to a standstill.

A pile of UXB reports was already waiting in the bomb disposal office when Carroll arrived. Several 50kg GP bombs lay among the rubble at the heart of the commercial district: three in St Paul Street, another at the Royal Hotel and a fifth in Ordnance Street, just yards from Carroll's home – all relatively routine jobs. More time was needed to unearth another, which had dug itself two feet into the top of the St Barbara Bastion, overlooking Grand Harbour. On the other side of Valletta, a 50kg GP was hidden under four feet of rubble in New Street, Marina. Thankfully, enemy bombers stayed away while all seven bombs were dealt with. The moment they had finished in Valletta, squads were dispersed to locations across the Island. There were eight UXBs in the town of Mosta, famous for its impressive domed church, and within a mile of Ta' Qali airfield. Another squad was off to Tal Handaq, to dig for two larger bombs reported close to an anti-aircraft battery. No sooner was one lot of excavations finished than fresh ones were added to the list. Attacks on military positions surrounding Grand Harbour and Marsamxetto left two buried UXBs at Fort Manoel, six at the Dockyard School on the edge of Cospicua, and seven at San Pietru.

That evening, the Luftwaffe returned to pound the Harbour relentlessly for over two hours. Again bombs struck the heart of Valletta. Troops in town looking for entertainment just escaped a night to remember. While they strolled through Strait Street, Valletta – a narrow alley and renowned 'night-life' centre, known affectionately as 'The Gut' – an unexploded bomb lay unnoticed behind a wall. Reported next morning, the 50kg bomb was soon attended to and taken away, and the normal business of the street could be resumed. As each enemy bomber could carry several 50kg bombs in a single load, the UXBs were often clustered in a relatively small area. In Capuchin Road, Zabbar, eleven were retrieved from under the rubble of shattered houses. And while NCOs with teams of sappers were working on eight 50kg bombs in the Three Cities, they were told about five more.

Lieutenant Carroll was becoming aware of one very marked difference in dealing with bombs in Malta. In London, most bombs burrowed deep into the soft clay subsoil, which gave some protection for the surroundings should a UXB explode before the disposal team arrived. It was therefore standard practice to cordon off and leave all buried bombs to allow any possible clock to run its maximum course, except those in areas vital to the war effort. In Malta three-quarters of the unexploded bombs lay on the surface – those not on military premises were often at the heart of civilian communities. Splinter and blast effects from a bomb exploding in the open were much more widespread than those from a buried bomb. An exposed UXB could not be left for four days in a location where it might cause injury or damage to property.

Until the bomb was removed the whole community was disrupted. The bomb disposal officer had to order a large area to be evacuated. Depending on the size of the bomb, entire buildings within 50–100 yards had to be completely cleared, as well as any rooms with windows and doors overlooking the site for up to 300 yards. Vehicles were prohibited within 50–100 yards if screened by walls, and 300 yards if not. Although the stone structure of Malta's buildings and the pattern of narrow streets made it possible to adjust these regulations, a significant area still needed to be sealed off until the UXB was gone. All of these measures added to the fear. In densely-populated areas, such as those around Grand Harbour, it was vital that such restrictions were in place for as little time as possible. As a result, many unexploded bombs in Malta were seen as urgent – and the pressure was on for the bomb disposal officer to get rid of them as quickly as possible.

On the Home Front, Lieutenant Carroll was used to company head-quarters deciding the relative priority of a UXB. Jobs were then issued out to the bomb disposal officer leading each section, already classified by HQ according to a scale of four established priorities:

A: bombs whose immediate disposal was essential to the war effort
B: bombs whose rapid disposal was important but less urgent than A
C: bombs not necessarily calling for immediate action
D: bombs which could be left to be dealt with in due course, e.g. in open country[12]

In Malta, only bombs which would qualify as 'A' on the Home Front were marked 'Priority' by police or military commanders. All other UXB reports within the Army's remit were prioritised by the bomb disposal officer. He alone assessed them, to determine quickly and decisively what action must be taken, and to allocate his limited resources to best effect. And with so many of the Island's unexploded bombs falling in sensitive locations, the more efficient option of exploding 'in situ' was rarely possible. For unburied bombs, that method could normally only be used in remote locations. In the first quarter of 1941, only fifteen per cent of Malta's UXBs were destroyed this way. Lieutenant Carroll began to realise that a far higher percentage of the unexploded bombs than on the Home Front would have to be defuzed, or removed fuzed, and dumped – operations which were more hazardous and time-consuming for the bomb disposal men. The challenge facing him was becoming apparent. He would have a large number of unexploded bombs to manage, the majority in conditions where they needed prompt action.

When a large unexploded bomb was detected under rubble at Bofors House in the dockyard zone of Corradino, it was the turn of the Royal Navy to ask the Royal Engineers for help. The sappers burrowed through five feet of debris to expose the 500kg GP bomb. The fuze was jammed in position, leaving the BD officers with a thorny problem. It was tricky enough to move a fuzed bomb across an open airfield to be exploded. Here in the dockyard it was a different matter: they were surrounded by important buildings and the nearest water was congested with vessels. Lieutenant Talbot turned to the Navy for a solution. It was an opportunity for him to introduce Lieutenant Carroll to the RN personnel in Malta, including Bomb Safety Officer Lieutenant C. Rowlands, RNVR.[13] A firm believer in close co-operation between the three armed services for bomb disposal, Rowlands willingly helped get rid of the bomb from Bofors House. It was loaded onto a boat, towed out of the harbour and ditched at sea.

Their paths soon crossed again – and this time the roles were reversed. The enemy were dropping parachute mines and two were reported to the Royal Engineers as unexploded bombs. One lay close to Tad Dawl , near the southern perimeter of Luqa airfield; the other was at the family home of the attorney general, Sir Philip Pullicino. It was found by his daughters in their garden beneath the bastions of the ancient City of Mdina. Strangely, by the time the Army bomb disposal officer arrived to inspect the reported UXB, all traces of its parachute silk had mysteriously disappeared! In accordance with War Office policy, the unexploded mines were referred to the Royal Navy. Once they were made safe the Royal Engineers could be called on to take them away for final disposal.

After days of strenuous activity, the sappers of bomb disposal returned to barracks on Saturday 3 May, looking forward to a night out on the town. All at once a formation of 30 aircraft roared over Grand Harbour and struck at Floriana. What appeared to be a large bomb crashed into Casemate Barracks adjacent to Lintorn. As they watched the aircraft wheel away, a group of NCOs from 24 Fortress Company spotted what they thought was an enemy pilot parachuting down towards the RE pavilion opposite their barracks. They ran to the spot hoping to capture a prisoner, only to be met with a massive explosion – their intended captive was a parachute mine. Within minutes, devastating news reached the sappers back at Lintorn Barracks. It took time for the scale of the tragedy to sink in. Eight NCOs of the Royal Engineers and one civilian were killed in the two explosions; five other servicemen were seriously injured. Then Sapper Tom Meager learned that two of his friends, Lance-Sergeant William Bodiam and Lance-Corporal Peter 'Blondie' Webber, were among the dead.

Still shaken from the night's events, the bomb disposal men were back at work on Sunday morning. Two teams were off to Safi, adjacent to Luqa airfield, where there were signs of another cluster of UXBs. The sheer quantity suggested that successful anti-aircraft fire had forced the Germans to jettison their bombs before target. The thought raised a few wry smiles amongst the sappers despite the hard slog in front of them, unearthing a dozen bombs. After yet another raid on the Grand Harbour area that morning, six more UXBs were reported in Valletta: two 50kg in Hastings Gardens overlooking Floriana and three on the other side of the city's bastions in Lascaris Ditch would all be straightforward. The final bomb was far from easy.

Just as Lieutenant Carroll was getting used to so many UXBs in the open, or under the rubble of a collapsed building, he was presented with a bomb in conditions more common in London than in Valletta. The location was one of the ornamental gardens between the city's main gate and Floriana – a popular area for a Sunday stroll. He inspected the entry hole and concluded that it was a small bomb, probably no more than 50kg, yet it appeared to have penetrated some distance into the ground. He was surprised – evidently the ground of the gardens was abnormally soft for the area. There was no way of knowing how deep the bomb might be, nor how far or in which direction it had travelled. And there was no certainty of its size, or the fuze it carried.

Carroll knew he must get the bomb away as soon as possible. He ordered his sergeant to return to Lintorn Barracks and assemble an excavation squad, on the double. Carroll turned to a policeman standing a few feet away and asked him to make sure that no-one apart from his bomb disposal men entered the area of the gardens and that no heavy-wheeled vehicles came within 50 yards. Leaving his sergeant to command the squad, Carroll moved on to the other UXB reports in Valletta. It was early afternoon by the time he returned, when the shaft was several feet deep. He decided to wait. Within minutes the NCO was at his side. They had reached the bomb – a 50kg with an impact fuze. Carroll decided to defuze it himself.

He was about to approach the shaft when he noticed a group of people standing a short distance away on the far side of the gardens, gazing into the hole. What on earth were they doing there? It seemed that nothing would deter them from enjoying this spectacle to liven up their Sunday afternoon. Lieutenant Carroll looked around him: where were the police and ARP? Telling his sergeant to hold it for a moment, he started moving towards the civilians when he spotted a familiar peaked cap out of the corner of his eye

– Special Constabulary. He marched towards the man and asked him in no uncertain terms to get the people away and make absolutely sure no-one else came near the bomb.

As soon as they were gone, the squad and sergeant withdrew behind a suitable wall and Carroll descended into the shaft. Very gently with a small trowel he eased away the final clumps of grey limestone from the head of the fuze. He attached his fuze discharger and counted away the seconds, repeating the process until it had done its work. Carefully he unscrewed the retaining ring, and the locking ring. The fuze was free. Wiping his hands clean and dry to prevent slipping, he gripped the head of the fuze and gently withdrew it from the bomb casing. He paused for a moment, then grasped the gaine at the base of the fuze and gave it a turn. Resisting at first, it finally gave way so that he could unscrew the small cylinder and detach it from the fuze. It was safe. Holding the fuze and the gaine, he climbed the ladder out of the shaft.

Although it was now possible to allow traffic back into the area, Carroll decided to finish the job and get the bomb away first. People could then resume their Sunday, reassured that the danger was gone. He called his sergeant and gave the order for his squad to retrieve the carcass. Carroll looked around him, intending to thank the uniformed man for his help: he spotted him in conversation with a regular policeman. The 'special constable' introduced himself; he was Philip Pullicino, superintendent of the Special Constabulary. And he was a member of a distinguished family – his father was Sir Philip Pullicino, the Attorney General of Malta. The two joked about Carroll's error of identification and 'Philo' explained that he had been promoted from inspector only a couple of days before. The two officers arranged to meet for a drink as soon as their duties allowed.

Next day there was a macabre reminder of the tragic events of Saturday night for one squad from RE Bomb Disposal, sent out with a report of eight UXBs at Pieta Military Cemetery. The prospect of digging in a graveyard was not a pleasant one. To their relief, none of the eight bombs recovered was more than a foot deep. The sappers of 24 Fortress Company were allowed only a brief respite to mourn their own dead – buried in the very same cemetery – before it was back to business as usual.

There had been over 100 air raid alerts since the beginning of April. The Luftwaffe continued to hit residential areas around the harbours at least as often as military targets. As well as frequent night-time raids, attacks were coming at unpredictable times of the morning and afternoon, disrupting the work and rest of the population. With the final handover to Lieutenant Carroll and his new team fast approaching, all available manpower was mobilised in an effort to finish off any outstanding unexploded bombs. While the NCOs and sappers handled the digging, the two bomb disposal officers divided the reports of larger bombs between them. In little more than two weeks since Carroll had arrived, he and Lieutenant Talbot had received 220 UXB reports. The combined forces of RE Bomb Disposal had dealt with a total of 143 high explosive bombs of 50kg and over – an average of ten per day – and more than in the entire three months to 31 March. The sappers had completed over 50 excavations between three and eight feet in depth, most in tough, rocky terrain. Yet no sooner had they cleared outstanding UXBs than more fell – and still dozens lay waiting for them.

Notes

1 Frayn Turner, J. (1961). *Highly Explosive*. London: Harrap and Co.
2 In January 1941, bomb disposal officers and volunteers were detached from the Quarrying Company to form a separate No 24 Bomb Disposal Company with its headquarters at Mill Hill.
3 Lieutenant G.D. Carroll, 2005
4 Lieutenant Carroll's Army Service Record shows that he was posted to 'HQ Fortress Company, No 2 Bomb Disposal Section, Malta. The number suggests that a need for two BD officers and sections was anticipated following the 'Illustrious blitz'. However, the decline in enemy bombing from the end of May 1941 meant that one BD section could handle the demand. The Fortress Engineers War Diary and other relevant records refer always to 'the bomb disposal section' in the singular, consistent with the handover of a single BD section from Lieutenant Talbot to Lieutenant Carroll. This remained the situation until the end of 1941.
5 Lieutenant G.D. Carroll, 2007
6 Lieutenant G.D. Carroll, 2005
7 Pankenham-Walsh, Maj. Gen. (1957). *History of the Corps of Royal Engineers*, Vol VIII: 1938–48. Chatham: Institute of Royal Engineers. The chapter on bomb disposal, Malta, explains that 'to give relief from the strain the personnel were changed over periodically with volunteers from the fortress companies.'
8 (1983) 'Correspondence from former Sapper W.D. Scott'. Camilleri, A. Collection of documents relating to UXB in Mosta Dome, 9 April 1942. The term 'bomb happy' was used to describe the state of nerves of those who had served in Malta for an extended period.
9 Lieutenant G.D. Carroll, 2005

10 Micallef, J. (1981). *When Malta Stood Alone (1940-1943)*. Micallef, Malta.

11 Now Triq ir-Repubblika (Republic Street).

12 Ed. (1942). *Manual of Bomb Disposal*. WO 287. National Archives, London.

13 Galea, F. (2008). *Mines Over Malta*. Malta: Wise Owl Publications. Lieutenant C. Rowlands, Bomb Safety Officer (BSO), was supported by Sub Lieutenant C. St. J. Ellis, GM, RNVR. In April 1941, T/A Elect Lieutenant A.G. Rogers, GM RNVR joined Commissioned Boatswain Lord J.H. Sheldon GM at HMS St Angelo in the Royal Navy's specialist task of 'Rendering Mines Safe'.

CHAPTER 5

LUFTWAFFE ALL OUT

Anyone working on a bomb in an area evacuated of its population is by necessity lonely and on occasions afraid.[1]

After seemingly endless bombing raids, on Friday 9 May 1941 the skies over Malta fell ominously silent. The uneasy peace continued through the weekend allowing the bomb disposal section to take its first break in two weeks. The lull was timely: the day had come for Lieutenant Talbot to stand down from active service as a bomb disposal officer. Responsibility for all Army bomb disposal in Malta now transferred to Lieutenant Carroll.

The calm was short-lived; enemy bombers were back on Sunday evening, attacking on and off through the night and into the morning. Bombs were dropped on Grand Harbour, Valletta and the airfields of Luqa and Ta' Qali. For three more nights the raids hammered on, as the Luftwaffe spread their attacks to include Hal Far. Now that the Island's defenders were scoring greater success during the day, the enemy concentrated on bombing under cover of darkness, disturbing sleep and heightening the sense of fear among the population. Reports were coming in to RE Bomb Disposal at an average of ten per day. With so many UXBs to inspect across the Island, Carroll needed to get around quickly. Instead of using his BD officer's motor car, he took to riding a motorcycle. It was the only way to keep up with his itinerary.

Setting out with a fresh batch of reports on Monday morning, Carroll arrived at Luqa airfield to find several holes made by bombs evidently larger than 50kg. Enemy bombs were getting heavier. For the past month nearly all UXBs had been 50kg; now almost every one he inspected was either 250kg or 500kg. Although in Malta the NCOs were trained to work on bombs up to 50kg when necessary, it was policy for all those of 250kg and over to be tackled by a bomb disposal officer. It was a policy that Carroll firmly adhered to – but now he was on his own. While his men got to work with their pick-axes, he rode over to the military camp a mile away at Tal Handaq to defuze a 250kg SC before returning to Luqa for the first two uncovered bombs. After a sleepless night – including one five-hour raid – he was back in Luqa on Tuesday morning. Two unexploded 250kg bombs lay near the Xlejli Tower, a look-out post used by observers plotting bombs and damage to the airfield. On the way he took a detour to inspect reports from Zabbar and Ghaxaq.

On Wednesday morning he was back at Tal Handaq in response to an urgent report from the military: a 500kg AP bomb lay near one of their buildings. As soon as he had finished he rode south again to follow up reports from Gudja and Kirkop. His final report took him past Hal Far air-field and along tiny dirt tracks to the southern tip of the Island and the cave at Ghar Hasan. Then it was back to barracks, only to be called out again for newly-reported bombs at Vittoriosa and Qormi.

Thursday brought a change of direction as he headed inland to the rural farmland of Lija, to inspect two reported bombs. Having arranged for them to be cordoned off for 96 hours, he set off for Lintorn Barracks. A dramatic daylight raid unfolded as he rode towards Floriana. Over a dozen aircraft crossed the coast at different points and dropped more bombs around Luqa. They brought more reports of UXBs from the airfield and from Marsaskala – plenty of work for him next morning. With several squads out digging on Friday, Carroll was kept busy touring the sites to defuze each bomb as it was revealed. This time he went with his sergeant in the car; he needed equip-ment to explode a bomb in fields near the Hompesch Arch, which stood astride the main road to Zabbar. Although he was now familiar with several of the impressive constructions left as a memorial by each of the Grand Masters of the Knights of Malta, Carroll could not help thinking how odd the imposing structure looked surrounded by open fields and little else.

As soon as the dust had settled from his explosion he was ready for his next appointment, defuzing a 250kg bomb on the edge of the stone quarries at Tad Dawl, adjacent to Luqa airfield. There were three more 250kg to defuze at Luqa, and a fourth to blow, before he was finished for the day. On Saturday he had another bomb to explode at Ghaxaq so he took with him reports of three UXBs at Gudja. While he was checking one of them, two more were reported nearby. The five inspections done, his final destination was Kirkop, for his last bomb of the day.

He had just enough time to return to his billet in South Street, smarten up and meet his friend Edward Talbot. They were going to a tea dance at the British Institute in Valletta. After such a busy week, Carroll was only too pleased to take time out to enjoy himself. His pleasure was increased when Talbot introduced his new friend to a large group of society Maltese, including some very attractive young ladies. It was a welcome afternoon of entertainment and good company for Carroll – but it was to have unforeseen consequences.

A quieter day on Sunday gave the officer an opportunity to embark on a special expedition. Disposing of the carcasses of so many bombs had become a real problem for Malta's bomb disposal section. The War Office originally intended that bomb casings should be kept, as a source of scrap metal to be recycled for the war effort. But bomb disposal units were soon working at full stretch – and the sheer numbers of empty bomb casings presented a storage problem. The order was issued that a suitably remote but accessible area should be used as a 'bomb cemetery' where bombs up to 500kg could be taken and blown up. In Malta, with such limited resources, it was not feasible to transport bombs several miles into the countryside to explode them. An alternative solution was tried, with almost fatal results:

> There were so many UXBs stocked that we had to dispose of them through deep-sea dumping. Once we were being towed out to the 5-mile buoy by a minesweeper when we were attacked by a German aircraft; we were set adrift, floating about in the rough sea on a flat-bottomed barge with bombs rolling about.[2]

Apart from Luqa and Hal Far, where bombs could be dumped close by, carcasses were being taken to Lintorn Barracks. There they remained, waiting for the explosive filling to be washed or steamed out, to leave a harmless empty shell. It was a long and messy process, especially when the bomb was large.

The high grade TNT filling … was almost as hard as the local stone and would require high pressure steam to remove it. We … took the bomb to our barracks in Floriana, and employing steam from the troops bath house boiler, well stoked up for the purpose, we went to work on it at the back of the boiler house. Though this took several days it proved to be very successful. The smell of steam-heated TNT permeated the barracks, as the molten TNT together with the condensed steam ran out of the bomb along a gulley to the drain. We segregated the smelly mess in the gulley as it cooled, and gathered up the TNT into sand bags, allowing only the water to run into the drain. In this way we obtained some useful additions to our depleted stocks of explosives.[3]

What began as a useful recycling operation when there were just a handful of bombs was now impractical. Since January there had been far too many coming in day after day; a backlog of defuzed bombs full of explosive was piled up in the barracks, and according to Harry Turner one had exploded unexpectedly.[4] Lieutenant Carroll needed a new way to dispose of the redundant carcasses. He was aware that several bombs recovered from Hal Far airfield had been rolled into the sea over nearby cliffs. He needed a similar cliff-top location – preferably reasonably central to the Island, with good road access but away from any large military or civilian centre. His final chosen site was a cove with vertical cliffs on the west coast between Hal Far and Dingli, with views across to the Island of Filfla.[5] The job of removing the defuzed UXBs to the cliffs and tipping them into the sea was given to a driver and a couple of sappers. They included Harry Turner, now a married man. Harry's new job worried his young wife, Mary – a local girl whom he had married in December 1940. She was not reassured when he called in at their flat occasionally during his working day, casually mentioning that he had bombs in the back of the lorry parked outside. In fact Harry himself could feel far from safe in a vehicle full of bombs loaded with TNT out on the open road, knowing the enemy might strike at any moment.

On Monday morning the entire bomb disposal section was back in action sinking shafts in locations across Malta, while Carroll followed up reports of larger unburied UXBs. Then on Tuesday 20 May 1941, their work was brought to a sudden halt in the face of fresh emergencies. Valletta and St Julians had been badly hit by bombs and mines in a series of heavy enemy attacks which started at four in the morning. Unable to sleep since the first bombs struck the city, Carroll arrived early at Lintorn Barracks. A Priority UXB report was waiting for him. Two of the bombs had hit St Augustine's Church; one had not exploded. Ordering his sergeant to muster a squad, he hurried to the church. He had a special reason to be concerned: he was a Catholic, and St Augustine's was the church where he attended Mass.

The UXB was on the roof. Guided by directions from one of the church helpers, Carroll made his way up to where he could get a good look at it. The bomb was lodged at the very top of the church wall, in the angle where it joined the roof. From below it looked like a 50kg. Even so, an explosion could not only bring down the church roof, it would shower debris across the narrow streets of the tightly-packed area of Valletta. It was certainly high-priority.

He had to get at the bomb, and that meant getting up onto the roof. Emerging from below, he recognised the small decorative tower of St Augustine's: he had seen it from the roof terrace of his pension in nearby South Street. The bomb was on the far side of the tower, where it had damaged part of the roof. The surface was fairly flat but it could be unstable; he would have to move carefully. Slowly, he inched forward until he was close enough to identify the fuze. It was an impact type – relatively harmless on the ground but if the bomb was dislodged and fell any distance it could explode. He needed the bomb to be wedged in position so that he could work on the fuze. He was about to call for his NCO to organise some sandbags when the familiar tones of the air-raid warning wailed out. He looked across the rooftops to see a formation of enemy aircraft heading for the coast, on course for Luqa. There was no point in taking any chances; he decided to take cover until the raiders passed.

As soon as the sky was quiet again, the sandbags were carried up to the roof and packed around the bomb. Now he could get to work, discharging and removing the fuze. Unscrewing the gaine from the fuze he carried both down. The bomb was now stable but it still had to be brought to the ground – and it contained several kilograms of TNT. A 50kg was small enough for a man to carry on his shoulder at ground level but manhandling it down a ladder from a high point was not safe. One slip could have serious consequences. Carroll and his sergeant looked at the structure of the roof. They decided the best option was to lower the bomb to the ground using ropes. A harness was tied tightly around the carcass and tested to check that it was secure. While they worked, another air-raid alert wailed out, but again Valletta was spared. Finally, the bomb was dislodged from its bed of sandbags and lowered steadily towards the floor, and into the arms of waiting sappers. It was driven away to the sound of a third air-raid alert.

There were two more alerts before lunchtime, then another in the afternoon. It was lucky that no attacks had hit Valletta, and not only for the bomb disposal men. Recently confirmed in post as Governor of Malta, Lieutenant-General Dobbie had chosen that morning to tour the bombed areas of the city and show his personal support for the Island's people and its defenders.

Next day the section returned to the task of digging up bombs in Luqa and its surrounding villages. One squad was hard at work close to the runways when the alarm sent them scurrying for shelter. Suddenly the sky was full of roaring, sweeping aircraft. Over a dozen Me109s approached from different directions and dropped bombs across the airfield. The Heavy Ack-Ack fired constantly at the raiders but could do little to stop them striking at valuable planes on the ground; two Wellingtons were destroyed, one Blenheim and a Hurricane damaged. The Me109 was normally a fighter, but it was being used over Malta as a fighter-bomber, with terrifying effectiveness. It could dive steeply from a great height, release its bomb load and climb sharply away. Its sheer agility made it difficult for the defending gunners to retaliate.

The morning of 22 May brought a Priority UXB report from Luqa. As the bomb was in the open, Carroll went alone on his motorcycle. He defuzed the 250kg SC, then rode down to the coast at Ghar Hasan to demolish two more. Next it was back up to Gudja, where squads were toiling away to reach two large buried bombs. Digging out bombs was the most time-consuming part of bomb disposal work. One of the main challenges, especially in Malta, was in working out the exact location of the bomb in relation to the point where it had entered the ground, in order to decide where to position the shaft. While there were average figures for the 'depth' and 'offset' (angle of penetration) of bombs in British soil, the ground in Malta was very different – and an unknown quantity in the early days of bomb disposal there. The direction of travel was more difficult to predict in this uneven, rocky ground than in the smooth clay of London.

As time went on, the bomb disposal officers came to know what type of terrain they might encounter in any particular area. The depth of each UXB recorded in the Weekly Bomb Disposal Reports gave them some idea of what to expect in that location. The penetration of a bomb depended on its size, shape and weight, and the height from which it was dropped. In May 1941 the information for Malta was still limited, but patterns were starting to emerge. Depths on the Island were normally less than the UK averages (from 9 feet for a 50kg to 22 feet for a 1,000kg bomb). Malta has a thin layer of topsoil covering a bed of limestone which varies in density from north to south. The ground in the southern half of the Island is harder and most UXBs reported there were on or near the surface. To the north, the softer ground allowed a deeper, longer travel for bombs – often 10 feet or more – and demanded a lot of spade work.

Examining the site of each bomb at Gudja, Lieutenant Carroll and his Sergeant considered carefully the hole of entry, estimated the size of the bomb and then calculated the most likely direction and distance of travel. Once they had decided on the bomb's probable location, work could begin. A cautious approach was essential. Even though the UXBs were more than 96 hours old, any careless jab with a pick or a man jumping into the shaft might trigger a booby-trap or cause a jammed clock to restart.

Aware of the Luftwaffe's changing tactics, and especially the recent introduction of 250kg and 500kg bombs, Carroll knew they might begin using Type 17 delayed-action or Type 50 anti-handling fuzes at any time. These were particularly effective weapons on airfields, where a 'time-bomb' on the runway would bring operations to a halt until it was rendered safe – and it might explode before or during any attempt to do so. The NCO and the sappers digging for a bomb were also aware that every unexposed bomb potentially held a lethal fuze that might activate as they were working. As far as Tom Meager was concerned, they just had to get on with the job. 'There was no possible way of knowing what the fuze was. You just dug until you uncovered enough to know.'[6]

The job was physically tiring, especially in the hot weather. The sappers worked by hand with picks and shovels, hacking away until gradually an eight-foot square shaft was sunk into the ground. The spoil was constantly carted away from the edge of the hole by wheelbarrow, to make it easier for new spoil to be thrown out. Though much of the digging was into solid ground, if the soil was soft and the sides of the shaft became unstable, they had to be lined with timbers as work progressed, to ensure it did not collapse. This was where the 'tradesmen' of a bomb disposal section came into their own. A carpenter and joiner like Harry Turner would find his skills put to good use when timbering of shafts was needed.

It took several hours of hard toil in Gudja before the first of the two bombs was located. It was a 250kg SC – the bomb which most often held one or even two Type 17 fuzes. Lieutenant Carroll was informed: rather than take any more chances by uncovering the bomb completely, he decided on a controlled explosion. He ordered the squad away to shelter, collected his equipment and walked back alone towards the bomb.

> I wasn't afraid going down the ladder into a shaft – but I was *concerned* – if the bomb went off I might stay alive but be terribly injured. Therefore when I got to the bottom I sat on the bomb. That way, if the bomb exploded, at least I would know nothing about it.[7]

Sitting astride the bomb's carcass, he attached his charges. Then playing out the fuze wire as he went, he climbed the ladder and retreated to the safe point. Giving the final warning, he blew the bomb. Within a short time the second bomb had been revealed as a 250kg SC and he repeated the entire process. The section could return to barracks with the prospect of two whole days off.

That Sunday morning, Carroll was back at St Augustine's Church as usual. His daily devotions were about to bring an unusual request. As soon as Mass ended, a young boy approached and asked him to come to the dormitory next door because a priest wished to see him.

> I went to the presbytery and was shown into his room to wait: it had whitewashed walls, with a mat on the floor, an iron bedstead, a small wooden table and chair, with a shelf of books above, a crucifix on the wall and a wicker armchair to one side. I sat in the chair, twiddling my round service cap on my finger as I waited. Finally, the priest came in. As he had asked to see me, I expected him to speak first, but he didn't. He walked [back and forth] diagonally across the room looking at me, and I was looking at him. Eventually, he spoke: 'You know [Signor X]?' You see,

in Malta, lots of people have the same name, not necessarily because their families are connected at all. I reeled off two or three whom I knew but he said 'No, no!'[8]

The priest explained: he was talking about the owner of a well-known building nearby.

The building was about 140 yards long, about 60 yards wide and six storeys high. He was obviously a rich man. I was staggered, as I began to realise what was happening. The priest looked at me again; I didn't respond. He said, 'He wants you to be friends with his daughter.' I now knew what was afoot: I must have looked aghast … I was sure that I was being offered marriage, and all before I'd had any breakfast!

I paused, as I knew that in our dealings with the Maltese, it was important not to offend. There were many more of them than there were of us, many were being injured; the Germans were attacking the island. So I had to tell a lie: I said, 'Well I'm sorry, but you see – there is someone else.' The priest seemed really displeased and said, 'All right, all right.' I offered to see the gentleman and explain but the priest refused, saying he would tell him. He dismissed me and I left …

Soon afterwards I saw a notice in the paper of the engagement of a young woman of the same name. I wondered whether, having been unsuccessful in my case, she had married another man of her father's choosing.

Lieutenant Carroll soon had other reasons to feel relieved: enemy action seemed to be abating. At the end of May raids gradually dwindled to one or two per day, often involving only a single aircraft. And after two more day shifts at Gudja, the sappers had exposed the final two buried UXBs – both 500kg – ready for him to demolish.

The total number of high explosive UXBs of 50kg and over dealt with by RE Bomb Disposal in just six weeks since Carroll's arrival had reached 177. It was more than his entire former company had tackled in four months of the London Blitz.

Notes

1 Hogben, Major A (1987). *Designed to Kill.* Wellingborough: Stephens.
2 Letter from Major Reginald Parker GM dated 1 May, 1980. National War Museum Archive, Malta.
3. ibid.
4 Maurice Turner, 2007
5 Evidence suggests the most likely location was at or near Ghar Lapsi. Lieutenant Carroll was concerned to find out years later the importance of the Neolithic monuments close to his chosen location.
6 Cyril Thomas Meager, 2008
7 G.D. Carroll, 2005
8 ibid.

CHAPTER 6

CHANGING ENEMY

I was looking after the civilian population. I was the one they'd call if they found a bomb … that's why I was called 'Ta'l bomba' (the bomb man) – and I became a friend to them.[1]

On Wednesday 28 May 1941, Lieutenant Carroll arrived at the site of a UXB report to find a large high explosive bomb with a very long tail-fin. There were no fuze pockets in its flank, the normal position for German HE bombs. This one had a fuze in its 'nose' and another in the base. It was a 500lb Italian bomb, and his first. Carroll had studied examples of Italian HE bombs stored at Lintorn Barracks. He knew their fuzes were mechanical, operated by a simple firing pin. It should be a relatively easy job to unscrew each fuze in turn. Nevertheless, he would take no chances, especially with his first one. It was some minutes before he declared the carcass ready for removal.

The Luftwaffe had all but vanished from the skies. In a major change of strategy, Hitler had withdrawn his air forces from Sicily to support a planned attack on Russia. Since April the German strike force seemed to have thrown everything they had at Malta in a last-ditch attempt to neutralise the Island. But while they had weakened its defences, they had not destroyed them. Now the task of leading the campaign was handed back to the *Regia Aeronautica*. Hopes were raised that bombing might reduce to the levels of the previous autumn. But while the Italians may have lacked aggression, they were not about to make life simpler for the bomb disposal men.

That Wednesday night a single enemy plane passed over Valletta and Floriana then turned south-west and dropped bombs on the community of Qormi. A UXB report from the local police was telephoned through for the bomb disposal officer. Taken to the site by a local guide next morning, Carroll was presented with a scene which puzzled him. Clearly two bombs had entered the ground. What interested him were the pieces of an alloy material around the holes of entry. They suggested some sort of tail fin – but not one he recognised. He had no idea what type of bomb he was facing.

Carroll stayed close at hand as his sergeant and a team of sappers began to uncover the bombs, with strict instructions to collect every scrap of material as they went. As the fragments of alloy were laid out on the ground, they began to take shape, suggesting a tail fin some two feet long. Bit by bit, the first bomb was unveiled and the BD officer could take a closer look. It was an incendiary, definitely Italian, and about four feet in length; its nose was covered by a twelve-inch cap. This was certainly a new bomb to Carroll, and not one he had read about in any of his manuals or bulletins. He called the work to a halt. Before going any further, he must check whether there was any prior knowledge of the bomb. He soon received his reply: he had discovered a new type of incendiary. Bomb Disposal HQ in London required a physical and technical description of the bomb and its function, to be distributed to bomb disposal personnel in the field. If the Italians were dropping these on Malta, they were likely to do so elsewhere, especially in the Middle East.

Lieutenant Carroll's task now was to make the bomb safe and recover all available parts to take back to Lintorn Barracks. There he got to work painstakingly dismantling the bomb's carcass and fuze mechanism. Examining them item by item, he dictated information to his sergeant who noted down every detail. The incendiary weighed in at 70kg. It was designed to ignite on impact, triggering the burning of its Thermite filling, which affected anything within a radius of ten yards. Like the 43lb incendiaries already in use, the 70kg was a hazard to fuel stores, as well as aircraft and shipping – if it hit target. But it seemed that when this bomb had entered the ground, soil had choked the gas escape holes and prevented the burning filling from blowing out. It soon emerged that a third of those dropped on Malta so far had failed to ignite. There would be many more in the months to come.

Enemy air activity did seem to be easing. There was still some night bombing but daylight hours were relatively quiet, with only sporadic bomber or fighter raids between occasional reconnaissance flights. When there was a raid, there were far fewer aircraft, and even those were noticeably less effective. Carroll noticed a marked difference in the Italians' style of attack. Their aircraft were often observed circling for long periods out to sea before finally making their approach over the Island. Even then they seemed reluctant to travel far inland.[2] 'We used to say that the Italians would fly towards Malta at high speed, then when they got close they would go into a steep turn and open the bomb bays, and the bombs came out sideways.'

Certainly an unusually high number of unexploded bombs were being reported around coastal defence posts. On Wednesday 4 June Carroll received a message from one of his NCOs asking him to come up to a coastal battery at St Paul's Bay. The squad had been sent to unearth two small bombs, expecting to find German 50kg. They turned out to be smaller – and evidently Italian. Each had a single fuze fitted to the base – normal for Italian bombs of less than 100kg. Yet despite their size, they had both plunged three feet into the ground. Could this be another new type of bomb? The lieutenant examined each of them in turn. In both cases the fuze was broken – the bombs were in a highly sensitive condition. He must not even attempt to extract a fuze in such an unstable state. Any movement could cause the fuze to function. It was impossible to take an example back to barracks for examination. He had no choice but to note what details he could from the two bombs, and then explode them.

He hoped for better luck next day, when there were five more of the small bombs – two at Tal Papa and three at Fort Benghisa. To his frustration, every single one was in the same state and had to be demolished. It was not until three days later that he found two bombs in a suitable condition to take back for a proper examination. The bombs weighed 15kg and their carcasses was of a thickened semi-armour-piercing design. That explained why so many were found deeper than expected. The heavy construction was designed to penetrate a target more effectively than was normal for a bomb of this weight. The Italians were evidently trying to overcome the strength of Malta's limestone. These small bombs could be carried in large numbers by a single bomber. Like the German 50kg bomb, the Italians seemed to be using them for maximum coverage, aiming them mainly at military targets. They soon became a common sight across the Island: the majority of UXBs in June 1941 were this new type. In many cases, the outer part of the fuze had snapped off on impact and the bomb was blown in situ.

Apart from the challenge of new bombs, for Lieutenant Carroll and his section work was beginning to feel more manageable. Inevitably as air attacks diminished the number of UXBs eased back, to between three and seven each day. After the frantic activity since his arrival, for Carroll the change brought the opportunity to restore some semblance of order. He could work just six days per week, and more reasonable hours, unless a Priority UXB brought a late-night call or a Sunday outing.

> You have to have some sense of routine, even in war: you can't spend all your time tearing from here to there, from this to that … I would have breakfast and report to the barracks. There would be work to be carried on from the previous day which hadn't been finished and any new reports that I had to arrange for the men to go to, and then deal with. If there was a bomb dropped which was a priority – an emergency – it had to be dealt with straight away.[3]

Carroll put his time to good use, developing good contacts in the community as he had in London. So much of his work was carried out among the civilian population of Malta's cities, towns and villages. Working alongside the police, the Special Constabulary and the ARP organisation, he was getting to know the Island and its people. And his friend Philo Pullicino had introduced him to a new social life.

> As is the way of the Maltese, he invited me to meet his family: I was pleased to go. They lived in Mdina towards the north of the island, in a lovely house with views from the ramparts.[4]

Just as life was becoming a little easier with a less fearsome enemy, a visit to Malta by General Haining on 8 June brought intelligence warning of a possible invasion. Military commanders recognised a need to review and strengthen the Island's defences in readiness for a possible seaborne attack. The Island's aerodromes were considered too vulnerable to enemy parachute landings. It was decided that in the event of an imminent airborne invasion mines should be laid to intercept the enemy. Military commanders decided to try out naval depth charges for the purpose. As an officer used to handling explosives, Carroll was called on to assist. The trial was scheduled for Saturday 14 June in the quarry at Luqa – the final resting place for so many UXBs in recent months.

The military authorities had received a delivery of depth charges by submarine from England. The objective was to test the potential of these to blow an enormous crater in the airfield and so hamper any proposed invasion from the air. My job was to create a chamber below ground to put in a depth charge. Under my instructions, my men dug down to provide an appropriate cavity for the charge.

I was told that I would not be required to carry out the actual explosion: the senior officers wanted to take charge of it. I put the depth charge in place, arranged the fuzes and so on, and handed over to the senior officer who was to co-ordinate the explosion. The Chief Engineer and other interested parties were invited to inspect the set-up. They stood in the field near the bombs, to be briefed on what was happening. On a given signal, they were supposed to retreat to the other side of a wall some distance away. In the belief that everything (and everyone) was ready, the order to fire was about to be given. However, some officers were still inside the wall. They were shouted at to 'get out' and they dived over the wall just in time. Even so, the blast threw stones etc and rocks into the air, a lot of which fell on their heads.[5]

Only too aware of the risk of inexperienced personnel handling high explosives, Carroll hoped that next time senior officers might prefer him to complete the job. He enjoyed telling the story to Lieutenant Talbot when they met next day to go swimming. His friend had his own news: he would not be returning to bomb disposal after his respite. He was transferring to a new job.

A new Air Officer Commanding (AOC), Hugh Pughe Lloyd, had arrived in Malta at the end of May and immediately reviewed the resources at his disposal for the successful defence of the Island. Having already secured help from the Army with repairs to the airfields, he turned his mind to strategic operations. His experience of Bomber Command in London had shown him the importance of reconnaissance and military intelligence, as well as good communications between the three armed services. He requested an increase in operations room and liaison personnel. With little or no possibility of importing additional manpower to Malta, Lieutenant-General Dobbie looked among those already on the Island. Talbot had the qualities and track record to fit him for the work. Reduced levels of enemy bombing activity were expected to continue for the time being, and Lieutenant Carroll and his BD section were meeting the need for Army bomb disposal. Currently 'in reserve', Talbot was given a new appointment, as liaison officer between the Army and the RAF.

Despite Talbot's secondment, there was no question in the mind of Dobbie as to the need for two BD sections to be available, should circumstances require. In an exchange of telegrams with the War Office in July 1941 on the subject of the Fortress Engineers, he made it plain that 'no possibility of disbandment of any unit can be foreseen'.[6] As well as Carroll's active BD section of twenty men, Lieutenant Talbot and other ranks currently back on normal duties with 24 Fortress Coy RE could form the basis of a second BD section, should the need arise. The CO of the Fortress Engineers emphasised in the Company War Diary that 'the bomb disposal section [was] busy on unexploded bombs.'[7]

Attached to the War Diary was the 'Composite Summary of Bomb Disposal in Malta from April to June 1941'. It showed that 237 high explosive bombs of 50kg and above (not including shells and incendiaries) had been dealt with by the Army BD section, compared to 89 in the previous quarter. Very few were blown in situ: in five out of six cases bombs had to be defuzed, or carried away with their fuzes intact, and dumped. Since January, almost all UXBs had been German, with the exception of the occasional 43lb incendiary dropped by Italian aircraft operating alongside the Luftwaffe. Now the balance was reversed; in June 1941 more than 50 per cent of the unexploded bombs were Italian. By August it would be 100 per cent.

Although there were fewer enemy attacks to interrupt the working day, the Italians maintained a persistent campaign of nuisance raids at varying times through the night. Single aircraft would approach Malta, raising the alarm, but not cross the coast. They then pretended to turn back for Sicily, only to return ten minutes later to trigger the alarm again. The constant disruption of these night-time alerts was taking its toll on the population, both civilian and military. For three nights, from 24 to 26 June, there were raids almost continuously from ten in the evening until three in the morning.

Shortly after midnight on Saturday 28 June, one Italian pilot ventured a lot closer than usual to the shoreline before dropping his load and turning away. First thing next morning Lieutenant Carroll was on his way to investigate the report of an unexploded bomb near the waterfront at Pieta Creek, a promenade overlooking the Royal Navy submarine base – and a popular walking area for the locals. The UXB had been reported by Royal Navy divers who found it during a routine operation to clear the waters surrounding their vessels. A buoy marked the exact location, some ten yards from the shoreline. To inspect the bomb, Carroll had to swim out to it and dive down for a closer look. Fortunately the water was clear and he had little difficulty identifying an Italian HE, weighing in at 130lb. It was about ten feet below the surface. Getting to and working on a bomb in this position would not be easy.

By the time his squad arrived, the sun was already hot: it would be a scorching day for working out in the open. As there was little for them to do until he had decided how to tackle the bomb, Carroll told the sergeant to give his men leave to cool off in the waters of the creek, with a reminder to keep well clear of the UXB.

We took our time over that one. It took us a whole day to deal with it – we took the opportunity to go swimming. We had to hold our breath of course to deal with the bomb. But we also enjoyed ourselves for once.[8]

Meanwhile, Carroll pondered the question of disposal. He swam out to the marker buoy, took a deep breath and dived down. The bomb had a single fuze in its base, but at this depth he would not have time to unscrew the base plate and remove it without special breathing equipment. For the same reason, it was not practical to attach ropes and recover the carcass from the sea bed; nor could it be left there with its load of TNT intact.

Carroll considered a controlled explosion. There were no buildings or vessels within 100 feet and the water would absorb some of the blast. Yet the sea presented a further problem: normal explosives would not work effectively in water; instead he had to use a special technique. Normally a man of few words in his Weekly Bomb Disposal Report, this time Lt Carroll gave a detailed description of the action he took: 'Depth: approx 10 feet. Bomb demolished by means of proximity charge of 15lbs Ammonal and G.C.' (gun cotton).[9]

The *Regia Aeronautica* were changing tactics. They began to use large high explosive bombs, giving Lieutenant Carroll another challenging UXB a short distance from the 'dark cave' of Ghar Dalam above St George's Bay. Used as a dwelling by Malta's very first inhabitants in prehistoric times, the 470-foot cave was adopted as an air raid shelter at the start of the war. Now it had been taken over by the military and housed a vital fuel storage depot. The Army unit on guard had survived a near miss, and a 500lb Italian bomb lay dangerously close to the stored fuel.

Lieutenant Carroll hurried to take a look and saw immediately that one of the fuze holders was partly detached. Any disturbance might detonate the bomb and set off the entire depot along with its massive stores of fuel. There was no time to lose. Steadying himself for an instant, he grabbed hold of the entire fuze mechanism and wrenched it away from the bomb. The remaining fuze came out easily and the bomb was relatively harmless. But there was still the problem of disposing of the carcass. He could not abandon a 500lb bomb packed with explosive just yards from the cave, in case another enemy bomb or stray shell exploded it – and for the same reason he could not explode the bomb. It should be removed, but the bomb disposal lorry was miles away on another job. There was one possible solution: to burn out the filling. The process took time, but once it was done the harmless empty casing could be abandoned to the elements.

The Italian pilots were getting bolder. In the early hours of Monday 7 July 1941 they dropped several bombs on the dockyard residential area of Paola. Seven exploded but two were reported next morning as Priority UXBs and Carroll responded straight away. While his squad uncovered one bomb, he examined the other which lay on the surface: it was an Italian 250lb HE. This time both the nose and base fuzes were partly broken. In this precarious state they could easily fire if any attempt was made to extract them. A bomb in this condition should ideally be blown in situ, but in such a busy place it was out of the question. There was no option but to get it away somehow and then deal with it, but where? All around him were dockyards, ammunition stores, forts and gun positions – not to mention civilian homes. What if he could get the bomb to the coast? Then perhaps it could be ditched in the sea.

It had to be somewhere nearby which could be reached by a road well clear of the built-up areas. The road must have a good surface so as not to jolt the bomb on its journey. He decided on San Pietru. It would be a delicate operation. He had to ask the police to clear the route so that the public were kept at a safe distance while the bomb was transported. While that was being organised, Carroll went back to the buried bomb – another Italian 250lb, another pair of broken fuzes. Now there were two highly sensitive bombs to be got away somehow. A large bed of sandbags was prepared in the back of the lorry. The process of winching up and loading each bomb was a risky business. Any disturbance of the fuzes could spell disaster. Once in place the carcasses were wedged in position and then covered with more sandbags before being driven slowly and gently away. It was a job the lorry driver and his mates did not enjoy.

A week later there was another abrupt change of tactics by the *Regia Aeronautica*. Carroll and his men were called out to towns and villages, searchlight batteries and gun positions far and wide, from Malta's sister island of Gozo in the north to Hal Far in the south, and from Mgarr in the west to Marsaxlokk in the south-east. Italian bombers had gone back to using the smaller 15kg HE bombs, which they were scattering liberally across the archipelago. The sheer spread of bomb disposal work was using a lot of manpower and petrol – resources in short supply. Carroll needed an alternative way to manage the situation; he decided to delegate authority to his senior NCOs. So many 15kg bombs had their fuzes snapped off. Although bombs with damaged fuzes were normally referred to the BD officer, he now knew that these 15kg were safe to pick up and transport, if it was done with care. He instructed his NCOs that if they came across a bomb in this condition they could go ahead with its removal. The new arrangements were timely: more bombs were soon reported in eight different locations; only one had to be referred to the bomb disposal officer.

Just after one o'clock in the morning of Monday 21 July, three RAF Wellingtons headed towards Malta, hot on the tail of three bombers from the *Regia Aeronautica*. One Italian pilot managed to release his bomb load over Luqa, leaving two unexploded bombs. The other two headed out over Grand Harbour and were seen to drop their bombs after they had passed the coastline. Next evening two more enemy aircraft tried a similar approach; one of them succeeded in attacking Grand Harbour from the east, dropping bombs on the Three Cities. A convoy was heading for Malta, and the enemy were using heavier weapons again.

Later that morning Lieutenant Carroll picked up a UXB report from the weekend's raids: a large UXB lay in a street in Senglea, just above French Creek. He was somewhat taken aback to find it was a 500kg German bomb – only the second he had seen since the beginning of June. Inevitably, sticking out beyond the bomb-casing was an extension cap. As usual the cap was badly distorted and it would be difficult, if not impossible, to get at the fuze. Here was a large German bomb – the first in a long while – with a fuze which could not be identified and which must be treated as a possible delayed-action type. Leaning forward again to place his ear close to the fuze pocket, Carroll could detect no audible sign of ticking. He had to be sure. He gave orders for the electric stethoscope to be unloaded. A microphone was attached to the carcass of the bomb, its cable played out as far as the safe point from where an NCO could listen for any ticking via headphones. Carroll paused a moment to weigh up the odds: DA fuzes were less common in 500kg than 250kg bombs. He looked around him at the location: the bomb was too close to a main road to be exploded in situ. There was no alternative but to shift it, complete with fuze. Yet again, the lorry made a perilous journey to San Pietru.

Returning to Lintorn Barracks with news of his find, Carroll learned that rumours were circulating about an Italian pilot flying a Luftwaffe bomber and dropping German HE bombs: it was not long before two more turned up as UXBs. The other disposal jobs from Monday's raid were Italian – one 200lb bomb at Qormi and another at Luqa. They were the last high explosive bombs the RE Bomb Disposal Section would face for almost six weeks. They were about to encounter a different kind of challenge.

The incoming convoy docked in Grand Harbour on Thursday 24 July, bringing further reinforcements to the Fortress Engineers. Seven officers and 223 other ranks of No. 173 Tunnelling Company had arrived, and were billeted in quarters at Msida Bastion, beneath the main Lintorn Barracks.

It wasn't only the approaching convoy which seemed to have attracted the interest of enemy aircraft. They had been spotted making reconnaissance flights over the Island for some time. In the middle of Friday morning, Malta's Hurricane aircraft engaged one SM79 and an escort of Macchi fighters as they approached Grand Harbour; two of the Macchis were shot down into the sea but a third crashed into the ruins of a house in Valletta's main street, Kingsway. The events were witnessed by a stunned group of Royal Engineers, some of whom were later placed on duty to guard the site.

The drama was but a prelude to one of the most remarkable events of the second siege of Malta. Like many residents of Valletta, Carroll was kept awake through the night of Friday 25 July thanks to constant raids, including a full-scale attack on the city and its surroundings, which was met by equally determined defensive fire. Then at about 5am a fresh barrage rattled out from the harbour guns. The Italian Navy had assembled a miniature fleet with the aim of launching a seaborne attack on the newly-arrived convoy. At 4.30am a flotilla of vessels assembled off Grand Harbour, including two fast torpedo-boats, nine explosive boats (MTs) and two manned 'Human Torpedoes'. Their objective was to destroy the protective net suspended off Fort St Elmo which prevented access to the harbour. The explosion of two MTs brought down the barrier but in doing so blocked the path of the remaining vessels. Having made their presence known, the would-be invaders were met with a resounding counter-attack by the defensive gunners of the Harbour Fire Command, who had been looking for just such an opportunity to show their increased strength and skill. None of the MTs escaped their fire. Roused by the immense noise almost everyone in and around Valletta – including Lieutenant Carroll – crowded on bastions or rooftops to watch the exchange. They were rewarded with a blazing display of criss-cross fire intermingled with searchlights illuminating the sea and sky – and a feeling of immense pride to see the attempted invasion resoundingly overcome, in what seemed like a matter of minutes.

Just as dawn was breaking on Tuesday 12 August, nine aircraft passed over Grand Harbour and spread out as they headed inland. Observers watched with alarm the trails of flames given off by countless clusters of small bombs as they fell to earth. Within seconds, dozens of fires flared up all over the Island. In the heat of summer, tinder-dry wooden structures and crops began to burn. Hundreds of incendiary bombs had been showered onto towns, villages and countryside. The central information office issued an urgent warning notice to the public: 'All householders are reminded that temporary fittings or structures of an inflammable nature should be removed from housetops to minimise the chance of fires taking a hold as a result of falling incendiary bombs.'[10]

Inevitably many did not ignite, and by mid-morning Carroll was look-ing at one of the dozens scattered across the village of Zejtun. Another new weapon had joined the arsenal of the *Regia Aeronautica* in their campaign against Malta – a 2kg incendiary. Lieutenant Carroll and his sergeant recov-ered a number of examples for analysis. Their findings were noted in the War Diary of the Fortress Royal Engineers:

> A new incendiary bomb dropped on night 11/12 August. The bombs have no markings or numbers of any sort. Each batch dropped consisted of over 40 mixed up with a larger number, estimated at 200, of small H.E. bombs marked TRITOLO SAV 937. Each batch fell roughly in a line about a mile long. The resulting fires on stone or earth lasted about 10 minutes. It is obvious that the objective was aircraft or petrol dumps.[11]

More details were added in a further report forwarded to the War Office by cable from Malta's governor and commander in chief:

> Comprises two cylinders joined end to end. One cylinder apparently steel casing containing fuel oil other cylinder electron casing containing thermite. Overall length 12″ diameter 2¾ ″ painted dark grey. Actuating mechanism contained under phosphor bronze cap screwed on end of thermite cylin-der. Mechanism armed by arming vane which unscrews safety pin from cap. Flashes seen in mid-air behind enemy planes during raid make it seem likely that several bombs are loaded into one container which explodes and discharges them in mid-air. Further investigations are in hand.[12]

It took two days to clear 56 unexploded incendiaries from the initial attacks. The raiders had dropped their loads along a six-mile route from Zejtun, through Marsa and Hamrun to Birkirkara and Lija. In nearly every case the fuze fired but failed to ignite the filling. Once he confirmed that the bombs were harmless if handled gently, Carroll could delegate the job of clearing them to his NCOs, each leading small squads of two or three sappers. They spent the rest of the month removing incendiaries from all over the Island. Thankfully it meant there was no digging to do under the hot August sun. Then the end of the month brought another welcome change – a whole week free of disturbing night raids.

The luxury of quiet nights could not last. In September 1941, the Italians reverted almost entirely to night bombing. The repeated intrusion of single bombers, usually over the most densely-populated areas around Grand Harbour, deprived residents of much-needed sleep. What the *Regia Aeronautica* may have lacked in aggression, they were making up for in unpredictability. The incendiaries did not achieve the desired destructive effect: the Maltese limestone had once again proved impervious to enemy weapons. With offensive actions from Malta-based forces becoming increasingly successful across the Mediterranean, the Italians began using heavier HE bombs again. And after alternating between incendiary and HE bombs, they began to drop both types during a single raid.

On the morning of 9 September Carroll was called out to Dingli by one of his NCOs. His squad had revealed the first of two small bombs, six feet under the narrow strip of fertile farmland overlooking the sea, below the Island's radar station. The NCO did not recognise the bomb. Carroll climbed down the ladder to take a look: from its size he estimated it at 50kg, but from its markings it was Italian – and certainly not one he had seen before. The NCO had reported that the bomb's base fuze was broken – so with any luck it might be harmless. But if the central part of the fuze was still in place, it could be in a highly-sensitive condition. Carroll's worst fears were confirmed; any attempt to take out this fuze could detonate the bomb. Better to set a charge himself and have a controlled explosion. Unfortunately they were too close to the radar station, especially if the second bomb went up as well. What if that one could be got out of the way first?

Carroll walked across to take a look: the lads were making good progress and the bomb was already exposed. He climbed six feet down the ladder into the shaft and squatted down beside the bomb: another damaged fuze. Now he had two bombs that were too unstable to move. Nor could they be exploded this close to the radar station. He had just one more option – but it meant putting himself at risk. The entire base plate would have to be unscrewed from each bomb. It was possible, but it had to be done without disturbing the broken fuze. Twice.

He gave the order for the men to retreat. This was a job for the bomb disposal officer alone. As soon as his sergeant signalled that they were out of range, Carroll began to unscrew the base plate of the first bomb, taking care to avoid touching the vulnerable fuze. Grasping it firmly, he gently eased it away from the carcass and climbed the ladder with his prize. Soon the second base plate was off and Carroll could afford to relax. However, there was the matter of yet another unknown bomb to consider. He ordered the parts of both bombs to be carried back to Lintorn Barracks. He had a report to write.

By the end of the day Carroll would have a second report to prepare. That afternoon an NCO discovered an unfamiliar UXB lying in the rubble of a ruined building in Hamrun. It was an unusual shape – about 32 inches long – and only 4 inches in diameter. It was an Italian anti-personnel bomb, weighing in at 12kg. This time it was possible to neutralise the fuze so the bomb could be taken back to the barracks as a specimen.

Thanks to the *Regia Aeronautica* the number of new bombs needing to be examined and kept as examples was increasing daily. Carroll was finding it difficult to manage. He needed a secure workshop and store, somewhere within the barracks but far enough from the main buildings in case of any explosion. He submitted a request to the CO. No.173 Tunnelling Company had been busy since their arrival in the summer but the construction of the new facility for bomb disposal was soon well underway. It was not long before Carroll moved into his new premises, hollowed out from the rocky bastions beneath Lintorn Barracks, close to the Polverista Gate.

Working so often alone, out and about across the Island, friendships were very important to Carroll. It was a while since he had seen his friend Edward Talbot, now busy with the RAF. In between his bomb disposal duties Carroll made the most of his contacts in the Maltese community. As a Catholic he was often referred to by the Maltese as 'one of us'. And with transport severely restricted, and community links fragmented, he provided a useful communication service for his friends.

> I was often out on my motorbike, working with my men up towards the north, beyond Naxxar for instance. When I was returning in the evening, I would pass the homes of Maltese friends, who might invite me to stay for dinner. For such families I became a carrier of news and gossip. They would ask me something like: 'When you next see the Preciosa's, would you tell them Millie's had her baby? They're both doing fine.'[13]

Early in September 1941 Lieutenant Carroll received a visit from the Royal Engineers Garrison's visiting priest, Father Orr. He was looking for a Master of Ceremonies to compere a charity concert, due to take place on 12 September at Dragonara Palace. The officer was pleased to help; the event would provide a welcome change from his military duties, as well as a chance to visit one of the most beautiful buildings on the Island. The host was the Marquis Scicluna, chairman of Malta's main brewery and husband of the Baroness of Tabria. Their concert was a great success and gave Carroll the opportunity to meet the Marquis and Marquesa, and particularly their two daughters and two sons, with whom he became good friends.

At the end of September, as a convoy approached from Gibraltar, Italian bombers redoubled attacks with incendiaries as well as high explosives. It seemed that the solo Luftwaffe bomber was still on the prowl: two reported UXBs turned out to be German 50kg. Then a 500kg German bomb was reported by the Gunners at Salina Bay. Carroll gave a wry smile at the competence of his Italian enemies when he saw the fuze had not been charged before the bomb was released from the aircraft. The War Diary of Malta's General Staff provided a possible explanation, commenting that the standard of enemy bomber crews appeared to be deteriorating.

With his workload reasonably under control, Carroll arrived at Lintorn Barracks on Saturday 11 October anticipating a relatively quiet weekend. But he could not relax until he checked whether any critical UXB reports had come in overnight. As he neared his office, the Company Adjutant came towards him, white-faced. Lieutenant Talbot was missing. George Carroll was stunned: how could this have happened?

The day before, Lieutenant Talbot had boarded RAF Blenheim ZL7638, one of four Blenheim aircraft from 107 Squadron based at RAF Luqa and sent to attack ships off the coast of Southern Italy. Talbot's plane was piloted by Wing Commander F.A. Harte, DFC.[14]

Some time later, two of the Blenheims returned, forced to turn back due to engine trouble. Hours passed with no sign of the other two aircraft. Eventually, the operations room at Luqa reluctantly chalked them up as missing. Then RAF intelligence monitoring picked up something from Italian radio. A report was saying that two RAF Blenheims were observed colliding in mid-air off the coast, while taking evasive action under enemy fire. If the Italian report was accurate, there was only one possible conclusion. The Fortress Engineers War Diary recorded the event in a few telling words.

No. 400411 A/Lt E. E. A. C. Talbot. RE, GC, MBE (attached RAF) reported missing, believed killed whilst flying over Sicily. For the last weeks he had been acting as liaison officer to RAF at the Bomber Aerodrome, Luqa.[15]

Malta's governor and commander in chief could waste no time in applying for a replacement for Talbot. When he cabled his request to the War Office on 16 October, he was called upon to explain the loss of a bomb disposal officer. Lieutenant-General Dobbie replied:

> Lieutenant Talbot attached RAF station Luqa for Intelligence duties … Army and RAF Intelligence officers exchanged periodically by local arrangements between AOC and GOC … In order to ensure adequate liaison with RAF I have found it necessary in the general interest of the Fortress to attach four specially selected officers for air intelligence duties. Three officers are attached to aerodromes and one does duty with RAF headquarters.[16]

The loss was of Edward Talbot was not only a blow to the Royal Engineers Bomb Disposal establishment, it was a personal tragedy to Lieutenant Carroll, who was deeply affected by the death of his friend.

> Because Edward didn't have a job any more, after I had taken over, he got attached to the RAF as an intelligence officer. He was taking in reports of returning pilots and he decided that, with this responsibility, he should know something about what it was like to be on a raid. So he volunteered and went off, in a Blenheim I think, and didn't come back. That was how he lost his life, after being in bomb disposal.[17]

Lieutenant Ellis Edward Chetwynd Talbot, GC, MBE was buried in the Catania War Cemetery in Sicily. He was 21 years old.

Notes

1 Lieutenant G.D. Carroll 2005
2 ibid.
3 ibid.
4 ibid.
5 Lieutenant G.D. Carroll, 2008
6 Ed. (1941) *Situation Reports & Operational Messages Out*. WO 106 National Archives, London.
7 Ed. (1941). War Diary Fortress Engineers, Malta. WO 169, National Archives, London.
8 Lieutenant G.D. Carroll 2005
9 Ed. (1941). War Diary Fortress Engineers, Malta. WO 169, National Archives, London.
10 Notice issued from Lieutenant Governor's Office, August 1941: Galea, M. (1992). *Malta Diary of a War 1940–1945*. Malta: Publishers Enterprises Group.
11 Ed. (1941). War Diary Fortress Engineers, Malta. WO 169, National Archives, London.
12 Ed. (1941) *Situation Reports & Operational Messages Out*. WO 106 National Archives, London.
13 Lieutenant G.D. Carroll 2005
14 Also in the crew were Pilot Officer C.O. Bloodworth as an Observer, and Flying Officer T. Wewege-Smith as wireless operator.
15 Ed. (1941). *War Diary Fortress Engineers, Malta*. WO 169, National Archives, London.
16 Ed. (1941) *Situation Reports & Operational Messages Out*. WO 106 National Archives, London.
17 Lieutenant G.D. Carroll 2005

CHAPTER 7

DEADLY THERMOS

I had to get them out. I couldn't carry them: depending as they did on vibration to explode, they could go off and destroy me.[1]

It had been a long and uncomfortable night. With no enemy encounters to stir their blood, a steady rain chilled the harbour Gunners to the bone. At 1.30am the sound of the air-raid alert jolted them into action. Before the searchlights could pick up the intruders, bursts of machine-gun fire rattled out in the distance, followed by the scream of an aircraft plummeting downwards. Got one! Some of the RAF lads must be out there. The Gunners sprang into action as the searchlight beams picked up three more enemy planes heading straight for the submarine base. They opened fire but could not prevent the Italians from dropping their bombs over Manoel Island, Lazaretto Creek and Valletta. Two hours later, the rising note of the air raid siren heralded another pack of four planes approaching the coast. This time the searchlights picked up only one – and he was heading straight for them. Managing to evade the defensive fire, the pilot made a sweeping dive over Valletta and released his load before turning back out to sea. As the morning light crept into the city, it illuminated hundreds of small metal cylinders lying scattered through the streets: bombs.

Leaving his pension in South Street that Saturday morning, 1 November, Lieutenant Carroll turned into Kingsway to find policemen trying to cordon off a large area. One of them recognised the bomb disposal officer and told him what had happened. They had already counted dozens of small bombs within just a few hundred yards and reports were still pouring in. Carroll asked the policeman to show him. The constable walked a dozen paces and pointed. The bomb disposal officer recognised the shape.

> I had [previously] received a report that the Italians were using bombs looking like Thermos flasks. They were small, pale coffee colour, and they had a cap on top which was split into a propeller. I believe an Italian professor of mechanics had designed the device for North Africa's airfields as a scatter bomb. It was designed to hit the ground but not to go off until it was disturbed. An aircraft starting up, or passing vehicles, would produce a vibration, causing it to explode suddenly and cause panic. The fragments would also be enough to damage an aeroplane. The bombs were designed to drop in the dust of North Africa, where they could lie undetected but, affected by vibration, to go off unexpectedly at a later time.
>
> But they didn't drop them on Hal Far or Ta' Qali; they dropped them on Valletta.[2]

The Italians had introduced a deadly weapon to their campaign against Malta and this time the target seemed to be the Island's people. Looking very like the harmless domestic flask, the Thermos bomb would easily attract the curiosity of innocent passers-by – especially children – who might pick it up unaware of the consequences. Although small, the bomb contained about 1kg of high explosive and could kill someone in the open up to 35 metres away. Released from the aircraft in canisters containing dozens of bombs, they scattered as they landed: each container-load could cover an area of up to 300 square metres. Lieutenant Carroll made his way quickly to Lintorn Barracks. His first priority was to issue a message via the police and the Information Office to warn the Maltese that if they came across anything looking like a Thermos flask, not to touch it, but to report it to the authorities straight away. The *Times of Malta* published the announcement with strongly-worded warnings to the public regarding the new and dangerous bombs.

The bomb disposal officer had to find a way of freeing the streets of Thermos bombs – and quickly. The task would be far from easy. Initially used in the Italian campaign in Libya, the delayed-arming AR-4 (*Armamento*

Retardato) model of the bomb was not fully armed until it hit the ground, where it lay waiting for any disturbance to set it off at random. Since it was highly sensitive to movement, as a UXB it was very difficult to deal with. To complicate matters, a proportion of Thermos bombs contained a delayed-action fuze, which could detonate, with or without disturbance, up to 80 hours after the bomb fell. There was no question of Carroll's men simply carrying them away, like the numerous small incendiaries. This bomb was designed to explode if it was disturbed. Nor was there any possibility of disarming them – the bomb disposal technical bulletin was definite about that. Every single one would have to be exploded. Arriving at the barracks, Carroll called up all available men for bomb disposal duties and assembled them for a briefing. The sappers were divided into small squads, each working under the command of a NCO, and given a batch of UXB reports of Thermos bombs for a designated area. The bomb disposal officer stressed the hazardous nature of these bombs and gave instructions on how to handle them.

The standard procedure was to blow up the Thermos bomb where it lay, following the usual precautions to protect people and property. In suitable locations such as open country this could be done by a shot from a rifle. If that was not practical, a noose on the end of a 100-yard cord was looped around the bomb, avoiding any contact which could disturb the mechanism. After retreating to cover, the cord was jerked swiftly and hard, to trigger the explosion. Sandbags should be placed around the bomb to localise the effect. If the bomb did not explode by this method, it must be reported to the bomb disposal officer to decide appropriate action. Inky Reeves was one of the sappers sent out to dispose of Thermos bombs. His first one lay in the window of a jeweller's shop in the centre of Valletta:

[The jeweller] begged us not to blow it up but to take it to the police station. This we could not do, so we asked him to take out his goods from the window but on no account to touch the bomb. He would not go near it, so one of the lads removed his stock for him and then we pulled the bomb. We made an awful mess but at least his stock was safe.[3]

Throughout the day reports of unexploded Thermos bombs poured in to Bomb Disposal HQ. By nightfall, the BD section had cleared 93 from

Valletta, plus another 35 from the countryside near Gharghur. In between, Carroll had other pressing work to do, answering a call from Manoel Island. A Priority UXB had been reported by the 7th HAA Regiment, Royal Artillery. The gunner who showed Carroll where to find the bomb had a disturbing story to tell. At 3am, while his comrades were asleep in their beds, two bombs hit their accommodation block. One exploded, killing five men. The second fell on a nearby room, landing on one of the sleeping gunners, killing him instantly. Yet it did not explode and his roommates escaped unharmed. Carroll was in a sombre mood as he entered the room to defuze the Italian 500lb bomb.

Checking on progress in the city that afternoon, the bomb disposal officer was beginning to feel satisfied with the way his BD section and the civilian authorities were rising to the challenge of the Thermos bombs. He had just returned to Lintorn Barracks, when 'I got a message: "We have several Thermos flask bombs in the police station," which was in the basement of the Opera House.'[4]

Lieutenant Carroll could hardly believe what he was hearing. He had been concerned that civilians might pick up the bombs; now it seemed that the police were ignoring his instructions and putting themselves in danger by doing so. He started out at a brisk pace for the Opera House to see for himself. The duty officer led him to a room behind the front offices, where the lieutenant was stunned to see some three dozen Thermos bombs and fuzes, lined up on a shelf on the opposite wall. Giving orders that in no circumstances were the bombs to be moved or touched in any way, he advised the station's senior officer of the consequences should even one of them explode. Carroll informed him in no uncertain terms that the entire Opera House had been placed in jeopardy, and that the police station ought to be evacuated with immediate effect.

Leaving the police to consider their predicament, and promising to return shortly, Carroll went back to Lintorn Barracks where he requested an urgent meeting with his commanding officer. As bomb disposal officer, Carroll told the CO that the only way to dispose of the Thermos bombs stored in the Opera House was to explode them where they were. Lieutenant-Colonel McMeekan was not slow to understand the gravity of the situation but he could not agree to the detonation of the bombs – with the implications for the Opera House – until he consulted further. He dictated an urgent letter expressing the advice of Lieutenant Carroll to the commissioner of police: it was delivered by dispatch rider the same day. The letter made very plain the views of the CO of the Engineers:

> This morning your Valletta policemen picked up about 35 Thermos bombs and carried them to a cellar under the Opera House. This is contrary to all instructions, and was either a very brave or a very foolish act. But it probably saved some lives as boys might have picked them up. They were lucky to get away with it – some civilians were not so fortunate.
>
> It cannot be too widely known that the 'Thermos' bomb is designed to become alive when it hits the ground. It only explodes when somebody moves it <u>after</u> it has landed. They are therefore NOT TO BE touched ...[5]

In the letter, Lieutenant Carroll took the opportunity to reinforce the correct procedure for reported Thermos bombs, for the attention of all police personnel and ARP wardens. In view of the high numbers of bombs being dropped, he added a new measure: in affected areas the 'All Clear' should not be sounded until those streets were cordoned off, and their occupants had been warned to look out for and report any suspected Thermos. Each bomb should be marked with a warning sign and surrounded on all sides with sandbags (or large stones). Traffic must not be allowed within 20 feet. The bomb disposal section would get to them as soon as possible.

The Chief of Police circulated the instructions, with a strong reminder of the dangers, to all police and civil defence authorities. The message reached Valletta ARP Superintendent C. Spiteri, who was alarmed when he realised its significance:

> When these first started to be dropped during late 1941, I did not realise how easily they could explode when touched and I instructed my men to pick them up slowly and deliver them to the police station. We picked up a good number of them and, strangely enough, none exploded. Later we received orders not to touch them, but to report their presence to the authorities.[6]

Their letter dispatched, Lieutenant-Colonel McMeekan and the bomb disposal officer returned to the pressing matter of the Opera House. The

Lieutenant Governor had been informed and contacted the Fortress Engineers to ask whether damage to the building could be avoided, for example by carrying the bombs out by hand. The reply left no doubt as to the unacceptable risk of attempting such an action.

Meanwhile, Carroll was pondering the situation, well aware of the symbolic importance of the Opera House. The elegant colonnaded building towered grandly over him as he walked to and from the barracks each day. He knew that everything possible must be done to try and save it. With his knowledge of mechanical engineering he believed he could devise a method of getting the Thermos bombs out. Returning to his CO with his proposal, he received the go-ahead to develop the necessary apparatus, and then to fix a date for the removal operation, as soon as other obligations allowed. Until then Carroll decided to surround the bombs with a protective shield of sandbags. Returning to the Opera House, he gave the police the news: there was no question of removing the Thermos bombs until a later date. He explained his plan for the sandbags and ordered his men to begin installation. Even this operation carried a high level of risk and had to be carried out in a controlled manner. Any violent movement close to the shelves could set off one of the bombs and explode all of them, with devastating consequences.

The situation in the Opera House did not escape the notice of the *Times of Malta*, which covered the story on 4 November 1941.

In a recent raid the enemy adopted cowardly tactics in attacking civilians. Well aware from the publicity given in the world press of the safety afforded by our rock shelters, an enemy raider, which met the fate it deserved, dropped a comparatively large number of mickie-mouse bombs or booby traps, which did not explode on impact with the ground as they fell, but which became highly dangerous when handled by inexperienced persons. Among their victims were two young boys and a woman.

It appears that the police during and after the raid found a large number of these small unexploded bombs … These dangerous missiles were picked up and carried to the police station, where they were lined up in a row … Indubitably the police exceeded their instructions when they handled these bombs; their quick clearance, however, fortunately without fatal accidents to the Force, undoubtedly saved life, for these bombs, lying about in the street, would have been a deadly trap for unsuspecting persons and children proceeding to and from the shelters during the night's air raids.[7]

It would be some time before Carroll could return to the thorny problem of the Opera House. Reports of Thermos bombs continued to stream in, as the UXBs were discovered in increasingly widespread locations – seemingly scattered indiscriminately across towns, villages and countryside. The bomb disposal section dealt with 20 or more around Mellieha on the northeast coast, plus others in Madliena and Gharghur, and closer to home in St Patrick's and Floriana. On Thursday 6 November they worked from 9am until 4pm on a batch at Ricasoli.

Exactly a week after the first attack, on the night of Saturday 8 November, a single aircraft again dropped Thermos bombs. This time the target was Rabat. Philo Pullicino was soon in touch with his friend Carroll, asking for help. There were dozens of unexploded Thermos bombs across the hilltop town. The bomb disposal officer lost no time in mobilising his men, and the entire BD section assembled in Rabat. Carroll joined Philo, local police and ARP wardens to co-ordinate teams of sappers in the long and difficult process of locating and detonating all 80 unexploded Thermos bombs.

One report given to Sapper Tom Meager and his mate was from an elegant private house, where they were directed upstairs to a bedroom. Gingerly, Tom opened the door and scanned the room: nothing. He stepped inside. Watching where he put his feet, he tiptoed slowly across the room. There it was – on the floor at the foot of the bed. He looked up, curious: the bomb must have come through the window somehow. According to instructions, Tom knew they should loop a string over the bomb and get out of here – exploding the bomb from under cover outside the building. But it didn't seem right somehow, to destroy a home. Using his initiative, Tom decided on a bold action. He called his mate in to help him:

I sat on the end of the bed and the chap that was with me was on the veranda, looking out … I said 'Check down there and make sure everybody's clear.' The police had been told beforehand to make sure everybody was either clear of the area or stayed indoors. I said [to my mate]: 'Are they clear yet?' and he said, 'Yes, all clear.'

So I bent down and picked this thing up like that [resting horizontally on two open hands] and carried it to the window. Just as I put my arms out of the window to drop it, [my mate] said, 'Hold it – a woman has just come out of the door up the road!' and I said, 'Well tell her to get back inside!' He yelled at her but she wouldn't go back in. She went on up the road, so I hung on there, thinking 'Come on, hurry up!'

I said, 'I've got to let it go!' and I did. And I'm sure to this day that it went off before it hit the ground. But the woman was safe enough.[8]

Next day there were even more Thermos bombs needing attention: 143 reports had come in from Birkirkara. They were scattered everywhere among the houses, military and government premises located in the growing town. Lieutenant Carroll and his men spent another long day scouring its streets, ensuring every single bomb was gone before they themselves departed. Day after day more were reported across the Island – sometimes singly, often in batches. Thermos bombs would keep them busy for the rest of November.

In the midst of all the activity for the bomb disposal section, night raids returned to disturb their rest. On the night of 10 November they were kept awake by a series of five raids – one each hour from ten in the evening. Now their work was not confined to Thermos bombs. Bombing with high explosive and incendiaries was stepped up, often hitting civilian targets. Carroll concentrated on the HE bombs, calling on detachments of sappers for digging when required. Friday 21 November was spent in Mosta, tackling a total of 66 incendiaries. While the sappers worked, the Italians carried out a series of the daytime raids which were becoming a feature of working life. Air raid warnings sounded at around 7am, 9am, 2pm, 5pm and 7pm, a pattern repeated on Saturday and Sunday.

Every now and then a reported unexploded bomb turned out to be a false alarm. An Ack-Ack shell hole, or a crater made by a smaller bomb which had already exploded, could sometimes be mistaken for the entry point of a UXB. While the bomb disposal section was busy tackling hundreds of Thermos bombs, one particular report received by Carroll was not at all what it seemed.

I received an urgent report of an unexploded bomb from a member of the Governor's staff. The location was away from the normal targets but naturally I attended immediately. I reported to a sentry at the gate, who showed me where the bomb lay. I walked over to the bushes and lying on the ground was an object the length of two cocoa tins, and a similar diameter, joined together and roughly painted in green which matched the Italian uniform, with a crudely drawn axe and faggots, the symbol of the fascists.

I believed it to be a hoax bomb. Nevertheless, it had to be treated with respect: I picked it up, with ceremony, took it away and reported that the bomb had been removed. No doubt the Governor was pleased.

I believed I knew who was responsible for the hoax. I had become friendly with a family ...and I had recently won a bet with one of the boys, that I could get a letter published in the newspaper. I won the bet. He had been quite annoyed about it and I was not surprised to think that he might have created a hoax bomb for me to deal with.[9]

Years later the real culprit may have been revealed as another adventurous young scholar, Ing. Maurice Mifsud Bonnici, who recalls the events of Saturday 22 November 1941 at St Aloysius' College, Birkirkara:

During the preceding night there were the usual raids. Round about 7.30 on that Saturday morning, after each division mustered in the college grounds under its Prefect, all boys proceeded for the usual morning mass. In church a rumour continued to be passed around that a bomb fell in the college ground near the entrance of the shelter. There were boys who like me said that they had seen it. The news got round like forest fire and when the boys got out of church, they darted towards the spot.

By Jove there was the bomb! There on a heap of rubble by the shelter entrance. At a safe distance the boys could see a green cylindrical object, long about two spans, with a coiled wire placed along it. It looked ominous and nobody dared to approach it further as children were repeatedly warned by their parents and the authorities against these strange objects that exploded when touched.

The bell rang and all the boys proceeded, in an orderly manner, to their respective classes. After a short time a policeman appeared on the scene and mounted guard on this dangerous object. In those dismal days, half of the college building was converted into an emergency hospital accommodating some 400 beds. By mere coincidence the Governor, Sir William Dobbie decided to pay an unofficial visit to that hospital on the very day of the incident. The Rector, Fr Joseph Delia s.j. thought it fit to inform His Excellency about the bomb ...

The military authorities were alerted, and having been informed that the Governor was around, took up the matter more seriously than they normally would have done ... By this time the Governor had left the hospital after requesting the Rector to keep him informed about the outcome. In no time the Bomb Disposal Unit were on site. The college hospital inmates, whose beds were in the rooms overlooking the college ground, were shifted to a safer place and all windows were opened wide ...

The officer in charge of the Unit lifted the object and discovered that the contraption was nothing more than two empty tins of meat and vegetables preserve, joined together at their open ends, painted green with the Fascist Symbol, serial number and date, '*gennaio ...*' in silver paint on one end and a coiled wire placed along its length terminating on a radio single-pin plug fixed to the other end, making the contraption look veritably ominous. It was a fake anti-personnel bomb which I contrived solely with the boyish hope that we would be given a day off from school while the 'danger' lasted![10]

In between organising the disposal of dozens of real Thermos, incendiary and HE bombs reported each day, Carroll spent time developing and testing his apparatus for removing the Thermos bombs from the Opera House. The room they were in was almost entirely underground but there was a window in one wall which opened on to a terrace outside. Opposite the window was an open space, in front of the entrance to the former railway station under the bastions of Valletta. He decided the best way to get the bombs out was through this window.

Yet it would have to be done without actually handling a single bomb, which could prove fatal. His knowledge of mechanical engineering had never been more useful: his life was about to depend on it. The challenge was to devise a method of picking up and transporting each Thermos bomb across the basement room to the window and then onwards into the space outside – all by remote control. Lieutenant Carroll decided on a suspended 'railway' of cords and pulleys, which could be operated from a position outside the room, to provide suitable cover in case of an accident.

So how could each bomb be taken up and away from the shelf? He hit on the idea of a mechanical grabbing device – like the ones used in penny arcades to manoeuvre tantalisingly over prizes – but this time, the grab had to collect its prey successfully first time, every time. Its jaws must open wide enough for it to be arched over the bomb on the shelf. Then it had to be closed gently, with minimum disturbance to the bomb. His design involved two horseshoe-shaped grabs, one at each end of a horizontal rod, linked so that they operated simultaneously with a single cord, which could be worked from a distance. After a number of prototypes, his final version went through several tests and adjustments before he was satisfied.

Now for the bomb's second journey, away from the building. The suspended grab would lower the bomb into a sand-filled tray in the window well. From there Lieutenant Carroll designed a second string railway, operated by remote control from outside, to hoist the tray with its bomb from the window well and transport it away from the building. Its journey would end in a sandbag emplacement, where it could be exploded. Carroll was ready to inform the Chief of Police that the Opera House basement could be cleared. Work would begin on Monday 1 December.

While Lieutenant Carroll and his sergeant installed the string railway inside the cellar, another NCO and working party constructed a sandbag emplacement in the street opposite the window well and lined it with steel plates to absorb the force of an explosion. The second string railway was erected, suspended between tripods in the square outside. Finally, everything was in place. A trial run was essential – any malfunction could be fatal. A dummy bomb was placed in the grab to test the system for any last-minute snags. To begin with, the railway didn't work smoothly and the cramped conditions in the basement didn't help: some of the rings and pulleys needed to be realigned. It was time for the real thing.

Because of the risks involved in the operation, only one person would remain in the cellar to operate the delicate mechanism – Carroll himself. He would control the cords from outside the storeroom door. At the same time he could monitor the effect of the operation on the remaining bombs. After one last check of the complete system, he was ready to begin. He pulled on the first cord to take up the slack, then manoeuvred the grab over and around the bomb, taking care to raise it in a horizontal position. Once it was free of the shelf, he operated a second cord to edge the suspended bomb several feet along the curtain railway and out of the basement window. Slowly, the bomb was lowered into the sand-filled tray in the window-well. Carroll gave the order to take cover and waited two minutes to see if the bomb exploded. Nothing.

The second manoeuvre could begin. Carroll made his way out to the square to oversee the operation. Taking up the slack on the second pulley system outside, the tray was pulled aloft – slowly to avoid any violent swinging – and carried up and away from the building. Finally it hung suspended over the centre of the well of sandbags. The order was shouted to take cover. Then a loop was pulled to tip the tray, dropping the bomb onto the sandbags at the bottom of the emplacement. Two more minutes: nothing. Carroll attached a charge and blew the bomb. One down, eighteen to go.

It was vital for each and every operation to be carried out with equal vigilance. Then it came to the final two bombs. They were lying at the back of the shelf and were the hardest to get at. As Carroll began to lift the first one, in a heart-stopping moment it slipped out of the grab and thumped down onto the shelf, sending him diving for cover. He counted off two minutes, impatient to get going again. On the second attempt he managed to get hold of the bomb and inched it safely out of the building. Then it happened again – the final bomb fell onto the shelf with a clatter. Two more minutes wasted. Picking himself up again, Carroll breathed slowly as he manoeuvred the grab once more over the bomb. At last he had it securely in his grasp, and it completed a trouble-free journey, to be exploded among the sandbags.

After two long days of nail-biting work, the job was over. Carroll was relieved, and gratified to receive a letter of thanks a few days later from the Lieutenant Governor. He submitted a detailed report which was added to the Fortress Engineers War Diary.[11] It was a task he would never forget, recalling the story in every detail more than sixty years after the event, as an example of his bomb disposal experiences in Malta. The danger confronted by Lieutenant Carroll and his men during work on Thermos bombs is underlined by the experience of Royal Navy Bomb Safety Officer, Lieutenant Rowlands, who dealt with four of them on 1 November 1941. Having tried unsuccessfully to blow one of the bombs using the 'string-pull' method, he placed it in a box lined with sand, to which he added two further bombs. He carried them to the sea wall, so he could drop them into the water. The first bomb again failed to explode, the second detonated on hitting the water and caused the third to fall into the water, where it too exploded.

> Apart from the risk of ... exploding due to violent handling, there was always the risk they were fitted with a timed self-destruct fuze which could have caused them to explode at any time, however gently they were handled. The fact that two did explode upon hitting the water emphasises the risks ... [12]

For Sapper Inky Reeves, disposing of Thermos bombs was 'the most disturbing and frightening part of our section's work ... I believe that each of the lads who covered those jobs deserved much more recognition than they received.'[13] The achievements of the Royal Engineers bomb disposal section were recognised by the *Times of Malta*, which featured a profile of Lieutenant Carroll and his men in its Sunday edition of 2 November 1941.

BOMB DISPOSAL

The 24th Fortress Company includes that which interests every civilian in this war – bomb disposal sections.

The men of these sub-units of the Engineers are responsible for the 'disposal' of unexploded bombs here, and dangerous as is their task, they are the last to claim any special merit for their job.

Quietly efficient, experienced in handling their dangerous charges, both here and in Britain, these soldiers take their orders in a routine manner.

MATTER OF FACT COURAGE

Their attitude is a commendable one. Trained and provided with the very latest information concerning the types of fuzes and explosives they are likely to encounter, they simply ignore any further danger. The bomb disposal officer, under whom they work, examines each new charge, and, when his decision is made and line of action decided upon, sappers of the bomb disposal section carry on as if with a parade-ground order.

Despite their reluctance to allow the factor of heroics to be associated with them, these sappers have, nevertheless, done sterling work here, amid breathtaking hazards. Readers will appreciate also that these risks are taken in a premeditated manner, without the exhilaration of actual battle to lend a spur to courage.

Nothing at any hour comes amiss to these soldiers. They are prepared to tackle at any time of the day or night any enemy missile from a small fire bomb to the heaviest high explosive. In Britain they have tackled all types of Nazi bomb, while their experience in Malta covers both German and Italian efforts.[14]

The bomb disposal section had worked right through the month of November without a single day off. They had received 418 UXB reports and dealt with a total of 533 bombs, including over 450 Thermos. The Italian Air Force had tried every possible weapon from their arsenal in their campaign against Malta, from small incendiaries to heavy high explosives. Despite their efforts, the Island had fought back, its bombers continuing to attack Axis convoys and targets around the Mediterranean. In North Africa, the tide was turning in favour of the Allies, as the Eighth Army advanced into Cyrenaica. In response, the Axis became doubly determined to win back domination in the Mediterranean. Malta stood in the way.

Notes

1 Lieutenant G.D. Carroll, 2005
2 ibid.
3 Hogben, Major A. (1987). *Designed to Kill.* Wellingborough: Stephens.
4 Lieutenant G.D. Carroll, 2005
5 Correspondence, Chief Secretary & Lieutenant Governor's Office, National Archives of Malta
6 Boffa, C. (1995). *Second Great Siege: Malta 1940-1943.* Malta: Progress Press.
7 Ed. (1941). *Times of Malta.* 4 November. British Library Newspaper Collection
8 Cyril Thomas Meager, 2008
9 Lieutenant G.D. Carroll, 2005
10 Personal recollection, Ing. Maurice Mifsud Bonnici, Naxxar, Malta 2007
11 See Appendix 4
12 Hogben, Major A. (1987). *Designed to Kill.* Wellingborough: Stephens.
13 ibid.
14 Ed. (1941). *Sunday Times of Malta.* 2 November. British Library Newspaper Collection

CHAPTER 8

BATTLE REJOINED

Finding what he thought was a bomb, a man would go to the ARP or the police. What could be done about an unexploded bomb? There were UXBs all over the Island, the Bomb Disposal Squad was dealing with them and this one would have to wait its turn or go off. It would be marked and ringed and would not hurt anyone as long as they kept away from it.[1]

Something about the sound and shape of the approaching plane made the searchlight operator at Ghar Lapsi hold his beam. Suddenly, the aircraft swooped down towards him, dropping a string of bombs as it roared overhead. A second before he dived for cover, the soldier registered its markings: German, Junkers 88. By breakfast time on Sunday 7 December, gun positions all along the nearby coast, around Fort Benghisa, Luqa and Hal Far had reported unexploded bombs. This was no tentative *Regia Aeronautica* attack. The Luftwaffe were back in Sicily. In response to events in North Africa, Hitler ordered major air forces from the Russian front to return to the Mediterranean, appointing Air Field Marshal Albert Kesselring in command. He had one key objective: to neutralise Malta. The Island and its inhabitants were about to experience the full terror of 'blitzkrieg'.

One UXB was reported at a military defence post near Luqa village. Lieutenant Carroll went out to the site early next morning to be confronted by a 250kg German bomb – the first he had seen since July. He paused, not sure what to expect. Experience reminded him that the 250kg was the bomb most likely to contain problematic fuzes. Preparing himself for the worst, Carroll scanned the bomb: one fuze pocket. He looked for the number stamped on the fuze head: Series 5 – impact. He could breathe easily again, for now. The returning Luftwaffe might start using time bombs at any point. He would have to be extra vigilant.

He knew he was facing the return of a formidable enemy. Attacks were coming thick and fast, every day and night. Bombs rained down on search-light positions, gun batteries, forts, airfields and harbours. The change brought a sudden and dramatic rise in the number of UXB reports for RE Bomb Disposal: from 14 in one week of December to 87 the next. And the majority were HE bombs – most of which Carroll expected to tackle himself. In seven months working single-handed he had never felt more alone. Edward Talbot was gone, and there was no other Army bomb disposal officer on the Island.

While the main Luftwaffe squadrons were still assembling, the *Regia Aeronautica* continued to work alongside the earliest arrivals. Attacks switched between all-out strikes by German aircraft and sporadic nuisance raids by single Italian planes. On Monday 15 December, Carroll was called out to the Madliena area, where he defuzed three 130lb bombs. They were the last Italian high explosives he would see for a long time.

The harsher raiding tactics of the German bomber pilots soon made their mark on Malta's communities. At just after nine on Saturday 20 December – the very time when the Maltese were out and about in town – 40 enemy fighters and bombers attacked, dropping bombs across Valletta and Sliema, and on Zabbar and Marsaskala. When the raiders struck, Carroll was on the road to Mqabba. Sited close to the southern edge of Luqa airfield, this small country village made its living providing much of Malta's finest lime-stone. Lying on the ground in one of its lanes were two large containers. They each held a number of long, narrow bombs, painted green at one end. According to his guide a large number of incendiaries had ignited across the area during the previous night's raids. These two containers had failed to do their job and now Carroll had several dozen bombs on his hands. They were harmless enough to pick up and cart away – but not before he had retrieved examples to take back to his workshop for analysis. They were German 1kg Electron Incendiaries, made of magnesium with a Thermite filling. Dropped in canisters containing 36 bombs each, they soon became an all too familiar sight in Malta.

On Monday 22 December 1941, Lieutenant Carroll heard that the bomb disposal officer to replace Lieutenant Talbot had arrived and reported for duty. Lieutenant T.W.T. Blackwell took longer than expected to reach Malta: with direct air routes to the Island suspended, he had to travel from England by ship. A former lieutenant and fleet air arm pilot in the Royal Navy, Thomas Walter Townsend Blackwell was retired on medical grounds following a flying accident in 1938. He volunteered for the Territorial Army in November 1939 at the age of 31 and was appointed as a driver for the Royal Engineers Motor Transport Depot in Aldershot. In December 1940 Sapper Blackwell was posted to 16 Bomb Disposal Company where he was soon promoted to Acting Lance Corporal. Recognising that his experience as a former naval officer could be put to better use, his CO put him forward for a commission, which was granted on 11 March 1941. Lieutenant Blackwell attended a bomb disposal training course before returning to 16 Bomb Disposal Company, with its new HQ in Cardiff.

At the time the company had ten bomb disposal sections under its command, including eight spread across Wales. The ten BD sections between them handled a total of 100 UXBs between April and June 1941, then numbers reduced to 40 for the following three months – with just six unexploded bombs dealt with in October 1941. In between tackling UXBs, bomb disposal officers ran training courses for civil defence personnel. It was on 3 November 1941 that Lieutenant Blackwell received news of his posting overseas. Reporting to the London District Transit Camp, on 28 November he embarked for Malta – and very different circumstances. Having had little opportunity to use his new bomb disposal skills in Wales, 33-year-old Blackwell was about to find them tested to the limit.

The arrival of a second bomb disposal officer could not come too soon for the hard-pressed Lieutenant Carroll. He described his new colleague as a 'straight-cap wearer – the kind of officer who did things by the book.' Unfortunately, there was little time for the two BD officers to get to know each other. The calls for Army bomb disposal were multiplying at an alarming rate, adding to the backlog of UXBs. Carroll was constantly on the move across the Island, inspecting and tackling unexploded bombs. It had become impossible for him to keep up to date with records of them all.

Christmas was approaching but in Malta the 1941 festive season brought no respite from the escalation of the war; there were 60 enemy raids during Christmas week alone. A series of attacks from 8.40pm on 22 December to 6.30am the next morning caused yet another sleepless night as bombs and incendiaries were dropped on Ta' Qali, Rabat and Mtarfa. Six more raids followed the next night, then four during the day. After his hectic schedule, Lieutenant Carroll was grateful for a brief respite over Christmas to recover his energies, as Lieutenant Blackwell temporarily covered his duties. On Christmas Eve he defuzed his first unexploded HE bomb in Malta, a German 500kg SAP, at the Dockyard School. The morning's work was interrupted just before ten o'clock when a formation of fighters accompanied four Ju88s as they dive-bombed Grand Harbour. One of the bombs fell on the Upper Barrakka gun position, burying gunners under debris. Sappers from 24 Fortress Company were called out to form a rescue party. Only two of the three men were recovered alive.

Christmas Day brought a little peace, with no air raids. Blackwell took the opportunity to get to know the Island, travelling up to a military defence post at Mellieha Bay to see to an Italian 70kg incendiary. He returned via Birkirkara, where he despatched a Thermos bomb. His initial entries on the Weekly Bomb Disposal Report described his actions in the sort of detail he was used to in his previous posting. He would soon realise that in Malta there was little time for more than the minimum information for each bomb.

Between UXB callouts, Blackwell went through the records to familiarise himself with the patterns of bomb disposal on the Island during the previous year. He was beginning to realise the scale of the task in Malta compared to his experience in Wales. And with so many Italian HE and anti-personnel bombs and incendiaries, he must expect to encounter a much wider range of bombs than before. Even armed with this information, Blackwell could have little idea of the challenge he and Carroll were about to face. The Luftwaffe's renewed campaign had barely started.

The Christmas 'truce' lasted a single day; that night enemy action resumed with a vengeance. During nine raids on 26 December, bombers struck Luqa, Qrendi and Safi, Grand Harbour and Gzira, Birkirkara, Salvatur and Hamrun, and west of Ta' Qali. Six raids next day were followed by ten more overnight, all on similar targets. Day after day the pattern was repeated. Over

200 aircraft attacked the Island in a week, bringing more than 70 reports of unexploded bombs to RE Bomb Disposal HQ.

Lieutenant Blackwell's arrival brought no reduction in duties for Lieutenant Carroll. With the return of Luftwaffe bombing, it was time for the Island's Army bomb disposal establishment to be brought up to full strength. Malta was about to have two active BD sections: Carroll continued in command of the existing section, while Blackwell led a new section to operate alongside them. They had new numbers; Blackwell had been posted to No. 127 Bomb Disposal Section[2] and Carroll's BD section became No. 128. All available NCOs and sappers from 24 Fortress Company with previous bomb disposal experience were mobilised to provide enough manpower for the additional section. New members had to be trained to make up the numbers.[3] Until No. 127 BD Section was up and running, Blackwell could assist Carroll by taking on a share of the larger bombs.

There was an ominous beginning to the New Year for the Fortress Engineers. Just before midnight on 1 January 1942, in bright moonlight, Lintorn Barracks experienced a near miss from a heavy bomb which roared overhead and exploded 30 yards from the Warrant Officers' and Sergeants' Mess. Next morning a messenger arrived with an urgent UXB report from the local ARP centre. Traces of two large bombs had been discovered in a busy part of Floriana, not far from the barracks. The first available bomb disposal officer took the report, summoned Lance-Sergeant Parker, and the two hurried to the site.[4] They were puzzled by what they found. There were two holes close together – so close that it seemed as though a bomb had entered one hole and then somehow passed out through the other. From the diameter of the openings, the bomb was a large one – possibly a 500kg.

There were no signs of an explosion in the vicinity so the bomb disposal officer must assume that somewhere there was still an unexploded bomb. It had to be found. The order was given for the squad to split up and make a thorough search, while the officer and his NCO concentrated on investigating the two holes. Exploring with a metal probe, they discovered that something was lodged between them – but if the bomb had emerged from the ground, what was this? The ARP warden had mentioned something unusual from the night before: an eye witness had apparently seen two bombs with flames several yards long trailing from the rear as they fell.

Perhaps they were connected to this bomb. But surely something of this size could not be an incendiary?

It was time to find out. The sergeant picked an experienced team for the job; their task was to unearth whatever remained of the bomb, with the minimum disturbance, in case of volatile fuzes. They set to work lifting away fragments of stone and rubble. Piece by piece, a puzzling array of debris was assembled on the ground.[5] Initially there were the usual fragments of a tail fin – but these were made from some type of alloy, much lighter than usual and painted in two shades of blue. Then they began to find sections of piping unlike any part of a bomb they had seen before.

The sergeant was ordered to make absolutely sure that no fragment was missed. At that moment a sapper approached at the double. They had come across something, although it was some distance away. Doubting that it could be from the same bomb, the BD officer followed the sapper back to the spot. Certainly this was more familiar; it looked like any other 500kg armour-piercing bomb but it had a screw-threaded section set into its base. Heavy scrape marks on the carcass did suggest that it could have bored its way through stony ground. But if so it must have been travelling with enormous velocity to penetrate and leave the solid pavement and limestone – and then to travel so far before it landed.

The BD officer looked all round the flank of the bomb, searching for a fuze pocket, but there was no sign. Instinctively, his eyes went to the base. There was the fuze but it was unlike the normal *Rheinmetall* design – it had no number, no collar or locating pin, and it had no plungers. Instead, a piece of electrical cable protruded from its centre. What type of fuze was it – impact, clockwork or booby-trap? One thing was certain: it was vital to make the bomb safe as soon as possible – but how? It could not be exploded in the middle of Floriana. Any attempt to defuze the bomb was ruled out and the casing was too heavy for a clockstopper to be fully effective. In any case, the fuze could very well be designed to operate if tampered with. Nevertheless it had to be disabled somehow. The only reliable option was to treat it as he would the most complex and highly-sensitive fuze.

Leaving a sapper on guard, the bomb disposal officer marched smartly back to his sergeant. He ordered a portable boiler to be brought over from the barracks. In the interim he could check on progress with the excavation. The main bulk of the debris was beginning to come to light and it was undoubtedly something highly unusual. The structure seemed to consist of a large cylinder, with tubes and other extension pieces attached. Part of it was threaded, which seemed to match the threading on the bomb that he had just seen. The bomb obviously formed the nose, and this appeared to be a completely separate rear section. It was totally different from any high explosive which the BD officer had encountered either in Malta or on the Home Front. This was evidently a highly-developed type of bomb – and an important find.

It took some time before the boiler was in place and steaming up. Eventually Parker sent word that all was ready and the officer returned to the main part of the bomb. His plan was to force a jet of steam into the fuze head which would heat its condensers and cause them to discharge. It was a tricky business; the boiler could only be operated from a distance. At the same time, the supply of steam had to be carefully controlled so as not to overheat the fuze, which could activate any trembler mechanism and detonate the bomb. He waited a full 40 minutes, to be sure that the fuze was completely discharged, then he allowed it to cool. Time to withdraw the fuze. As he did so, he saw a number stamped on its side: [49]BIII – not one he knew. And there was no 'gaine' attached to its base. Now the bomb was harmless it could be taken back to the workshop, along with all the components they had found.

Before he went any further the officer was required to report his find to the CO of the Fortress Engineers. He noted brief details for an initial alert to Bomb Disposal HQ in London. A top secret reply came by return: this was a completely unknown type of bomb and the extension parts were the subject of great interest. A detailed report was imperative. Back at the bomb disposal workshop, every fragment was itemised, dismantled, examined and photographed. On 4 January, a preliminary report was flown to London, followed by further details a fortnight later.

The first 'Rocket Bomb' recorded in the Second World War had been dropped on Malta. Its main body was a 500kg armour-piercing bomb but with added rocket-type accelerators. The rocket propulsion was intended to aid the bomb's penetration of warships and fortifications. It emerged later that five others fell during the same raids and exploded: the one in Lintorn Barracks, and others on the naval canteen at Corrodino, at Marsaskala Bay and at Gzira. On 16 February 1942 a detailed technical report was issued by the War Office for Allied commanders and all bomb disposal units, which explained the operation and fuzing discovered by the team in Malta.[6]

It soon became clear that this was part of a new Luftwaffe initiative aimed at more efficient destruction in Malta. Heavier HE bombs were becoming increasingly common. Large numbers of UXBs began to appear in the Weekly Bomb Disposal Reports as 'SD' (*spreng dickenwand*), thick-walled bombs designed to smash the Island's stone buildings and break through its rocky ground in a way impossible for the SC or GP general purpose bomb. The initial target for the SD bombs appeared to be Luqa, where the aerodrome was badly cratered and six nearby houses were destroyed. A Priority UXB at San Vincent[7] brought an early Sunday morning call-out for a bomb disposal officer. He defuzed a 500kg SD on the surface, followed by 250kg SD bombs in the village of Ghaxaq and in the elegant town of Haz-Zebbug, to the south of Ta' Qali.

Then the bombing abated, thanks to a spell of dense cloud, squalling winds and poor visibility. But as soon as the wind dropped enemy aircraft used the cover of low cloud to approach their targets unseen before swooping down to strike. Luqa suffered another heavy raid on 8 January which destroyed aircraft and demolished fourteen houses in the village, causing five civilian casualties. Four UXBs were reported between Luqa and the neighbouring village of Gudja. Two 500kg SC bombs lay in the open; another two had entered the ground nearby. All four had extension caps jammed in place and the BD squad faced the difficult task of removing the bombs with their fuzes intact.

Saturday 10 January was a rough and windswept day for one unlucky squad, working on a trench out in the open, at the bridge beside Marsa Sports Club. On his way back from Luqa Lieutenant Carroll decided to check on their progress.

I was passing the Polo Ground [in my car] during an air raid. Two teams were just going out to play football with their greatcoats on over their strip. Their coats were buttoned up to the neck: this was required as it was an inter-service match. Not far away (towards Luqa) there was a massive explosion – a 1,000kg bomb – or possibly an RAF bomb store had gone up.

The blast went up inside their heavy buttoned coats and lifted all twenty-two of them right off the ground![8]

Other storm clouds were gathering. Lieutenant-General Dobbie had received worrying intelligence from HQ in Cairo that Kesselring was moving many more aircraft from Germany and North Africa into Sicily for large-scale dive-bombing attacks on Malta's aerodromes. Among them were many of the hated strike aircraft, the Junkers 87, or 'Stuka'. An invasion of Malta looked increasingly likely. Battling against the gales, men from all three services worked tirelessly to make ready all anti-aircraft batteries, aerodromes and harbour defences. The authorities decided that a special alert was needed to give proper warning of an invasion. The practice of ringing church bells to signal the 'All Clear' was ended. From now on the bells would ring only to warn of imminent danger of a general attack by the enemy. The 'All Clear', or 'Raiders Passed', signal was changed to a steady note from a siren.

The four weeks which followed brought 107 heavy raids; a single raid often lasted for over eight hours. The attacks rained down 1,800 tons of bombs on the Island, many of which did not explode. At least there were two bomb disposal sections in place to meet the considerable challenge. Lieutenant Blackwell's No.127 Bomb Disposal Section was now up to strength and ready for duty and they could share the workload with Lieutenant Carroll and No.128 BD Section.[9] Manpower had almost doubled, and not a day too soon.

With both bomb disposal officers needing NCOs in their section, at least one sapper had the chance of promotion. Blackwell wanted a driver with skills in bomb disposal to accompany him on missions. Former driver to the CO of the Fortress Engineers, Sapper Cyril Thomas Meager had over a year's experience in the BD section. Blackwell was more than satisfied with his abilities and Tom could celebrate the start of 1942 with a stripe on his sleeve. He went home to tell his wife Maria the good news. She had a job to do: Blackwell had handed over his stripes with strict orders not to turn up for work next morning unless they were stitched onto his uniform.

Tuesday 13 January dawned fine and clear, but the blue skies brought heavy air raids – 14 in the space of 19 hours, lasting a total of 9 hours. That afternoon, attackers bombed the area around Grand Harbour, leaving large craters scarring the formal gardens and avenues between Floriana and Valletta. One unexploded bomb threatened to disrupt a lifeline for the Maltese people. It was preventing access to the Island's main bus station, outside Kingsgate (Porta Reale). Lieutenant Blackwell went to investigate and decided that only a heavy high explosive could have pierced the road so cleanly. Evidence of the large craters nearby confirmed his suspicions. Unfortunately, the UXB was right in the centre of the roadway and buses could not pass the spot while it remained. Not wishing to extend the hold-up any longer than necessary, Blackwell issued his orders and a squad got to work with their pick-axes. It was Tom Meager's first major job as a lance-corporal and he was keen to impress. Blackwell remained on hand to ensure that the bomb was constantly monitored for any sign of ticking. It was difficult to anticipate exactly where the bomb lay. Under the tarmac, the ground was rocky and uneven. As the light began to fade, the pit was already several feet deep, with no trace of metal. Blackwell had no alternative but to suspend work until next day.

The following morning Lieutenant Carroll was on Sanctuary Street in Zabbar looking at the remnants of a partially exploded 500kg bomb, when raiders roared across from the direction of the coast. With no time to take cover, he was relieved to see them fly on towards Luqa. The bomb's fuze had already functioned, so he made a note for it to be collected later. He was heading for the wireless station at Rinella to check the progress of one of his squads when a second formation of bombers loomed overhead on their way to the southern airfields.

At the bus station, Lance-Corporal Meager and his squad located their bomb, but only after opening a second trench at an angle from the original shaft. There was no possibility of exploding the 500kg without tearing up a considerable section of roadway. Thankfully a singe impact fuze was soon found and rendered harmless. Meager lashed a rope around the carcass of the bomb, ready for it to be winched out of the hole and onto the back of the BD section's truck, under the watchful eye of Lieutenant Blackwell.

Meanwhile, Lieutenant Carroll was busy dealing with bombs around the southern airfields. Sending NCOs and their sappers to two sites on the outskirts of Gudja, Carroll took a team with him to Hal Far, to make a start on digging for two Priority buried bombs. While they did so he went over to Ghar Hasan to follow up the other two Priority reports. The two 500kg SC bombs lay in full view. He walked towards the nearest of them and stopped. It had two fuze pockets. Although from experience in London he knew that 250kg SC and 500kg SC bombs often had 'twin' pockets, he had not previously come across any in Malta. He was concerned because often where there were two fuzes, one of them was a Type 17 – with a clock. He moved closer to the bomb, bending down to read the numbers stamped into the head of each fuze. Both ended with a '5' – impact type. Before he went any further, he decided to check the second bomb. Two fuze pockets – but again both were Series '5', so no booby-traps or clocks yet. When he got back to Hal Far his sergeant had similar news; another bomb with two fuzes, both impact. Although Carroll was relieved, he couldn't shake off a nagging feeling. The Luftwaffe were making changes. The next twin pockets might well contain a clockwork fuze and maybe even a booby-trap.

It had been a hard week. The sappers had toiled through rain and cold to complete eight excavations, bringing the total number of UXBs dealt with to 34; more than half of them weighed 250kg or more. While both bomb disposal sections took a break on Sunday there were dramatic developments in the defence of Malta. Aware of increased numbers of enemy bombers in Sicily, and with a convoy on its way to Grand Harbour, Malta's air forces went on the offensive. Wellingtons and Blenheims launched an extended attack on the air base at Catania. The Luftwaffe's response was swift. At dawn on Monday 19 January 1941 they retaliated with a heavy attack on the inbound convoy and Malta's aerodromes. The onslaught continued relentlessly until midday. During the morning's raids, a large bomb hit the quarters in Pieta of Major-General D.M.W. Beak, the Army's new General Officer Commanding (GOC) in Malta. It nearly split the once grand house in two, smashing through the central staircase and leaving Major-General Beak stranded on the top floor with no way to escape.

The bomb did not explode. Within minutes the emergency telephone rang at Lintorn Barracks and a bomb disposal officer hurried to the spot. Checking that everyone had already been evacuated, he picked his way through the ruins. At the centre of the building, under a heap of debris in what had been the hallway, lay a 500kg SC bomb. He eased away a couple of broken stair treads looking for a fuze pocket. It was a single, with a straightforward impact fuze. Wiping away splinters of wood and dust from the fuze head, he applied his discharger and counted down the minutes till it had done its job. He tried to remove the fuze from the bomb. No such luck; the locking ring would not budge. The force of the bomb crashing into the building had probably jammed it in position. The bomb would have to be carried away with its fuze in place – not viable while air raids were in progress. The officer paused; he had a decision to make. Although this was an important military location, the building was already wrecked. The bomb could stay where it was until the 'All Clear'.

Major-General Beak was not about to let the matter of a bomb on his quarters disrupt his plans. Having arrived in Malta only a short time before to assume overall command of the Army, he had already carried out a review of his forces and concluded that changes were needed in order to sustain the morale and condition of the men. He summoned all the officers in his command to a series of three lectures and the two bomb disposal officers joined their colleagues to hear his words. The GOC stressed the importance of improved 'leadership, endurance, discipline and the offensive spirit'. Towards this aim, he announced that physical training and cross-country runs were to be instituted for all ranks under 40 years of age. Lieutenant Carroll was informed that, as a bomb disposal officer, he was not required to take part.

The GOC was not the only one to escape catastrophe. On the morning of Tuesday 20 January the Luftwaffe launched another prolonged attack on the convoy in Grand Harbour. During a lunchtime raid, a bomb hit an ammunition store in the Ospizio, just a few yards from the workshop where Carroll examined and stored sample bombs. The Ospizio was barely affected but another heavy bomb demolished the clothing store at Marina Pinto, burying nine people. The Royal Engineers formed rescue parties, working throughout the night in shifts. Only one man was recovered alive.

The enemy were increasingly directing their efforts towards the southern airfields. They attacked Hal Far early in the morning of 21 January, killing and wounding military personnel and damaging aircraft. A second attack later in the day on both Hal Far and Luqa brought a Priority UXB report from a defence post further up the coast to the west, at Il Hnejja, or the Blue Grotto as it became better known. This time the carcass of the 250kg SD could be easily rolled over the nearby cliffs.

In the month to 24 January there had been 150 alerts during the day and 103 at night, including 132 bombing raids. Already badly cratered by the constant heavy bombing, both Hal Far and Ta' Qali airfields were waterlogged; only Luqa was operational. The AOC needed help with the repairs and with the building of hundreds of pens to protect his aircraft. With the help of Lieutenant-General Dobbie, an agreement was reached for an all-out effort by all three services. 24 Fortress Company joined other Army, Navy and RAF personnel, aided by Maltese civilians, in the work. The BD sections played their part by keeping the airfields and their surroundings clear of unexploded bombs.

As the Luftwaffe expanded the range of their bombing activity, UXBs were turning up right across the Island. Most were now 250kg or over and with the enemy's concentration on military targets more UXBs were given high priority, requiring the attendance of a bomb disposal officer. Despite the increase to two bomb disposal sections, it was already becoming impossible to keep up with demand. There would have to be changes.

Since June 1941, Lieutenant Carroll and his bomb disposal section had been able to clear away unexploded bombs endangering either the military or civilians within a very short time. He had to face the fact that it was no longer feasible. From now on, only UXBs marked Priority were likely to be attended to on the day they were reported. Instead of being tackled as they arose, many more reported bombs, including some in densely-populated areas, were put to one side until a bomb disposal officer had a vital job in the same area – if they had not exploded in the interim. The sheer numbers of UXBs made it increasingly difficult to keep a complete record of every one. It was decided that only details of HE bombs would be entered on Weekly Bomb Disposal Reports. Totals of smaller anti-personnel and incendiary bombs were added as a footnote. With squads from two BD sections hard at work all over the Island, Harry Turner and his colleagues were hard pressed to reach every location quickly to collect defuzed bombs for delivery to the cliffs. From now on their workload would be organised to make the most of each lorry journey – and to avoid unnecessary use of fuel. It could be some time before carcasses were taken away. One family at Ghar Hanzir near Qormi were relieved when the bomb disposal officer defuzed a massive 500kg SD bomb in their garden. Their comfort gradually turned to concern while they waited for it to be removed. Residents of Tonna Street in Mosta were evacuated while a stray 500kg SD bomb intended for Ta Qali found lying in the roadway was made safe and taken straight away by the Bomb Disposal men. A second buried bomb was quickly uncovered and attended to, only to lie in its shaft for two anxious days until the lorry could come and take it away.

Though the changes were unavoidable, they threatened to undermine the morale of Lieutenant Carroll and all members of RE Bomb Disposal, who saw the protection of civilians as an essential part of their role. Many of the enemy bombs aimed at military targets inevitably fell on nearby towns and villages. Any delay in disposing of these unexploded bombs could only add to the growing fear hanging over Malta's people.

One cold, wet afternoon Carroll had a batch of four large unexploded bombs to inspect on the outskirts of Luqa. He was returning through the village on his motorcycle when a group of fighters and bombers emerged from heavy cloud cover, heading towards the airfield. He was forced to stop and dive for cover as bombs crashed all around him. Finally the last of the aircraft wheeled away. As he emerged and the dust began to settle, a scene of devastation confronted him.

> There was a shelter nearby and there was a woman lying [near it] injured; her head was bleeding. I took off my Mackintosh and put it under her head, then I went to find someone to attend to her. I didn't normally see people very badly injured because, by the time I got there, the area had been cleared and the only thing remaining to deal with was the bomb.[10]

Lieutenant Carroll felt helpless. He had no choice but to leave the victim to the care of others. An unexploded 500kg SC bomb was waiting for him in another part of the village.

Notes

1 Hogan, G. (1978). *Malta, The Triumphant Years 1940–43*. London: Hale
2 Army Service Record, Lieutenant T.W.T. Blackwell, Army Records Office
3 Ed. (1941) *Situation Reports & Operational Messages Out*. WO 106, National Archives, London: telegram from War Office to Lieutenant-General Dobbie confirmed the 'establishment' (size, structure and trades) of two BD sections applicable to Malta as 'Lieutenant one, Sgt one, L/Sgt One, Cpls three, L/Cpls (Sapper) two, L/Cpl (driver I.C.) one, sappers nine, drivers I.C. five, att. Cook one, total all ranks 24 (half 48). Second. Trades of above group A-D fitter one Group E Pioneers RE seven engine hand I.C. one Pioneers RE for duty as batman one, sanitary one, timbermen four.' The two Sections would remain operational until October 1943. However, available resources meant that No.127 Section would be limited to 16 O.R. and No.128 would not grow above 20.
4 Lance-Sergeant Parker is identified as the NCO here, as descriptions of this bomb match characteristics he recalled in his 1979 account of dealing with a

bomb in January 1941. (See footnote Chapter 2.) There is no similar evidence to identify the BD officer involved.

5 See Appendix 5

6 ibid.

7 The Poor House: now known as San Vincenz de Paule

8 Lieutenant G.D. Carroll, 2008

9 There is no evidence that at this stage Army bomb disposal work was divided between the two Sections along any formal or geographical lines, as happened later; nor do the Weekly Bomb Disposal Reports identify the BD officer/section dealing with each UXB. Officers are therefore only named in connection with an action if there is supportive evidence available to confirm this or make a reasoned assumption.

10 Lieutenant G.D. Carroll, 2005

CHAPTER 9

RAIN OF TERROR

Anywhere else but Malta, an air raid warning would sound over a large area as the enemy aircraft moved towards their target; whereas when our sirens sounded we <u>were</u> the target.[1]

The weather was deteriorating. The winter was fast becoming one of the worst in living memory: cold and wet, with gale-force winds and pouring rain. February rainfall was double the average. Transport was difficult, towns and villages lay in ruins, roads and streets were blocked by mounds of rubble. Day after day, the RE Bomb Disposal men battled through driving rain, often on roads which were barely more than rough tracks, searching for, digging out and working on unexploded bombs. Whenever the weather did ease off the Luftwaffe took the opportunity to strike. The endless storms, combined with air raids of increasing frequency and ferocity, were taking their toll on everyone on the Island. Attacks persisted day and night, and lack of sleep became a serious problem. Military personnel arriving in the spring of 1942 remarked on the visible strain etched on the faces of comrades who had endured conditions in Malta for more than a few weeks.

During the London blitz Lieutenant Carroll had experienced one period of 57 nights of bombing raids with no break. He was about to face an even greater trial. There had been 1,300 raids in the past twenty months; a similar number would now be added in just five months. And whereas in London the bomb disposal officer had only to try and sleep during raids, now he must work through them. The constant alerts were disrupting many activities vital to the survival of the Island. Malta's chiefs of staff had to find a way for essential work to continue everywhere that was not in the direct line of fire. They decided that a red flag would be raised over the Castille, high up in the government district of Valletta, and above Fort St Angelo across the water in Vittoriosa, only if a raid was headed directly for Grand Harbour. From now on, when the siren sounded, everyone outside the main target area would carry on working. Carroll described the arrangements at Lintorn Barracks:

> … we had to work, even during air raids. There was a system of red and yellow alerts. The yellow alert was used when, for example, 'dots' were seen from the direction of Sicily. The barracks could not stop working so we had an officer and an NCO on top of the building. The red warning would come and at some time [they] had to determine whether that raid was going to affect us. [They] would then send the message downstairs and everyone would move quickly down to the shelters. Apart from that we were working all the time.[2]

On Friday 6 February, one bomb disposal officer and squad worked on through five morning raids uncovering a 500kg SC bomb in the town of Zabbar. At lunchtime dozens of Ju88 bombers accompanied by Messerschmitt fighters targeted Hal Far, damaging a number of buildings and leaving another 500kg SC at a Bofors gun position on the nearby coast. The Light Ack-Ack gunners at Kalafrana had done their best to thwart the efforts of the incoming enemy planes. After the raid a local farmer discovered a number of unexploded bombs scattered across two of his fields. Despite spending the day up to their ankles in mud, the bomb disposal squad were happy to report that a bomber had been forced to jettison his entire load of 50kg SC bombs in the face of defensive fire.

Next morning dawned bright and sunny – perfect weather conditions for the Luftwaffe. They carried out 16 raids in 13 hours 6 minutes, setting a new world record for the number of air attacks in a 24-hour period. In the evening raid Lintorn Barracks suffered a direct hit. Four bombs fell on one of the accommodation blocks, destroying half the entire building. It was Saturday and as luck would have it the men were enjoying a night out, so no-one was hurt. On any other evening there would have been serious casualties.

Day in day out heavy raids battered areas on both sides of Grand Harbour. Bombs dropped on Valletta and Floriana, Pieta, Lazarretto and Manoel Island. The residential area of Paola was pounded by seemingly indiscriminate bombing; whole streets were razed to the ground, with many civilian casualties. Valletta was rapidly becoming a ghost town, apart from service personnel going about their essential work. Carroll was forced to clamber over huge mounds of rubble just to get from his pension in South Street to the city's main gate.

On Wednesday 11 February a bomb hit the Phoenicia Hotel just outside the gate and failed to explode. Completed just before the outbreak of war, the Phoenicia had not yet operated as a hotel; instead it was put into service as accommodation for the RAF. As soon as the report came in to BD headquarters, Carroll crossed the short distance from Lintorn Barracks to the grand building. The UXB was evidently buried under rubble in the basement. By the afternoon a 50kg SC ten feet underground had been defuzed by an NCO and taken away.

Next morning Carroll received a call from the police in Valletta, reporting an unexploded bomb within yards of the Opera House.

When you look at the front of the Opera House, to the right a building ran across the present Square, with a balustrade on the top of it, which was part of a walkway. I was told that there was a bomb on this balustrade.

When I arrived, I saw that the bomb was hanging suspended over the street. The balustrade had a ledge extending towards the square. I edged along this parapet on my knees – knowing I could fall onto the pavement below. When I reached the bomb I found it was one which I hadn't seen before: it was small, made of metal, and on the top it had a rocking cap. The bomb was attached to a wire, which I had to carefully snip, so that I could deal with the fuze and then take the bomb away for examination.

I traced the wire back and found that … it must have stretched across streets and houses. Then I realised that, while I was on the ledge delicately holding the bomb, someone anywhere in Valletta could have found the wire and pulled it out of curiosity, banging the bomb against the balustrade and exploding it in my hands.[3]

As usual, Lieutenant Carroll hurried back to barracks to prepare a detailed report of this new bomb. He was stunned when he found out it was an Allied device being used in the defence of Grand Harbour.

> I was informed later that the bomb was sent up by the Navy. To deal with Stukas, they invented a system whereby they sent into the air a pot of explosive with a rocking cap on top – the fuze mechanism – attached to a thousand feet of wire, with a parachute at the end. It would probably be fired up by a mortar, to launch it vertically into the sky. As it was fired into the air, the parachute would separate and as a Stuka hit the wire, the parachute would pull across the wing. The pot would hit the wing and the rocking cap would set it off, destroying the wing and bringing the plane down.[4]

The bomb could have killed the bomb disposal officer – and others could easily fall into less expert hands with fatal consequences. Carroll promptly arranged for an information office announcement, which appeared on the front page of the *Times of Malta*.

> The Public are hereby informed that in the event of a low-level attack on the Grand Harbour by enemy aircraft a new type of barrage may be fired by our defences in addition to the usual anti-aircraft artillery barrage.
>
> The new barrage will take the form of a number of parachutes to which bombs and lengths of wire are attached. When the parachutes are floating down to earth, with the bombs attached, they should not be mistaken for parachutes used by parachute-troops. The bombs attached to these new parachutes are very small and it is easy to see that there is no man attached to the parachutes. Moreover, the parachutes used to hold the bombs are much smaller than those used by men.
>
> If any of the bombs reach the ground or sea unexploded they remain extremely dangerous and should no account be touched; nor should the wire or parachute be touched, as even the slightest pull may explode the bomb. If anyone finds one of these bombs unexploded he should immediately inform the nearest police station of the exact whereabouts of the bomb.
>
> The bombs are yellow and about the size of a one pound cocoa tin.[5]

Friday 13 February 1942 lived up to its superstitious reputation for one group of Valletta civilians. They had just taken refuge in an air-raid shelter in Theatre Street when a huge bomb crashed through the ceiling above and came to rest in their midst. When their screams subsided, they could only stare in terror at the silent bomb, with the dawning realisation that it had not exploded. The shelter was evacuated and a message was rushed to Lintorn Barracks. A bomb disposal officer was quickly on the scene and defuzed the 500kg SC bomb but the shelter had to stay closed for another day until it could be retrieved.

Despite the bombing, Valletta was still an attraction for military personnel and civilians seeking relaxation in its places of entertainment. 15 February was Carnival Sunday, and it was marked by almost constant raids. At just before six in the evening, Carroll was relaxing with fellow officers in the Union Club in Valletta when a fierce raid struck the centre of the city.[6] As the officers headed for shelter in the wine cellars below a terrible explosion rocked the ground above their heads. In the midst of the confusion a shout came from above. A massive bomb had hit the Regent Cinema a short distance along Kingsway. Minutes earlier a packed cinema audience had been enjoying an innocent afternoon's entertainment; now they were trapped under the collapsed building. Rescue operations were soon underway. The Royal Engineers joined the teams working through the night to try and find survivors. The many civilian and military casualties included 12 servicemen killed and 29 wounded. Among the dead were two men of 24 Fortress Company, RE.

The following Wednesday the Fortress Engineers were again in the direct line of fire, during one of four massive daytime raids:

It was the fourth raid that concerned us at 3pm ... planes [were] approaching... heading over Grand Harbour for the submarine base ... This was our first real taste of being in the target area and it was not so good.

Within an hour the siren went up again ... As the planes came in so did the bombs – rained around the area. Our cook-house had got a direct hit and there was only a small bit of it left ... The bath house had got it and a very heavy bomb had hit the Company's motor transport garage, killing five of the lads and completely wrecking four lorries. Six bombs, two large and four small ones, had fallen in front of our barrack blocks ... it was quite obvious that we would not be able to use them until they had been repaired.[7]

It was a particular blow for Carroll. He knew many of the sappers in the garage well, having been given the job of overseeing motor transport for a time during the previous autumn.

The violence of the attack was followed next day by equally violent weather. The stormy conditions turned Thursday 19 February into the first raid-free day of 1942. The weather was so bad it enforced a break from many military operations around the Island. Within their barracks, the Fortress Engineers could only survey the damage and try to sort out the mess. The raid depleted their already limited vehicle resources and other essential services.

Next morning despite more rain and gales lashing the Island the bomb disposal sections were back on the road. While one BD officer followed up UXB reports from as far apart as Gudja and Mosta, the other put a team to work exposing a large bomb at Zabbar. In the filthy conditions, progress was slow. Rain soaked into the sappers' denims and collected in puddles under their feet, making extra heavy work of it. A grim four days went by before the 500kg SC bomb was reached at the bottom of a nine-foot shaft and defuzed. As it turned out they were fortunate to be away working that Friday. Lintorn was hit again; this time a large bomb struck the barber's shop at the heart of the barracks. It missed the sheltering sappers by just 30 yards:

> The air raid shelters … [were] a series of walls built along the main bastion wall and slabs of sandstone placed across the top to form a roof … the boys … would not go to them until they were ordered to by the senior officers…However we were extremely lucky and up to this time we had not had any casualties. The guardian angel must have been above our barracks day and night. During the period of our heaviest attacks … we had our barbers shop hit … we were confined to our gun pit and it wasn't policy to go out, I later learned that the only casualties were minor ones, a few cuts and bruises caused by falling masonry. After the boys had inspected the crater it was generally agreed that it must have been a 1,000lb bomb [500kg].[8]

With much of Lintorn Barracks in ruins, there was no longer enough serviceable accommodation to house all of the Fortress Engineer companies. A new encampment was needed away from Floriana and a site was chosen further up the north coast at Bahar ic-Caghaq. Major de Piro Cowley took command of No.1 Works Company RE and moved them out to the new camp. The sappers could hardly believe their luck: the shallow bay was one of the most pleasant bathing areas in Malta. Major C.L. Fox took over as CO of 24 Fortress Company at Lintorn. For a whole month day to day routine in the barracks was disrupted while the Fortress Engineers adjusted to their predicament. The devastation had struck a blow to morale, but it would soon be eclipsed by even greater trials.

On the night of Saturday 21 February a number of enemy bombs fell in the area of St Paul's Bay. They did not detonate. Long after the 'raiders passed' signal had sounded, the restored peace was ruptured by a loud explosion, then another. As night turned to morning more seemingly random explosions echoed around the bay. A Maltese gunner was about to report an unexploded bomb he had just passed on the road, when he was knocked off his feet by a blast from the very same bomb. Early next morning, Bomb Disposal HQ received the news they had been dreading since the previous December: the bombs dropped at St Paul's Bay were delayed-action. The Luftwaffe had added a terrifying new tactic to their bombing campaign against the Island: unpredictability. From now on, anyone finding or working on an unexploded HE bomb faced the fearful prospect that it could be a time bomb and set to explode at any moment.

Both bomb disposal officers had experience of Type 17 delayed-action fuzes on the Home Front. Carroll remembered how their introduction during the Blitz on London in 1940 reduced the life expectancy of bomb disposal officers to a matter of weeks.

The Germans were amazed that their excellent bombs were not going off. The only way they could tackle the matter was to kill the people who were dealing with the bombs. They devised a clock, which would be set for any period between a few minutes and [eighty] hours. So from then on the first requirement was to listen to the bomb. If there was ticking, there was a clock inside which had to be stopped.[9]

Lieutenant Blackwell too had a reason to be especially wary of time bombs. While he was in Wales, in May 1941, five men of his company had been killed while tackling a 250kg bomb with a Type 17 clockwork fuze.

It was not long before the telephone rang again. It was the Royal Artillery at St Paul's Bay; a bomb had entered the ground near one of their main buildings. It hadn't exploded – yet. If this bomb held a clockwork-controlled fuze, it might already be ticking. If so, there was no way of knowing whether there were minutes or hours to go before the clock ended its run and detonated the bomb. A bomb disposal officer and squad set out on the long journey north, preoccupied with a single thought: they were about to encounter a time-bomb.

The site was on rocky ground overlooking the bay – too close to the building to leave for 96 hours. The bomb disposal officer realised there was no option but to dig down to the bomb immediately, even though the lives of his men were at stake. And they all knew that even if the clock had malfunctioned, any disturbance from a pick or shovel could start it running again – and then the bomb could go off within seconds. The work was slow and painstaking, to avoid jarring the bomb. Yet every minute which passed held the possibility of a clock reaching detonation point. The sappers were much quieter than usual as they worked. After what seemed like an eternity, the base of the carcass was revealed. It was a 250kg SC – the type most likely to be fitted with a DA fuze. The officer's reminder to proceed with care was hardly needed. At least now the bomb could be monitored for ticking. The electric stethoscope was ready, the cable was unreeled and the microphone applied gently to the exposed flank of the bomb.

The limestone and soil were gently scraped away. An eternity seemed to pass before a hoarse voice called out from the foot of the shaft. The fuze head had been located: a Series 5 impact type. But there was something else. It was nearer to the base of the bomb than usual. It was not good news. The position of the fuze meant only one thing: there were two fuze pockets. From experience, the officer knew that the fuze in the other pocket was probably fitted with a clock. This time his warning was more insistent: that only the lightest of movements should be made to uncover the second fuze pocket. More minutes dragged by, then at long last the call came that a second fuze had been found, marked 17A. The officer's response was instant: 'Everyone out of the shaft.' The rest was up to him. His only assistance would be from the man at the far end of the stethoscope, listening hard for ticking while his officer worked. Standing alongside him at the safe point, his comrades fell silent.

The bomb disposal officer lowered himself gently down beside the bomb – it was a 17A fuze all right. The preferred method of disposal for a DA fuze was to explode the bomb in situ – it was quick and required less manhandling. It was also reasonably safe, provided the clockwork mechanism did not start up. If it did, there was always a possibility that the bomb was set for only a few seconds' delay. He had already calculated that the blast from a 250kg would be acceptable in this location – especially while the bomb was still partly covered. The local military commander had also been informed. No need to hang about. The officer had brought his explosives with him and now attached them to the bomb. Taking with him the microphone of the stethoscope, he climbed slowly out of the hole and joined his men. He ordered everyone to take cover, and then detonated the charge. The explosion boomed out across the bay, and sprayed tiny fragments far and wide. One down – but how many more to go?

Another two reports of possible UXBs in the area had already reached HQ. Both lay in the flat open farmland further inland from St Paul's Bay. They could be cordoned off for 96 hours, only for a bomb disposal officer and squad to go through a repeat of Sunday's nail-biting experience twice, digging up and exploding both bombs. They were evidently from the same batch: both were 250kg with twin pockets, one impact and the other type 17A. News soon spread among the population that 'time-bombs' were being used on the Island. From now on, any cordoned-off site marked 'Unexploded Bomb' provoked an even greater sense of fear – and the constant threat of a sudden explosion.

On Thursday 26 February three daylight raids struck Luqa – and more DA bombs were used. Among several reported UXBs was a 250kg SC on the road by an RAF billet at the edge of Luqa village. One look at the fuze pockets confirmed the BD officer's suspicions: two fuzes again, the one nearest the nose marked 17A. In this location the bomb could not be left to its own devices, nor could it be blown in situ. Every passing minute brought the possibility of a sudden explosion – unless the clock could be stopped. At times like these Lieutenant Carroll was grateful for a flaw in the enemy's design.

The Germans thoughtlessly put steel components in their clocks instead of brass, because they were stronger perhaps. This enabled us to stop the clocks using a strong magnet. The bomb could be removed, with the magnet on it, to a place of safety. If necessary, keeping the magnet in position, we could take out the explosive without causing serious damage.[10]

The magnetic clockstopper could stop a clock, and keep it stopped, for up to six hours in 50kg SC or SD, and 250kg or 500kg SC bombs. The squad quickly unloaded the equipment from their lorry. It took two men to bring the magnet to the bomb. Painfully aware of time ticking away, they resisted the temptation to run. Under the supervision of the bomb disposal officer, the clockstopper was centred over the head of the 17A fuze and strapped in place. Electric cables were unwound from a drum and connected the magnet to large batteries back at the safe point. When all was ready, the men retired and their officer shouted the order for the clockstopper to be switched on. The magnetic force jammed the steel components of the clock. It was paralysed.

While the clockstopper stayed in position the bomb was harmless. Unfortunately, the bomb disposal officer could not extract the clockwork fuze. In their attempt to defeat bomb disposal efforts on the Home Front, the Germans fitted at least half of their type 17 fuzes with a booby-trap – an anti-withdrawal device underneath the fuze. It was designed to detonate the bomb instantly if the main fuze above was withdrawn even a few millimetres. This left the officer with two choices: to take the bomb away to a suitable place to explode it, or send it directly to be unloaded over the cliffs. As the coast was not too far away, he decided on the latter, especially as it would also save on the dwindling stock of explosives.

Moving the bomb was not an easy task. The magnetic clockstopper must remain strapped securely in position as the bomb was hoisted onto the tailgate of the lorry, transported to the coast and lowered to the ground. Its weight of 40kg, added to 250kg of bomb carcass, made it awkward to handle. At the top of the cliffs the clockstopper was switched off and there were anxious moments while the magnet was lifted off, before the bomb was finally rolled over the edge and plunged into the sea. The sappers dived to the ground as the bomb dropped, and lay still for a few moments, in case of an explosion. Nothing happened. Their NCO gave the thumbs-up and they were on their way, glad for once to be heading for another job.

A street in Senglea, Three Cities, January 1941, after the Illustrious Blitz. *(NWMA, Malta)*

Lieutenant Talbot.

The bomb in the foreground is of a similar size to that described by Major Parker in Chapter 2. The photograph may have been taken to record the successful recovery of this challenging UXB in January 1941. Personnel left to right (standing): Lt E.E. Talbot, L/Sgt R.C. Parker, L/Cpl R. Hilliar, Sprs Miller, McCarthy, Leonard and Reeves, Cpl C. Brewer; (seated): Sgt Piggott, Sprs H. Turner and Lockyer. *(NWMA, Malta)*

Fort Mosta *(NWMA, Malta)*

Hal Far accommodation blocks in ruins. *(NWMA, Malta)*

Royal Engineers at Lintorn Barracks demonstrate hoisting an unexploded bomb using a 'gin' or derrick' tripod. L/Sgt J. H. Lockett front centre. (NWMA, Malta)

Lieutenant G.D. Carroll, 1940. *(Courtesy of G.D. Carroll)*

Grand Harbour with Valletta to the left and the Three Cities on the right. *(Courtesy of Norman Tarrant)*

Members of RE Bomb Disposal Section, Malta, summer 1941, left to right: Lt G.D. Carroll; (unknown); Spr Laurence Miller; Spr Harry Turner; Spr Daniel McCarthy; (unknown). *(Times of Malta: NWMA, Malta)*

Above: In Malta's narrow streets bombs often had to be removed by handcart. *(NWMA Malta)*

Right: Finding a parachute mine. *(NWMA Malta)*

500kg German bombs lie camouflaged by trees in Sicily, ready to deliver 'iron greetings to Malta'. *(NWMA Archive, Malta)*

Officers and NCOs, Royal Engineers, Malta, 1941. Lt G.D. Carroll, front row, third from left; Lt E.E. Talbot, front row, fourth from right; Sgt J. Holland, centre row, right; L/Sgt R. C. Parker back row, third from left. *(Courtesy of G.D. Carroll)*

Italian 500lb bombs. *(NWMA, Malta)*

Officers of the special constabulary on 18 November 1940. Philip Pullicino is in the front row, fourth from right. *(NWMA, Malta)*

Above left: Pieta waterfront. *(NWMA Malta)*

Above right: Thermos bomb.

Left: Lieutenant T.W.T. Blackwell, Royal Navy (1921–1938). *(Courtesy of David Blackwell)*

Below: Cpl R. R. Cushen with the first unexploded German rocket bomb found in Malta, 1 January 1942, photographed for report to the War Office. A AP bomb 1,134lbs; B suspension band; C HE fuze and gaine holder; D side fuze pocket; E rocket holder; F tail fragments; G Venturi tubes; H tail locating webs; J end cap 118lbs; K rocket container 190lbs; L distance piece. *(EODTIC)*

A bomb; B suspension band; C fuze pocket; D fuze & exploder holder; E Rocket holder separator; F tail; G relief valve spring cap; H Venturi tubes; J weld; K distance piece screwed into rocket container.

Lieutenant Blackwell (left) oversees digging for the UXB at Valletta bus station 13 January 1942. *(NWMA, Malta)*

Lance-Corporal Tom Meager prepares to remove the unexploded bomb from its shaft. *(NWMA, Malta)*

The bomb is hoisted up onto the lorry. Lance-Corporal Tom Meager is third from left. *(NWMA, Malta)*

Left: The red
flag is hoisted
over the
Castille, Valletta.
(NWMA, Malta)

Below: The
Opera House
in Valletta with
balustrade
to right of
foreground.
See Chapter 9.
(NWMA Malta)

Remains of the Regent
Cinema in Valletta, 1942.
(NWMA, Malta)

Above: ARP Zabbar.
(NWMA, Malta)

Left: Searchlights over
Floriana. *(NWMA, Malta)*

The Opera House in Valletta after the bombing of 7 April 1942. *(NWMA, Malta)*

Above: Mosta. *(NWMA, Malta)*

Right: Penetration of the dome of Mosta church by the bomb of 9 April 1942. *(NWMA, Malta)*

Defuzing an uncovered bomb. *(NWMA, Malta)*

Lieutenant F.W. Ashall, 1941. *(Courtesy of Mrs Mary Ashall)*

Villa Fleri in 2008 *(Courtesy of Gaston Mifsud Wismayer)*

No 45 General Hospital (St Patrick's) showing in the foreground (left) the white circle with red cross. *(NWMA, Malta)*

Clearing debris from Kingsway, Valletta. *(NWMA Archive)*

Bombs strike Luqa airfield. *(NWMA, Malta)*

A defuzed bomb is rolled over the cliff at Hal Far, 1942. *(NWMA, Malta)*

Above: Thomas Whitworth, as Master of Hatfield College, Durham, 1957–79. *(Courtesy of Hatfield College)*

Left: German SD2 'butterfly bomb'.

Above: German 1,800kg 'Satan' ready for use and destined for Malta. *(NWMA Malta)*

Left: Lieutenant Henry Lavington 1940/41. *(Courtesy of Henry Lavington)*

Below: Unexploded bombs dropped early in 1942 were still being discovered in remote areas a year later. *(NWMA, Malta)*

While one bomb disposal officer had been busy at Luqa, his colleague had discovered a problem which could seriously compromise the capacity of RE Bomb Disposal to cope with DA bombs. They had only one magnetic clockstopper between them. Despite the enlargement to two active BD sections in January, no extra supplies had been sent out to equip a second section. In fact no new equipment had been received since early 1941. If the number of delayed-action UXBs continued to grow, how could they possibly manage? Until new supplies could be obtained, their only chance would be to borrow from their RAF and Royal Navy counterparts. But with an increase in DA bombs likely in all areas, the other services were unlikely to have equipment to spare.

Overnight, the task facing the two officers became significantly more hazardous and time-consuming. Already hard-pressed to cope with the increasing numbers and weight of unexploded bombs on the Island, Lieutenants Blackwell and Carroll were now constantly on the alert for possible DA bombs. In the four weeks following the 21 February raid, out of 177 UXB reports a dozen more bombs had DA fuzes. As bombs became more complex and dangerous, the officers had to be much more involved with each one of them.

But every single buried bomb would now require a longer and more delicate bomb disposal operation. The Germans did not need to drop a high percentage of delayed-action bombs to cause the extra disruption: once they started using them, the threat of an explosion without warning was achieved with every bomb that fell.

Notes
1 Henry Lavington (1990). *Family History*.
2 Lieutenant G.D. Carroll, 2005
3 ibid.
4 ibid.
5 Ed. (1942) *Times of Malta*. 14 February 1942. National Library of Malta
6 The former Auberge de Provence; now the Museum of Archaeology
7 Sppr Richard Walters. Personal account: *Story of Events Leading up to the First German Plane I Shot Down in Malta in 1942*, Royal Engineers Library
8 ibid.
9 Lieutenant G.D. Carroll, 2005
10 ibid.

CHAPTER 10

TRAIL OF DESTRUCTION

As far as I could tell, almost everyone else was in shelter or heading for
shelter – which I respected. I was on my own out there.[1]

March roared in 'like a lion', with a night of absolute terror. In one continuous succession of raids from ten in the evening until seven the next
morning, aircraft roared across the skies hurling bombs at targets all over the
Island, amid the booming echo of defensive barrages and heavy anti aircraft
fire. February's delayed-action bombs were merely the prelude to an even
more determined Luftwaffe bombing campaign. The mental resilience of
people struggling to survive in Malta was about to be tested to the limit. It
is difficult for anyone who has not experienced it to understand the effects
of relentless bombing:

> The scream of the planes, the whistle of the bombs hurtling down to their
> target, the incessant cracking of the Ack-Ack guns and the clouds of dust
> belching sky-wards as the bombs exploded on the white sandstone made
> the whole place rock.[2]

Enemy bombers seemed to have little concern for civilians. Around noon
on Sunday 1 March, when the avenues of Floriana were filled with people
enjoying some welcome spring sunshine, bombs struck at the heart of
the community, causing several casualties. On and on the attacks raged,

all through the following day and night, pummelling Grand Harbour and Valletta. Raids became so long that each day passed on almost constant alert, including more than 33 of the 48 hours from 7am on 5 March to 7am on 7th. One Royal Artillery officer suggested that the BBC would find it easier to report gaps between raids, such as 'During the last month, Malta had six all-clears, one of which lasted for twenty-five minutes.'[3]

Lieutenant-General Dobbie knew that the survival of Malta had reached a critical point. Visiting Floriana to view the effects of Sunday's bombing, he expressed a belief that the Germans were building up to a final assault. And he was concerned about public morale: many civilians had been killed, rations were already at less than half of normal levels and they were about to be reduced still further. Singling out the civil defence services for special praise, he stressed how essential Malta's people were to the security of the Island: 'the fortress stands on four legs: the three services and the civilian population.'[4]

The police and ARP services were certainly providing invaluable support to the work of Army bomb disposal. As soon as an air raid warning sounded, the Valletta Emergency [telephone] Exchange went into operation, connecting all police stations, ARP headquarters and centres. Roof-spotters at civil defence posts across the Island fed back details of bombs, damage and casualties via an ARP control room. This centre collected and channelled the information to co-ordinate the work to be done following a raid. Air raid wardens and superintendents were always standing by when a bombing raid was on and hurried to reach scenes where bombs were dropped, often before the raid ended. Reports of unexploded bombs could then be reported promptly to Bomb Disposal HQ.

On Monday 9 March the ARP centre at Rabat phoned through details of a UXB tracked down by one of their wardens in a field near the road to Bahrija. He was worried it might be a time bomb. The bomb disposal officer took one look and confirmed his suspicions: it was another 250kg SC with twin fuze pockets and the forward pocket held a type 17. But as he glanced across to check the rear fuze, the hairs stood up on the back of his neck. He leaned in to take a closer look: it was marked El.Z 50. A booby-trap. This bomb was intended to kill him. Lieutenant Carroll had come across this deadly device before:

The anti-handling fuze was introduced when I was in London, because so many German bombs which had not gone off were being easily rendered harmless. They knew about bomb disposal and saw an opportunity to attack us by causing the bomb to explode while we worked on it, moving it for instance. They conceived the idea of a booby-trap.[5]

The Type 50 anti-handling fuze was fitted in the second of twin fuze pockets and was only activated after the bomb landed. It was so sensitive that it would explode a bomb which was only lightly moved or struck. Even an attempt to place a magnetic clockstopper over the DA fuze in the other pocket would trigger the anti-handling fuze and explode this bomb.

The officer straightened up, thinking fast. If the clock was running, it could not be stopped until the anti-handling fuze had been disabled. He bent down again and carefully placed his ear near the front fuze pocket: no ticking. He checked again, just to make sure: nothing. He had to act quickly. If the bomb was in a sensitive area, he would have to do whatever was necessary to prevent an explosion. That meant discharging the anti-handling fuze first, even if the clock was already ticking. But because of the risk to the bomb disposal officer, this action was only required if the protection of the bomb's location was more important than his own life. The decision was his to make – and there was no time to mull it over. He stood up, thinking fast. To disable the Type 50 he would need a liquid or steam fuze discharger – and he had neither. He looked around him. The bomb was close to the road but there were no buildings nearby. This time he was spared: the DA fuze could be allowed to run its course.

When he did return four days later he still had an extremely delicate operation to perform, avoiding the slightest disturbance to the bomb while he positioned his explosive charges. He was very relieved to destroy the bomb, leaving himself in one piece. But who knew when or where the next booby-trapped bomb might fall?

The following morning a break between the clouds revealed a sight to bring a smile to the faces of Malta's besieged inhabitants. The first of the long-awaited RAF Spitfires had arrived during the weekend and now took to the skies. Civilians crowded outside their shelters to watch the agile aircraft sweep overhead. Their elation soon turned to dismay when they heard how these precious few were battered by ferocious enemy attacks.

Air Field Marshal Kesselring was ready to implement his ultimate strategy: to obliterate the Island as a base for Allied offensives in the Mediterranean. First, the airfields were to be put out of action to prevent any fighter opposition; next the dockyard, submarine base and essential harbour services must be destroyed, then all stores, barracks and communications rendered inoperable; finally all approaches to the Island would be mined so that no rescuing forces could reach it. The Luftwaffe had its deadly orders to bomb Malta as often as possible, day and night. During daylight, the Island was attacked by waves of bombers accompanied by Messerschmitt fighters. Disruptive 'intruder raids' followed throughout the night, dropping bombs over a wide area, to prevent repairs to the airfields and so put a stop to defensive operations. With typical precision, the enemy established a pattern of raids which became known by the Islanders as 'breakfast, lunch and tea', with frequently an additional raid at dusk. The extent of the onslaught can be seen from the Luftwaffe's own report of just one day of action, 16 March 1942.

0733 hrs 20 aircraft flew down the north coast, turned inland over Della Grazia and bombed Luqa.

0915 hrs 11 aircraft attacked and bombed Sliema from the sea.

1030 hrs 20 aircraft repeated the earlier bomb attack on Luqa.

1305 hrs A single aircraft attacked Valletta from the sea, dropping one 500kg SD and two 250kg SD bombs.

1320 hrs 20 aircraft made a third attack on Luqa.

1402 hrs 4 aircraft turned across the coast at Pembroke and headed for Ta' Qali, bombing the airfield.

1412 hrs 4 aircraft flew over Ta' Qali to Luqa and dropped bombs on the airfield.

1420 hrs 8 aircraft flew down the north coast, turning over the coastal forts below Della Grazia, and headed for Gudja, dropping bombs on the Safi strip.

1505 hrs 6 aircraft approached Malta from the north west, crossing the coast around Ghain Tuffieha and dropping two 1000kg, four 500kg, eight 250kg and sixty 50kg bombs on Ta' Qali.

1620 hrs 11 aircraft attacked and bombed Sliema from the sea.

1720 hrs 20 aircraft made a fourth attack on Luqa.

1725 hrs A single aircraft flew down the west coast over Dingli and attacked a Heavy Anti-Aircraft battery in the area of Qrendi/Siggiewi.
1740 hrs 8 aircraft repeated the earlier attack on the Safi strip.
1835 hrs 8 aircraft made a third attack on Safi.
1840 hrs 13 aircraft flew down the north coast and turned inland: one dropped bombs on Grand Harbour (one 1000kg and two 250kg), damaging the area of St Elmo; four aircraft bombed Luqa and four went on to bomb Ta' Qali.

As well as damage noted above, Luftwaffe pilots reported hits on the runways and quarters at Luqa, damage to runways and aircraft at Ta' Qali and hits on the runway, a workshop, dispersal pens and two aircraft at Safi.

Total bombing sorties: 151
Total bombs dropped: 258 (17 x 1000kg; 98 x 500kg; 74 x 250kg; 70 x 50kg)[6]

Not all the bombers reached their target. Picking up a UXB report which had only a map reference, Carroll found himself in open country to the south of Naxxar. He spotted his prey glinting in the sun: a large, fat, pale blue bomb. It was a Hermann – the first 1,000kg SC he had encountered in Malta. The fuze pocket had an extension cap, but after expending some effort trying to get it to budge, he gave up on identifying the fuze. He knew it was extremely unlikely it was a DA type; none had ever been encountered in a Hermann. Still, even with an impact fuze intact there was some risk of an explosion which in a bomb this size could cause serious casualties across hundreds of yards. Better to blow the bomb immediately. It took some time for the civil defence authorities to make sure the whole area was cleared. When Carroll finally detonated the bomb, even from a carefully calculated distance, the massive blast almost knocked him off his feet.

On the morning of 20 March, Carroll was on his way to a UXB when an ominous droning sound made him look up:

There was a red [flag] warning, I was making my way down the main street in Valletta, clambering over masses of rubble. It was a beautiful day, the sun was shining. Looking up at the bright blue sky between the buildings, I watched as some 30 or more German bombers went over my head… they seemed headed towards Ta' Qali.

It was that sort of life. As far as I could tell, almost everyone else was in shelter or heading for shelter – which I respected. I was on my own out there.[7]

He was looking at the forward party of the 50 aircraft which attacked that morning, followed by another 70 at teatime. The Luftwaffe had turned on Ta' Qali with all their might, using high explosive and anti-personnel bombs, as well as fighter machine-gun fire, to destroy the airfield's runways and write off all its aircraft. At sunset, 60 Ju88s plus ME10s and other fighters attacked again. The full-scale battle which followed was described in the General Staff War Diary for that day:

> 1919 to 2353: Very heavy raid on Ta' Qali developed. About 50 Ju88s came in from north in line ahead at about 10000 ft. Engaged at height control by HAA. All machines concentrated on aerodrome and heavily engaged by LAA once within range of Bofors. Many D.A. bombs dropped and numerous craters to aerodrome, though runways not appreciably damaged. Until dark AA destroyed 4 JU and damaged 1. Some bombs dropped outside main target area, Luqa, Grand Harbour; raid turned into normal night attacks by enemy a/c singly and in 2s and 3s with coming of darkness. Mil[itary] casualties Ta' Qali nil, 2 RAF wounded. Normal night raids continued at intervals throughout the night.[8]

In just 24 hours, the Luftwaffe dropped over 1,000 bombs, totalling 296 tons, on Ta' Qali – an area the size of a small English village. In a similar period 500 tons of bombs were used across the entire city of Coventry in England. Here was the first ever instance of carpet bombing on such a scale against a military target.

DA bombs were scattered all over the airfield, holding up repair work on the runways. RAF bomb disposal needed the help of the Royal Engineers to cope with the sheer number of unexploded bombs. In two days RE Bomb Disposal received over 70 UXB reports. Among them was a Priority UXB at an RAF billet in Rabat. The RE Bomb Disposal officer and squad who attended were saddened to hear that five off-duty pilots had been killed during the raid.

The raids continued with the same force the following day. The communities surrounding Ta' Qali suffered badly; there were casualties and shattered buildings in Mosta, Balzan and Mtarfa, as well as Rabat. 24 civilians were killed and 45 wounded in Mosta, where a large percentage of the bombs fell. The police at Rabat had several UXBs on their patch, including three at the Concezzione Church. Two of the bombs were marked Priority: they had entered the ground very close to the building. A bomb disposal officer ordered a squad to follow him to the church right away. Although he estimated the bombs were no more than 50kg, one of them gave him particular cause for concern. From the angle of entry he suspected it could undermine the foundations of the building. He gave the order for the squad to start digging.

Days went by with no sign of the bomb. The NCO on site was puzzled: smaller HE bombs did not normally bury themselves so deeply in Malta. Wondering whether it could be a new type, he consulted his bomb disposal officer. His comment was noted; still there was no choice but to keep at it. It took seven days to reach the bomb, yet it was only a 50kg. Even though it was the heavier SD type, the NCO was amazed that it had travelled 22 feet into the ground.

The second bomb took another week to uncover. It too was a 50kg SD, and even deeper at 24 feet. Hearing the news, their officer concluded that both must have been dropped from an exceptionally high altitude. An enquiry to the airfield's HQ revealed that observers had seen enemy planes approaching at 10–16,000 feet and releasing their bombs from varying heights. If they continued with this tactic, the men would have a lot more digging to do.

As the Luftwaffe extended their campaign, information began to circulate warning of new types of anti-personnel bomb. Carroll received a UXB report which suggested something unusual.

There was a notice to the effect that the Germans were dropping 'shaving stick' bombs and 'fountain pen' bombs … I had a message from an Ack-Ack unit over towards Vittoriosa that they had found a fountain pen bomb. I had to go and deal with it.

I had an open-topped Austin 8 tourer, camouflaged. I got my sergeant to put sandbags in the back seat, we put helmets on (because you must treat any such report seriously) and we drove over to the Ack-Ack detachment. I walked in and asked for the duty officer and was told, 'He's having a nap, sir.' He told me where and I found the officer asleep on his bed. I woke him and said, 'I gather you've got a fountain pen bomb here. Where is it?' He answered, 'On top of the cupboard over there.' I said I would deal with it and climbed up to get it … I put it on my [open] hand and carried it [to the car], put it carefully on the sandbags, covered it with more sandbags, put up a red flag on the car, and we drove back to [Floriana].

I dealt with it some time later, as it was rather small and not as important as others. We had a bench with a vice and there were some sleepers nearby left from the old railway. I asked my Sergeant to get the sleepers and lean them up against the vice, to get some boxing gloves for us (they would at least reduce any injury), goggles and steel helmets. We went down [to the workshop].

In dealing with a new bomb like this, you had to have a witness and recorder. My sergeant was there [outside the door] with a pencil and notebook and I called out to him. 'I'm putting the barrel of the fountain pen in the vice so that the cap can be freed.' 'Yes, sir,' and he wrote it down. Now I had to wait two minutes. 'I'm attaching a piece of surgical tape to the cap, wrapping it round so that, if I pull, it will unscrew.' 'Yes, sir,' he wrote it down and I waited. 'Now I'm going to pull the tape to loosen the cap.' 'Yes, sir,' and he wrote it down. I pulled it and it unscrewed, and I waited. 'I am now going to pull it off.' 'Yes, sir.' I pulled it off and it was a fountain pen! But I treated it as it had to be treated – I couldn't do otherwise.[9]

It was extra work which the hard-pressed bomb disposal officers could do without. With only two of them to manage so many UXB reports, it was vital to reduce the number of false alarms. They approached the Chief Engineer with the problem, and a circular was issued to the police, special constabulary, ARP wardens and others involved in the reporting of UXBs.

Great care should be taken to verify whether reported unexploded bombs really exist before making a request for the attendance of a bomb disposal officer who has been called out on frequent occasions only to find that the reports were incorrect and no such bombs were to be found. Journeys thus involved have incurred a considerable waste of petrol. Always ascertain whether a bomb is exposed or buried.

Two other important points to be observed in connection with bombs are:-

a) Fragments of exploded bombs must not be moved.

b) Instances of bombs having been dropped with delay action fuzes have occurred recently. It is therefore dangerous to approach near unexploded bombs and the risk of explosion persists at least four days after the bombs were dropped.[10]

Somehow a convoy managed to struggle through the Mediterranean to reach Grand Harbour on Monday 23 March, to the usual Luftwaffe welcome. Raiders lashed the Dockyard for 20 hours out of 24, at ten times the intensity of the '*Illustrious* blitz' just over a year before. The attacks raged on for three days, from noon and all through the night, bombarding Grand Harbour and the aerodromes. The fast supply ship *Breconshire*, a lifeline of supplies and military personnel for so many months, finally succumbed to enemy attacks and sank in Marsaxlokk Harbour. Again the Three Cities bore the brunt of the bombing; civilian areas suffered most. Unexploded bombs in the rubble waited for long periods until it was possible to get men to them. Another air-raid shelter – this time in Tarxien – suffered a direct hit from a bomb which failed to explode. It was dealt with by Carroll along with two other UXBs in nearby Temple Street.

The Luftwaffe were not escaping entirely unscathed. With Spitfires now among them, RAF defences were better equipped to fight back. Enemy fighters and bombers were beginning to fall victim to counter-attacks. In response, the Luftwaffe's dreaded Ju87 'Stuka' reappeared in force. This agile dive-bomber, with its notorious screeching roar, struck fear into the hearts of everyone within earshot. The night of 25 March 1942 saw one of the fiercest battles so far between the opposing air forces. All night the sky over Grand Harbour was lit up by enemy parachute flares, searchlights and exploding shells from harbour gun positions. Carroll and his fellow lodgers in the South Street pension were irresistibly drawn to witness the fighting:

Some nights after dinner we went up onto the roof to watch bombing raids which made flashes of light. This particular night we were up there and thought it was a bit unsafe so we went downstairs into the hall for protection – the front door was closed. Suddenly, there was a blinding white flash, with complete silence, and then tinkling of glass. The house next door had just blown straight up and disappeared, just a few feet away. The houses were built of big stone blocks, four floors perhaps. The bomb had gone down and blown the whole lot out between the walls. I don't remember whether anyone was hurt – a lot of people had moved out of Valletta. It was strange being so close to a bomb and hearing nothing: it was like a funnel and all the sound went up into the air.

That was a curious thing about bombs when they went off. If you watch what happens when a stone drops into water, the water mushrooms up. The same thing happens with bomb explosions – sometimes people were so close to an exploding bomb that they were blown over and their clothes were ripped off but they were left physically unhurt.[11]

At daybreak the Luftwaffe returned, only to launch their most intensive raid of the war yet. Immense formations of bombers, dive-bombers and torpedo-carrying machines, all accompanied by swarms of Messerschmitt fighters, attacked the Island. For nearly six hours, massive waves of air-craft dropped hundreds of tons of bombs on the Grand Harbour area. Kesselring's plan was taking its toll: his main target areas were already unbelievably wasted. Three-quarters of the buildings around the once-populous Grand Harbour had now been partly or completely destroyed. The number of military and civilian casualties rose sharply. By the end of March, Malta had suffered 117 days of continuous raids. During the month the Island's inhabitants had spent nearly 372 hours under air raid alert – the equivalent of more than 15 days of constant fear and apprehension. The strain of round the clock air raids and casualties, combined with the pressure to maintain their defence of Malta, was increasingly affecting the morale of military personnel. Concerned that some might buckle under the pressure, military commanders decided to post a warning notice at all gun emplacements.

• Fear is the weapon which the enemy employs to sabotage morale.

• Anxiety neurosis is the term used by the medical profession to commercialise fear.

• Anxiety neurosis is a misnomer which makes 'cold feet' appear respectable.

• To give way to fear is to surrender to the enemy attack on your morale.

• To admit to anxiety neurosis is to admit a state of fear which is either unreasonable or has no origin in your conception of duty as a soldier.

• If you are a man, you will not permit your self-respect to admit to anxiety neurosis or to show fear.

• Do not confuse fear with prudence or impulsive action with bravery.

• Safety first is the worst of principles.

• In civil life, anxiety neurosis will put you 'on the club'. In battle it brings you a bayonet in the bottom and a billet in a prisoner-of-war camp.[12]

Looking back on this period, the British Army Medical Services ultimately acknowledged the inevitable impact of the relentless air raids on Malta's forces:

> The conditions in Malta in 1941 and 1942 were such as to expose even the most stout-hearted among its garrison to the risk of a breakdown. Violence continually descended from the skies and, save for the gunners and the fighter pilots, there was no means of retaliation. It had to be endured. To the endurance and to resilience of everyone there is a limit; no wonder then that anxiety neurosis, though not labelled as such, came to figure largely among the causes of sickness.[13]

The arrival of Spitfires had brought some hope – but there were too few to make more than a small dent in the Luftwaffe's command of the skies. When Malta's defenders did achieve some success, enemy aircraft jettisoned a large number of bombs over the Island, resulting in many more UXBs for RE Bomb Disposal. Bombs released from a great height travelled further into the ground, forcing the sappers to sink deeper shafts before any sign of their quarry. And every strike of a pick or shovel brought them closer to a possible time bomb.

In one month, the weight of bombs dropped on Malta had more than doubled, from 990 tons in February to 2,170 in March. The total number of unexploded bombs reported for the same periods had trebled, from 90 to 270 in a month. Malta's two RE Bomb Disposal sections were scarcely able to keep up: their workload was now greater than entire BD companies of a dozen sections had managed on the Home Front.

Notes

1 Lieutenant G.D. Carroll, 2008
2 Sppr Richard Walters. Personal account: 'Story of Events Leading up to the First German Plane I Shot Down in Malta in 1942', Royal Engineers Library
3 Ministry of Information (1944). The Air Battle of Malta. The Official Account of the RAF in Malta, June 1940 to November 1942, London: HMSO.
4 Ed. (1942). Situation Reports & Operational Messages Out. 1942. WO 106, National Archives, London
5 Lieutenant G.D. Carroll, 2005
6 Information compiled from Vella, P. (1985). *Malta: Blitzed But Not Beaten.* Malta: Progress Press.
7 Lieutenant G.D. Carroll, 2005
8 Ed. (1942). *War Diary General Staff Malta 1942.* WO 169, National Archives, London
9 Lieutenant G.D. Carroll, 2005
10 Correspondence of Chief Secretary and Lieutenant Governor's Office. National Archives of Malta
11 Lieutenant G.D. Carroll, 2005
12 Army Medical Services. *Official History of the Second World War*, National Archives, London.
13 ibid.

CHAPTER 11

IN THE LINE OF FIRE

... all of us during the siege were only doing what we were trained to do and, if it helped in any way, that's what life is all about.

Sapper C.E. 'Inky' Reeves[1]

Yet there was worse to come. The German bombing campaign had not even reached its climax – Malta was about to become 'the most bombed place on earth.'[2] In just one month another 6,728 tons of bombs would be dropped on the small island, more than over the entire mainland of Britain in any month of the war. In the first week of April 1942, another 158 UXB reports reached Bomb Disposal HQ at Lintorn Barracks – nearly four times as many as in the previous seven days. There were tough decisions to make. From now on, all but the most urgent bombs would be put on hold until manpower was available. With so many UXBs affecting military operations, those in town centres waited even longer than before. Buried bombs, especially remote ones, were deferred until several had accumulated in an area: only then could digging parties be allocated to them.

At dawn on 1 April, the first beams of daylight flickered as a swarm of black objects loomed towards Malta from the east, silhouetted against the rising sun. A steady drone grew to a roar as 100 aircraft swept across Grand Harbour, and on towards the airfields, unleashing bombs as they went. Within an hour ten UXB reports were telephoned in from the southern airfields, another eleven from Grand Harbour and Sliema, and two from

Rabat. The RE Bomb Disposal officers divided the reports between them and prepared for another busy day – one mustered his section and headed south while the other deployed his squads to work in Valletta, Sliema and Rabat. Then rescue teams working in Zabbar reported five unexploded bombs among the rubble. The officer attending reluctantly informed them that both bomb disposal sections were fully occupied. As the bombs were among buildings already in ruins, they would have to wait.

The squads made their weary way back to Lintorn Barracks that evening, to be met with more bad news. During the afternoon raid, a bomber had struck the Fortress Royal Engineers Garage with a direct hit, for the second time. Nine more men were killed, including one from 24 Fortress Company who had worked with Lieutenant Carroll. Before the officer could take in what had happened, a messenger rushed towards him. A 250kg bomb had fallen on the bastions at the rear of the barracks administrative block, and failed to explode. The site was just yards from Carroll's bomb disposal workshop and store.

> Under the bastions there were arches where they created some storehouses. One of the bombs that came down landed in the rubble on the top of the arch. It was stuck there. As the officer I had to deal with it on my own. So I crawled across the arch with my trowel, like an archaeologist. I was scraping away gently to find the fuze about half way up the bomb.
> Then suddenly the bomb fell, right in front of my eyes … I died!
> It hit the ground … and I died –
> and it bounced – and I died –
> and it rolled – and I died -
> but I didn't die.
> That was the feeling, when that happened in front of you.[3]

There was no time to contemplate anything but the job in hand. Next morning, RE Bomb Disposal squads were off to start excavations in Vittoriosa, Ta Mehrla and Hal Far. While they worked, another 26 UXB reports came in to their HQ. Overnight the bombs had become heavier: nine of the high explosive bombs reported were either 250kg or 500kg, all lying on the surface. Every one was likely to contain a clockwork fuze – or maybe two.

It was Easter, and for the second year in a row the people of Malta would be celebrating their most important religious festival under enemy bombardment. This time, the annual weekend of peace and reflection became the prelude to a particularly violent period in their already harsh ordeal. Good Friday, 3 April 1942, marked the start of seven days of saturation bombing against Valletta. With the crash of falling bombs echoing in the distance, the officers and men of the Fortress Royal Engineers stood in silence at Pieta Military Cemetery mourning the loss of comrades killed two days before. Bomb disposal went on as usual. Lieutenant Carroll and No.128 Section spent the day working in and around the Three Cities, while Lieutenant Blackwell and his section were busy down at Luqa airfield.

The sappers did have something to look forward to: a day off. It was long overdue. Despite the growing backlog of unexploded bombs, the officers needed to consider the mental and physical well-being of the men in their command. They had been working for weeks without a break, under the added strain of round the clock bombardment. For sappers as well as officers the work of bomb disposal required a cool head and constant adherence to correct procedures; any momentary loss of concentration could be fatal. If the current level of effort was to be sustained, the men must have some respite. Lieutenants Blackwell and Carroll decided that their NCOs and sappers would take it in turns to rest during the Easter weekend. A core squad attended to the most critical jobs, led by one of the two bomb disposal officers each day. The other officer could have some rest but remained on call for any urgent UXBs as necessary.

ARP Superintendent Spiteri also decided to give his second in command a deserved day off, so he was working alone in Valletta on Easter Saturday. Suddenly, a large formation of bombers swooped in and fanned out to attack both sides of Grand Harbour, bringing down dozens of buildings. On his way to survey the damage, Spiteri was approached by an ARP warden who had spotted suspected unexploded bombs in a shattered building. A quick inspection confirmed at least two UXBs. Leaving the warden on guard, the Superintendent hurried back to his control room to telephone Bomb Disposal. He barely had time to finish the call: a crowd of civilians and ARP wardens were clamouring for his attention elsewhere. Carroll was quickly on the scene and before long two 50kg SC bombs were crossed off the list of 30 reported to Lintorn that day. But as the bomb attacks raged on through the afternoon, Spiteri found it increasingly difficult to keep up with his duties. 'I had 21 bombs on Valletta and [still] had to go on my usual reconnaissance …'[4]

On into Easter Sunday the raids persisted; each one seemed heavier than the last. Over 140 bombers attacked the Island. The first UXB report of the day came early in the morning from the huge ramparts of St Clements Bastion, part of the southern outer defences of the Three Cities. The fragments looked familiar to Blackwell: it was a rocket bomb, the same construction as the one back in January. Removing the fuze from the base of the bomb he took it with him to add to the samples already collected in the workshop.

The Luftwaffe saved the heaviest raid of the day until after lunch, when 40 Ju88s and 14 Stukas attacked Grand Harbour. They were obviously becoming even more determined to destroy all in their path. Carroll was taking advantage of a precious few hours on standby to fit in a game of tennis with a friend, Lieutenant Clark:.

> Within the barracks at the base of the bastions there were tennis courts. We were playing on the side nearest the bastion – it was towering above us. The sky was absolutely clear blue and while we were playing we heard aircraft approaching. We looked up and there were about five Hurricanes overhead. Shortly afterwards another aircraft came from the same direction, following the fighters. It was heading over towards the built-up area. As it went over our heads a bomb dropped from underneath. It was blue – it was a 'Hermann'.
>
> Clark dived into a hole in the bastions and there wasn't room for me. I belaboured his backside with my tennis racket and said 'Bloody well move over!'. I watched helpless – and saw the bomb disappear over the top of the buildings before it went off.[5]

The bomb was one of several massive 1,000kg SCs which smashed into buildings around Grand Harbour and military defence positions inland that day. Two unexploded Hermanns were reported at the Dockyard School and another on the coast near Xghajra. It seemed that dozens of the huge and powerful bombs were being dropped on all kinds of military and dockyard installations – many landing in the midst of nearby civilian populations. 28

were reported as UXBs in April, all except one in built-up areas. Many had extension caps jammed in place, and were hauled aboard the bomb disposal lorry with their fuzes intact, to be driven cautiously to the coast. It was perilous, tough and time-consuming work for Harry Turner and his mates.

On Easter Monday morning both bomb disposal sections were back to full strength, with new UXB reports from Birzebbuga in the south, as well as the Three Cities, Sliema and Tigne. Then late in the afternoon, the initial wave of a massive raid launched a direct attack on Hamrun and Marsa leaving a 500kg SC close to the extensive Army camp and prompting a late call out for one bomb disposal officer. As he headed for home, three more waves of bomber and fighter formations roared in. One group peeled off to hit the dockyard and Hal Far, the next aimed for Grand Harbour and Luqa, and the final one targeted the dockyard again, leaving more UXBs in their wake.

As if to mark the milestone of Malta's 2,000th raid, on Tuesday 7 April the Luftwaffe executed its most violent attack yet on Valletta, pummelling the tiny peninsula with 280 tons of bombs. Raids thundered on continuously all day. The enemy seemed hell-bent on completely destroying the city and nearby Floriana – few buildings were left standing, and almost none were still intact. Attacks seemed to approach Grand Harbour from a different direction each time, as well as targeting the three aerodromes. Just before three in the afternoon, 120 Ju88s and Stukas swooped down again on Valletta and Grand Harbour, causing more extensive damage and leaving behind another 30 unexploded bombs.

While attacks thundered overhead, the two bomb disposal officers did their best to keep on top of the large number of heavy bombs. While one worked in the heart of the dockyard district, the other headed for Tarxien, to find a community still reeling from a tragedy the day before. Seventeen civilians had been killed by a bomb which struck a private air raid shelter. As the raids rumbled on into the afternoon, a UXB report came in from the RAF. A very large bomb had landed close to the airfield. It was Carroll who picked up the report:

> We had a Hermann to deal with near Luqa, just outside the perimeter of the airfield … It was on the surface … I went off with my Sergeant and four or five men to take a look and decide what we were going to do about it. We had just [reached the bomb] when suddenly there was

an attack. A fighter-bomber – came down, swooping across towards us, machine-gunning the airfield. We had literally nowhere to shelter, so I shouted at [the men] to dive under the bomb. Fortunately it wasn't hit and once the planes had passed over we crawled out, dusted ourselves down, and carried on with our work.

We didn't have an alert out there. I was on my own, in a sense: I wasn't on the airfield – they had no responsibility for me. If we were dealing with a bomb, and there was an air-raid, we just had to make the best of it.[6]

The attacks raged on relentlessly until dusk. Then, at just before 6pm, bombs smashed into the Opera House. The building which Carroll had worked so hard to save the previous December was utterly destroyed, along with many others – several close to his pension in nearby South Street, including the premises of the Malta Amateur Dramatic Club. The raids made it unsafe for Malta's seat of government to remain in Valletta and it was decided to evacuate to Hamrun, two miles inland. Next day the Governor himself retreated to the relative safety of his residence at San Anton Palace in Attard. And after another lucky escape from an unexploded 1,000kg SC bomb near their HQ at Pieta, Army general staff were on the move to Tal Virtu, on the south side of Rabat. They were just in time to avoid a fresh attempt by the enemy to cause havoc among military personnel and civilians alike.

On Wednesday 8 April 1942, the number of Luftwaffe sorties against Malta in a single day doubled again: 261 aircraft took part in fourteen air raids. During an attack in late afternoon, several fires broke out in and around Lintorn Barracks. The sappers were quick to respond, managing to extinguish every blaze with no casualties or significant damage to buildings. Word soon spread that the fires had been started by small incendiary bombs. Within minutes of the All Clear, messages started to arrive at Lintorn: small unexploded bombs lay spread across Floriana.

Led by their BD officers, all available NCOs from Bomb Disposal were deployed to investigate. As Lance-Corporal Tom Meager crossed the parade ground heading for the centre of town, he could see dozens of the bombs, some still burning. He sped across the square, with only one thought on his mind. In her flat opposite the barracks, Tom's wife Maria opened the door to the sound of her husband's footsteps, surprised to see him coming home at this time. Not even pausing to explain, Tom pushed her firmly back inside, telling her in no uncertain terms to close the door and windows and to stay put. Maria did as she was told but could not resist the temptation to peep out of the window to see what was going on. Looking out over the top of nearby buildings she spotted Tom, jumping from one roof to another, clearing away small bombs.

The enemy had started to drop hundreds of 1kg incendiaries in large batches, from canisters. Scattered across densely-populated areas, they formed a trail of hazards every few yards, a menace especially to the young and elderly – and to anything flammable, including vehicles. Once again NCOs and squads of sappers travelled miles to and fro across the Island tackling incendiary bombs. There were so many that it was impossible to keep complete records for the Weekly Bomb Disposal Reports. But at the same time there was no let-up in the use of heavy HE bombs, which enemy aircraft also seemed to be deploying indiscriminately. Many more were landing in civilian areas, with the inevitable terrifying outcome.

After the emergency of the previous afternoon, on Thursday 9 April both bomb disposal sections went back to their various outstanding jobs. For once they enjoyed a relatively quiet morning. Only the occasional small formation of aircraft crossed the coast and few UXBs were reported, none of them critical. One bomb disposal officer had a report from a military defence post to check on: this time the description suggested a very large bomb. The hole of entry was so wide he even considered whether it was the crater from an explosion by a smaller bomb. He inspected the surround-ings carefully: there was no indication of any blast but the ground had been compressed downwards – signs of a large UXB. Having discussed with his sergeant the most likely position of the bomb, he gave the order to open a trench. By mid-day the squad was making good progress. Small fragments of blue tail fin confirmed first suspicions – another Hermann.

At noon, the day suddenly took a dramatic turn. A formation of Stukas swept across from the north-east coast towards Luqa, unleashing a hail of bombs – not on the airfield but on the village itself, destroying many houses and badly scarring the beautiful parish church. Worse still, one heavy bomb scored a direct hit on an air-raid shelter in Pope Innocent Street, killing 25 people who had fled there for protection. More bombs struck the neigh-bouring village of Gudja, damaging houses and the police station. Seven villagers died when a large bomb hit a private shelter. At nearby Mqabba, three civilians were killed and six injured as bombs destroyed dozens of houses and partly demolished the village church. News of the tragedies was quickly brought to the notice of the Governor, Lieutenant-General Dobbie, who arrived as soon as he could to show his support for the stricken villagers. One unexploded bomb at the heart of Luqa village demonstrated the ferocity of the raid: it was a Hermann. A bomb disposal officer was also soon on his way. Two more 1,000kg bombs were reported as suspected buried UXBs in the streets of Marsa, and a fourth on the surface near Hompesch.

At 4.30pm the Luftwaffe returned. Their target appeared to be Ta' Qali. Instead, another community was in the line of fire. At this time of day, Catholic parishioners of Mosta were attending Mass in their magnificent church, the massive dome of which was a highly-visible beacon, dominating the landscape to the north of Ta' Qali. Two enemy aircraft roared across the sky over the landmark, releasing bombs onto the town. One penetrated the dome and crashed to the floor of the church in front of the terrified congregation. Rev Salvatore Magro, then a young priest at Mosta, described what happened.

> At about 16.40 hours one of the bombs pierced the dome, bounced twice off the wall, skidded the whole length of the church and finally came to rest without exploding. At the time there were about 300 people attending the service and, while the majority [had] sought refuge in the side chapels, some remained kneeling. The dome was damaged but inexplicably no one was injured.[7]

Recovering his senses, the priest saying Mass took command of the situation, shepherding his parishioners out of the church and into an underground shelter. He then sent a messenger to the police asking for the bomb disposal squad to be called. In the meantime, a second unexploded bomb was spotted outside the church and was added to the police report telephoned through to Lintorn Barracks. The report had the highest priority. An important symbol for the Maltese people was in danger. A report of this status and sensitivity must be brought immediately to the attention of a bomb disposal officer – either Lieutenant Blackwell or Lieutenant Carroll. Whoever was available first would head for Mosta straight away; an NCO and squad could join him there. Met at the scene by representatives from the civil defence authorities and the church, the bomb disposal officer established the whereabouts of the two bombs, then thanked them, asking them to leave the area.

The bomb outside the church was a 50kg SD, lying close to a wall. Unless there were complications, this one could be delegated to his NCO. The bomb inside was a job for the bomb disposal officer alone. Walking up the aisle, he could see piles of stone and debris strewn across the floor; then he caught sight of the bomb. Looking up, he was surprised to see how cleanly it had pierced the dome, making a neat hole high up in the cupola, not much greater than its own diameter. Remarkably, it seemed as though the bomb had been travelling on such a trajectory that its nose was at a perfect angle to pierce the dome head-on.

Time to focus on the bomb. It was a 500kg SC: he braced himself for a possible delayed-action fuze – if it was, the church could still be in jeopardy. Moving nearer, he saw that there was only one fuze pocket, which was a good sign. Then he bent to look for the number stamped into the fuze head: Series 5 – impact. The fuze was easily discharged and he could unscrew the rings and lift it free. It was over.

Back in the fresh air he found his NCO and told him that the bomb was safe, although his men would have to shift some rubble before the carcass could be moved out of the church. Then it could be handed over to Harry Turner and the lorry team for its final journey to the western cliffs. The NCO also had news: the 50kg bomb outside the church had been defuzed but the police had reported another four unexploded bombs lying in nearby streets, all 50kg. The bomb disposal officer decided that they might as well finish them off. By the end of the day, all six UXBs were on their way to the coast to be dropped into the sea.

The community was keen to express its gratitude for the actions of the section. One letter appeared in the *Times of Malta*:

AN APPRECIATION. MOSTA.
May I through the medium of your paper voice a word of sincere and heartfelt thanks to the Bomb Disposal Squad who so promptly and so gallantly removed the unexploded bombs from the Mosta Church – a church so dear to the heart of the people of this Island. In so doing, I am sure I am expressing the feelings of every Maltese and, more so, of the

people of Mosta who are justly proud of their magnificent dome.

Joseph M. Cassar Torreggiani[8]

But the story of the bomb in the Rotunda at Mosta did not end with that memorable day in April 1942. Down the years, the tale has been continually told and retold in many different ways. A display and example of the bomb in an ante-room of the church have become a powerful symbol of survival in Malta through the trials of the Second World War. Yet despite much speculation there is no reliable way to identify who actually worked on the bomb, or even which of the two Army bomb disposal sections was involved.[9] Instead, the events have come to represent the achievement of all members of RE Bomb Disposal who worked through the blitz on Malta. As one of them said in the 1980s, when asked about the Mosta bomb: 'It was just one of many.'[10]

Regardless of the unsolved mystery, the true miracle of Mosta surely lies in one unquestionable fact: on a day when the Luftwaffe evidently launched direct attacks on the innocent civilians of Malta, one large bomb landed among a congregation attending Mass, and failed to explode.

Notes

1 Letter from C.E. 'Inky' Reeves (1992). Camilleri, A. Collection of documents relating to UXB at Mosta on 9 April 1942
2 Moorehead, A. (1965). *The Desert War.* London: Hamish Hamilton.
3 Lieutenant G.D. Carroll, 2005
4 Reports and correspondence, ARP Malta, National Archives of Malta
5 Lieutenant G.D. Carroll, 2005
6 ibid.
7 Rev Salvatore (Don Salv) Magro, interviewed by NWMA, Malta (1975). Vella, P. (1985). *Malta: Blitzed But Not Beaten.* Malta: Progress Press.
8 Ed. (1942). *Times of Malta.* 16 April.
9 See Appendix 6: apart from specific quotes where indicated, the account of the action taken inside the Church is the author's own, based on available evidence and RE Bomb Disposal policy in Malta during the Second World War.
10 Hogben, Maj A (1987). *Designed to Kill.* Wellingborough: Stephens.

CHAPTER 12

NCOs INTO THE BREACH

The head of the fuze was caked with soil and he hadn't given it a second thought as he took it out. It was only when he went to unscrew the gaine that he noticed anything amiss.

While the community of Mosta was still reverberating with news of the miraculous escape, the UXB report No. 2175 was returned to Bomb Disposal HQ marked simply 'defuzed & removed'. It was added to the 54 other high explosive UXBs listed in the Bomb Disposal Report for the week ending Saturday 11 April 1942. Two thirds of them had required the attendance of a bomb disposal officer. Between them, the sappers of both BD sections had dug up sixteen bombs, two of them more than 20 feet below ground. For some of them, the effort brought a weekend free from digging.

That Saturday morning, Lieutenant Blackwell was out on bomb disposal duties, and Lieutenant Carroll was on standby. But there was no opportunity to rest: he was taking his turn as duty officer in the observation post on the roof of Lintorn Barracks. His job was to decide whether an incoming attack was on a direct course for the barracks and, if so, give the order to retreat to shelter. The enemy had been coming over on reconnaissance raids all morning and an attack was expected at any time. The senior NCO on look-out duty with Carroll was describing 'one hell of a blitz' on Floriana the evening before when two bombs had fallen on the barracks.

The NCO fell silent at the sound of an aircraft engine approaching them from behind – a Ju88. Carroll turned and looked up in dismay to see the plane heading straight for them, no more than 40 yards above their heads. Instinctively, the two men dived to the floor. Nothing happened. Scrambling to their feet and dusting themselves off, they watched the bomber head out to sea. The bomb racks were empty: the payload had already been released inland before it reached them.

Suddenly, Carroll felt a familiar sharp pain in his abdomen. He was sure this couldn't be the 'Malta Dog'[1] for which the doctor was treating him. He sat down with a thud, doubled up in pain. The NCO asked what was wrong. From the officer's reply, the NCO thought it might be a stomach ulcer; he suggested Carroll should go to the medical officer. Within an hour, Carroll was at No 45 General Hospital, where he collapsed in agony. He was rushed to the operating theatre just in time for life-saving surgery. It was a perforated duodenal ulcer: 20 minutes more and the resulting peritonitis would have killed him.

One of Malta's two Army bomb disposal officers was out of action. Lieutenant Blackwell learned the news when he returned to Lintorn Barracks from Hal Far that afternoon. He was called to a meeting with his CO to discuss what should be done. The CO did have some good news: Carroll would reach the end of a year's service in Malta on 22 April 1942. A replacement bomb disposal officer had already been identified in the Middle-East and warned to expect a transfer. With a bit of luck, he could be on his way sooner than planned. Until he arrived, Blackwell was on his own. Even with the resources of both BD sections, it would be impossible for him to cope with all of the large UXBs across the Island – even more of them would have to be put on hold.

There was no time to dwell on the problem. On Monday there were more bombs to unearth at Hamrun and Mqabba as well as plenty of incendiaries to see to. The sappers worked on while the boom of exploding bombs echoed in the distance. Instead of attacking in the usual close formations, single enemy raiders seemed to be operating almost at random, especially targeting gun positions.

One gun-site on the east coast near Xghajra had a near-miss: a bomb sliced into the ground just a few feet away and failed to explode. The Gunners' call to RE Bomb Disposal was followed by three more from gun positions: one to the south of Hal Far, another at Marsa, and a third on the ground above Rinella Creek near Fort Ricasoli. Sending NCOs and squads to work on trenches at Marsa and Xghajra, Blackwell jumped into the lorry alongside Lance-Corporal Tom Meager. They drove first to Rinella and defuzed the 250kg bomb, then down to Hal Far. They reported in to the main gate and a guide climbed on board to show them where to find the UXB. It was much nearer the end of the runway than the report had suggested; Blackwell decided it should be rendered harmless right away. As it was a 50kg, he could let his lance-corporal see to it. Tom Meager went ahead and removed the fuze from the bomb. Then he had a shock:

I just pulled [the fuze] out, and I noticed there was only one booster charge at the bottom of it. I then checked on the top of it – and lo and behold it was a 17 fuze, the clockwork fuze. I got a surprise, and quickly unscrewed the gaine, so if it went off it would only just flash. It had never been known for a time-delay fuze to be put into a 50kg bomb – it was always impact fuzes – and so we never used to look much at them. I just took it out and it happened to be a long-delay fuze.[2]

It was a lucky escape. This time the Luftwaffe had delivered the unexpected, and it could easily have cost the lives of the two bomb disposal men. The fact was not lost on Lieutenant Blackwell, though he would not let his lance-corporal see how much it affected him. The delayed-action fuze had rarely been found in a 50kg UXB anywhere – and it was certainly the first in Malta. But he was only too aware that it was probably not the last.

What about the bomb at Marsa? Although he knew the men were always careful, they too would be less alert to the possibility of a clockwork fuze in a 50kg. Lieutenant Blackwell called Lance-Corporal Meager back to the lorry and told him to drive over there fast. Tom put his foot to the floor and the lorry bounced along the rough roads as they sped northwards to Marsa, covering the six miles in record time. When they pulled in, the NCO and his squad were talking in a huddle. The senior man turned to the approaching bomb disposal officer; there was evidently something on his mind. The NCO reported finding a 50kg bomb ten feet down, which he had defuzed. Blackwell was about to feel relieved, but the NCO had something to add: the bomb had a clockwork fuze. The head of the fuze was caked with soil and he hadn't given it a second thought as he took it out. It was only when he went to unscrew the gaine that he noticed anything amiss. He was out of the hole pretty fast and in the brighter light he saw the number: 17A.

Two near misses in one day. Blackwell knew they now had to expect a Type 17, or indeed any other dangerous fuze, in every unexploded HE bomb. As soon as he could assemble the two bomb disposal sections together, he gave them a stern warning. He acknowledged how keen they were to get the job done but they could take no further chances. Things were stretched enough; he could not afford to lose any one of them. From now on, every fuze must be fully identified before any attempt was made to extract it from the bomb.

Severe storms over the Island on Wednesday made the work even harder going, although they brought a welcome break from heavy air raids. After a day out slogging through the bad weather, the men soon found the energy to celebrate the news which greeted them on their return to barracks that evening. His Majesty King George VI had awarded the George Cross to the Island Fortress of Malta. *The Times* newspaper in London expressed the significance of the much-deserved award:

> ... Malta – the first part of the British Commonwealth to be so decorated – has received the George Cross, 'to bear witness' as His Majesty said in his telegram to the Governor, 'to a heroism and devotion that will long be famous in history'. No-one, least of all our enemies, will deny that an honour had never been more richly deserved. Nor will there be doubt that the Islanders, much as they have borne and have yet to bear, will fulfil the determination expressed in the Governor's reply, 'that by God's help Malta will not weaken but will endure until victory is won.'[3]

The Royal Engineers could share with Malta's civilians a sense of pride at having survived so many months of relentless enemy action, combined with increasing deprivation and hardship.

On Friday 17 April Lieutenant Blackwell and Lance-Corporal Meager made an arduous journey through stormy weather to the Ghadira military camp in Mellieha Bay, where two more 50kg bombs had been reported lying in full view of the accommodation huts. After the events of recent days they were not sure what to expect as they approached the nearest bomb. The fuze marking was plain: a series 5, impact. This should be a straightforward job for Meager but memories of the previous Tuesday made Blackwell tell him to wait while he checked the second bomb for a DA fuze. He did not want it exploding unexpectedly while Tom Meager worked on the other one. The head of the fuze was visible but – Blackwell blinked and looked again – there was no identifying number. He could be excused a curse at that moment. Common sense dictated that it would be a dangerous fuze.

The Germans introduced the unmarked fuze to kill any bomb disposer who might attempt to deal with it, despite its lack of identification. However, there was a flaw to their plan. The bomber crew on board the aircraft had to know which fuzes had been fitted – especially if they might be forced to turn back to base without releasing their bomb load. In that case, the Allies concluded, only one type of fuze could be unmarked. It stood to reason that the enemy would choose a dangerous fuze for the purpose, so it was assumed that all unmarked fuzes were delayed-action. Blackwell put his ear to the bomb: no ticking. There was always the chance it might be an entirely new type of fuze, in which case he needed to know how it operated. That meant getting it out. But first he must make sure that any possible clock was paralysed. He called to Meager to bring the clockstopper and the two men placed it over the fuze head and switched on. Now for the fuze. Removing a delayed-action fuze was normally contrary to best practice: on the Home Front, half of them were fitted with an anti-withdrawal device underneath. This bomb had one thing in its favour: as a 50kg, its girth was too small to allow space for a normal anti-withdrawal device. Nevertheless, with no markings who could tell what fuzing system was inside this bomb? Blackwell could take no chances so he decided to take out the fuze by remote control. While Meager prepared the fuze extractor, Blackwell carefully unscrewed the locking and locating rings from the fuze pocket. Then a threaded tube was screwed onto the fuze head. The tube was attached to a drum wound with cord. Unreeling and playing out the cord as they went, the two men withdrew towards their lorry and took cover. Blackwell pulled steadily on the cord. Slowly, the drum rotated, unscrewing the threaded tube holding the fuze. As soon as he felt the tension on the cord relax, he knew the fuze was free. Once it was away from the bomb, he could approach and see what they had: it was a type 17. His relief was mixed with a touch of disappointment: no new fuze to discover today. Nevertheless, the job was finished – and no harm done.

Blackwell had another order to issue to the NCOs. Any unmarked fuzes they encountered must be referred directly to him. The situation placed an increased burden on the solo bomb disposal officer. Already struggling to cope with so many large bombs single-handed, he now faced the possibility that any number of 50kg bombs might have Type 17 or unmarked fuzes. And he had just heard confirmation from Lieutenant-Colonel McMeekan that Lieutenant Carroll would be out of action for at least a month and there was no definite date as yet for the arrival of a replacement. Lieutenant Blackwell needed help right away.

The only possible solution was to delegate more work to the NCOs. Fortunately some of them, such as Lance-Sergeant Parker and Corporal Brewer, had been trained and begun working in bomb disposal in 1940. It was decided to authorise these experienced NCOs to handle bombs up to 250kg, as long as they had straightforward impact fuzes. For even greater efficiency, they could inspect reported UXBs, and only refer them to the bomb disposal officer when necessary. The largest bombs, those with delayed-action or other difficult fuzes, and all Priority UXBs, would still be down to the BD officer himself.

Lieutenant Blackwell called the NCOs together for a briefing to outline their new duties. For an added precaution, in the light of the recent use of unexpected fuzes by the enemy, he instructed them in removal by remote control. There was no time to test the new arrangements; they would start right away. Now that the NCOs would be taking on many more bombs, they ought to be properly equipped for the job. Something had to be done about the continuing shortage of bomb disposal equipment. For months now Lieutenant Blackwell and Lieutenant Carroll had been struggling to cope with very high numbers of unexploded bombs, and many DA fuzes, with just two electric stethoscopes and only one clockstopper. Borrowing from the Royal Navy or RAF was almost impossible in these times of high demand for bomb disposal. The situation was critical. Blackwell reported the matter to his Commanding Officer, who agreed that immediate action was needed. Within a day, a message from Lieutenant-General Dobbie had reached the War Office and received a prompt reply. It seemed that a set of equipment had been sent out some time before but was lost due to enemy action. Another clockstopper would be despatched by the next available flight, with the remainder of a complete set of bomb disposal equipment to follow soon after. Blackwell hoped it would arrive before the new bomb disposal officer did. Until a second clock-stopper was available, the NCOs were reminded to ensure that their men took appropriate precautions, and monitored a bomb constantly. At the slightest indication of ticking, work must be stopped, and the bomb cordoned off for another 96 hours before any further action was taken.

Lying in bed at No 45 General Hospital, St Patrick's, recovering from his emergency operation, Lieutenant Carroll was very conscious of the bombing raids continuing all round him – and frustrated that he could do nothing to help. Little did he know that his Bomb Disposal colleague was about to start work just yards from where he lay. Early on the morning of Sunday 19 April the hospital reported a 500kg bomb, lying in its grounds. Marked Priority, it brought an instant response from Lieutenant Blackwell. Thwarted by yet another UXB with a jammed fuze, he no longer had to order the hazardous removal of the bomb. One essential item of his bomb disposal equipment had arrived: a BD discharger. Serving on the Home Front in 1941, Blackwell was accustomed to using the discharger, considered the most reliable way to disable impact and anti-handling fuzes. It consisted of a container of a sugar and water solution and a vacuum pump. The apparatus was fitted over the head of the fuze, then pumped to create a vacuum in the fuze pocket. A tap was turned to allow the solution to enter the pocket and so disable the fuze.

While Tom Meager assembled the equipment, Blackwell carefully cleaned off the head of the fuze. Bringing the liquid up to the correct pressure, he then attached the discharger, screwing up a wing-nut to secure it. Calculating the amount of liquid required, he pumped it steadily into the head of the fuze, making sure there was no leakage. That done, he allowed 25 minutes to be sure that the fuze was fully discharged. Leaving the harmless bomb for the lorry squad, he had time to polish off two more before the end of the day.

Back at Lintorn Barracks there was good news: Carroll's replacement had finally arrived. Lieutenant F.W. Ashall had originally taken off from Heliopolis Aerodrome in Cairo, at 4pm on Saturday 18 April, on board an aircraft of 267 Squadron, bound for Malta. Approaching the Island during the early hours of Sunday morning, the RAF pilot saw ahead of him formations of enemy aircraft about to launch an attack on the Island. It was his first flight to Malta and this was no time to experiment with an alternative approach. Rather than endanger the lives of his passengers and crew, he turned back to Egypt. Next day, they tried again: this time with more success. Lieutenant Ashall landed in Malta under cover of darkness early on Monday 20 April 1942.

Frederick William Ashall was a trainee quantity surveyor at the Lancashire County Council offices in Preston when war was declared. Although married, he saw it as his duty to volunteer for the Army, and joined the Royal Engineers as a sergeant in a construction company. Sergeant Ashall's company was instantly posted to St Nazaire in France, where they worked for some months, unaware of the events unfolding at Dunkirk. Suddenly the order came to head for the nearest coast and evacuation to England. A brief spell of service in Yorkshire brought him just close enough to Preston to dash home and see his baby daughter. Then he was posted again – to an officer cadet training unit. He was appointed 2nd Lieutenant on 18 January 1941, at the age of 28, and assigned to bomb disposal. His first posting as bomb disposal officer was in Portsmouth, during a period of heavy bombing. Working on one of the largest bombs in use at the time, he was to discover that his new job could have unusual rewards.

> The bomb had gone straight through the brewery and it hadn't exploded. We got the fuze out fairly easily, then we had to steam the explosive out of the bomb. We made the job last a week: they were lowering brown ale to the boys! The manager would call down to us saying: is everything all right? Have another beer.[4]

Before long Lieutenant Ashall was on the move again: on 2 October 1941, he joined 18 Bomb Disposal Company, one of two BD companies covering the Middle East, with its HQ in Cairo. The company ran training courses for personnel from other RE units in North Africa, as well as disposing of UXBs. The Company had fourteen officers and some 400 other ranks. Its bomb disposal sections covered the coast of North Africa and into the Nile delta.[5]

Ashall commanded a section of 25 NCOs and sappers. Work was much less eventful in the Middle East than in Portsmouth, a change which was not particularly satisfying to him. His main task involved blowing up Allied and Axis bomb dumps in turn, as Rommel's and Montgomery's armies fought their way back and forth across the desert. By January 1942 Ashall and his No 34 BD Section were located in Tobruk, where they tackled twelve unexploded bombs over two months. On 21 March they relocated to Sarafand but before he could deal with any more bombs the message came through warning of his transfer to Malta. It would bring a significant, if not welcome, change. Axis operations in North Africa had fortunately given him experience of Italian as well as German bombs of all sizes. The knowledge would prove very useful in his new role.

Lieutenant Ashall began his journey from Luqa to Lintorn Barracks that Monday morning just as dawn was breaking. In the distance Valletta's bastions and bell-towers seemed to rise up from the mist, as the sun began to light their limestone facades with a rosy glow. But the reality of his new posting was soon upon him: at 8am enemy aircraft roared in and attacked Floriana, dropping bombs on many of its streets and squares. The whole area was already largely in ruins, and even within Lintorn Barracks several buildings had been razed to the ground. Ashall had seen nothing even remotely like it since his time in Portsmouth. Reporting in to the Adjutant's office, he was given details of his billet and told to get some rest.

Conscious that he had already missed one day of service, the new officer made sure he was on time to report for duty at noon as arranged. Lieutenant Blackwell arrived a few minutes later, explaining that he had already been out to six UXBs that morning, three of them Priority. He gave Ashall a brief but intensive introduction to the work of Army bomb disposal in Malta – including the range of bombs he could expect, and a terrain which affected their behaviour very differently to the soft sands of the Egyptian desert. Handing over copies of previous Composite Summaries of Bomb Disposal for him to study in due course, Blackwell suggested that they get on the road. There were plenty of practical examples to demonstrate what the job involved.

After a fairly uneventful time in North Africa, Ashall was plunged into relentless activity from his first day in Malta. With an improvement in the weather, the enemy pounded the Island throughout the weekend; 30 unexploded bombs in built-up areas were added to eight already outstanding from previous raids. The two officers climbed on board the lorry with Lance-Corporal Meager to begin their working tour of the Island. Blackwell decided to start in the dockyard and the Three Cities. Not even the destruction he had seen that morning could have prepared Ashall for the scenes of devastation which now met his eyes: nothing but ruins in all directions. Still, there was work to be done.

They were heading for St Joseph's Flour Mills, the site of a Priority UXB report. A 1,000kg SC bomb had crashed into one of the buildings; part of the casing had been ripped open and the explosive was exposed to the air. It was a tricky one. They needed to get the fuze out but, as Blackwell expected from experience, it was jammed. The bomb could not be moved in its present condition. The only alternative was to scrape out all the explosive before the bomb was disturbed. For Lieutenant Ashall it was a near repeat of his experience in the Portsmouth brewery, except this time there was no beer on hand to compensate the sappers for an unpleasant job. Next port of call was St Edward's College, high on the bastions of the Cottonera Lines looking out towards Zabbar. Here it made sense for the bomb disposal officers to handle one each of the two UXBs. Then it was on to the Dockyard School, where Blackwell could concentrate on discharging a jammed fuze in one bomb, while Ashall defuzed the other two. On the way back to Lintorn, they called in at the Hornworks in Floriana to clear two bombs unearthed that morning at the heart of a Royal Engineers facility.

Back at barracks, there were messages from two NCOs with problem UXBs: a jammed fuze needed to be discharged near the stores at Marina Pinto on the Valletta waterfront. A 250kg bomb at 209 Tower Street, Sliema was found to be broken; a BD officer removed its fuze and the empty carcass was carried across the road and dropped into the sea. Late that afternoon another urgent report came in, a 500kg bomb in the grounds of the main military hospital at Mtarfa, high on the hills to the west of Ta Qali. Blackwell decided it could not wait until morning and Ashall joined him on the journey inland. They were relieved to find the bomb had a single impact fuze – and this time it came out easily. As they drove back through Floriana towards Lintorn, they heard the roar of enemy aircraft over their heads, followed by two enormous explosions. Smoke and dust were still drifting across the barracks yard as they drove in. There was one large crater in the North Square and a second bomb had hit one of the air-raid shelters under the bastions. Incredibly, there were no casualties. A visit to the officers' mess was in order: Ashall had just completed his first day as a bomb disposal officer in Malta.

The two BD sections had dealt with 20 UXBs that day – but 20 more had been reported to HQ. Ashall began to realise just how pressurised his new job was going to be. Next morning, the two officers could split the outstanding UXB reports between them and cover more ground. Lieutenant Ashall went north. The town of Mosta was in the firing line again, with six reported unexploded bombs. He toured the sites and put in place a programme of work to clear the streets. As he drove back out of Mosta, he suddenly spotted movement to his left: a formation of enemy aircraft roared across from the coast towards Ta' Qali, followed moments later by the crash of bombs on the airfield. He was staggered to see how little time it took for the incoming raiders to reach and drop bombs on their target.

Getting rid of the bombs was another matter, especially now that the enemy were releasing them from greater heights. Unearthing one buried UXB was going to prove a long, slow process. Late in the afternoon of Wednesday 22 April, a bomb disposal officer responded to a call from Tigne about a large UXB within the barracks. The commanding officer had assigned it top priority. Sure enough there was a large hole in the ground – broad enough to have been a crater caused by an exploding bomb. Nearby structures were cracked but there were none of the tell-tale signs of blast damage. The evidence pointed to a heavy unexploded bomb. A squad was ready with picks and shovels in hand, awaiting orders. The BD officer briefed his sergeant: it was a Priority bomb – and at least as big as a Hermann. His men would have to work in shifts round the clock to get at it as soon as possible. Having confirmed the proposed direction of the first investigative trench, the bomb disposal officer left them to it, with orders to let him know as soon as the bomb was reached. He would have a long wait.

After three days of relentless activity, another 34 unexploded bombs had been made safe. By Thursday, the backlog had been sufficiently reduced to allow the two bomb disposal officers to meet with the CO of the Fortress Engineers and discuss plans for the future. To increase efficiency and maximise resources, they decided to divide Army bomb disposal operations into two zones. Lieutenant Ashall and No. 128 BD Section would cover the northern area, Lieutenant Blackwell and No. 127 BD Section the south. The exception would be at weekends when – enemy activity permitting – one officer might be given a day off on Saturday and the other on Sunday. The bomb disposal officer on duty would cover the whole Island, assessing all incoming reports and tackling bombs as necessary. As in the UK, the resting BD officer would remain 'on call', contactable at all times in case of emergency.

The two bomb disposal sections were assembled next morning to hear about the changes. It was an opportunity for Blackwell to show his appreciation for the support of the NCOs and sappers of both BD sections during his ten days as solo bomb disposal officer. The NCOs had taken their extra duties in their stride: fewer than half the reported bombs had been referred on to him. Their achievement had helped to keep the number of outstanding UXBs to a manageable level until Ashall's arrival. For two of the NCOs the additional responsibility would be followed by promotion. By June 1942, Lance-Sergeant Parker became Sergeant Parker and Corporal Brewer became Lance-Sergeant Brewer.

There was other news affecting them all: the men of both bomb disposal sections were on the move. 24 Fortress Company was leaving Lintorn Barracks and relocating to the Royal Engineers encampment at Bahar ic-Caghaq. At the same time, new accommodation had been arranged for the NCOs and sappers of the company currently seconded to No. 128 BD Section. While Blackwell remained at Lintorn Barracks with No. 127 Section, Ashall and his men would be moving to new accommodation at Villa Fleri in the Msida valley – a pleasant former family home, taken over for military use. The announcement was met with mixed feelings: a mile inland from Floriana, the new billet was less convenient for the nightlife of Valletta but, on the other hand, it was probably further from the line of fire than Floriana. The move was scheduled for the end of the month. However, the geographical division of bomb disposal work could begin right away.

While Lieutenant Blackwell and his NCOs went south to finish off their backlog of UXBs, Lieutenant Ashall's squad journeyed north across the Victoria Lines to a remote hilltop Army station at Bidnija, where four bombs had been reported. The officer then took off towards Rabat, where he had unfinished business at Concezzione Church, seeing to the last of the three bombs unearthed by his men. He could report back to Floriana, satisfied with his first week's work in Malta. The two bomb disposal sections had disposed of 24 tons of bombs between them. But no sooner had Ashall arrived back at Lintorn Barracks than the order came from the look-out post to head for the shelters. Within seconds of reaching cover, he heard the deafening rumble of a massive formation of bombers over-head, followed by the boom of explosions echoing around Grand Harbour, interspersed with the thud and rattle of anti-aircraft fire. Suddenly a huge explosion shook the ground, followed by a roar. A bomb had hit Casemate Barracks next to Lintorn and an oil store had burst into flames. As soon as the 'raiders passed' signal came, the RE personnel dusted themselves off and returned to their stations.

Lieutenant Blackwell had worked for too long without a break. Lieutenant Ashall could take over as duty BD officer on Saturday 25 April allowing his colleague to take things easy for the weekend. At 7.30 that morning Lieutenant Carroll was wide awake in his ward at No 45 General Hospital, St Patrick's:

After a while, the dressings were all removed and I was told I could get up. I dressed in the morning and, with my new freedom, I went out onto the balcony in the sunshine, looking out over the sea. As I looked out I saw the silhouette of a Stuka dive-bomber, headed directly towards our hospital. I saw two black objects, released by the plane and obviously bombs. This was clearly an attack on the hospital.

I ran into the ward and picked up one of two helmets and gave it to the naval officer in the bed opposite mine whose leg was in traction, and I dived under the bed in the corner. The next moment, all the windows came shattering across the room. He was hurt but I was unharmed. The matron came round to check if there were any casualties. She put her head round the door into the ward and asked, 'Anybody hurt?' I said, 'I'm all right but my friend here has been cut by glass, I think.'

It was particularly surprising that the hospital was bombed, although the enemy might claim it could be a store in disguise. But right outside our ward there was a huge circle of white stones with a red cross – about 30 feet across. He was diving down towards the hospital with the red cross right in front of him. One can only conclude that it was deliberate; some Germans (and British) acted in disregard of who or what was damaged.[6]

As he realised the impact on the hospital, Carroll decided he need not take up a valuable bed in one of the few wards that was still serviceable. He went to find his surgeon, and volunteered to discharge himself and return to Valletta. With no transport available, he set off on foot carrying his suitcase. He needed a working telephone and Dragonara Palace, home of the Marquis Scicluna and his family, was about a mile away at St George's. The Marchioness took one look at George Carroll and insisted he must go no further. He could convalesce with them.

St Patrick's was not the only target: similar heavy bomb attacks were aimed at No. 39 General Hospital in nearby St Andrew's, demolishing two wards – despite a large red cross on the roof of the building. All of Malta was in shock at the news. Lieutenant-General Dobbie was appalled and sent a wire to the War Office in London notifying them of the atrocity, with the comment 'suggest this be given wide publication'.[7]

By the time Ashall reported for duty that morning calls had already come in from both hospitals. He was soon heading for St Andrew's and a reported 1,000kg bomb. The fuze pocket had an extension cap, and it was jammed firmly in place. He would need specialist equipment and plenty of time to discharge the fuze. The 'Hermann' was unlikely to explode if undisturbed so he would return to it next day. Three smaller 50kg bombs lay among the ruins of the bombed hospital wing. While the building was unstable it was not sensible to try and get at them on his own. He would have to abandon them for now, until he could spare a squad. Just as he was leaving, a messenger hurried towards him. Two more bombs had been discovered in the wreckage – including another Hermann. He examined the smaller of the two; as a 500kg it might contain a clockwork fuze. Relieved to find an impact fuze, he was frustrated when it refused to budge. His expectation that the 1,000kg might present similar problems was proved right. There would be plenty of work to do at St Andrew's next day. The 50kg SD at St Patrick's was an easy job and he returned to Lintorn Barracks, only to find three more UXB reports. Within minutes he was on the road to Marsa. The trip proved worthwhile, as one by one he set about three 250kg SD bombs with impact fuzes. Still his work was not over. There was an urgent report from Hal Far of an unexploded 500kg bomb lying just outside the perimeter of the airfield. It was dusk before he had neutralised the bomb and arrived back at HQ, finally finished for the evening.

Fortress Engineers HQ at Lintorn Barracks had been hit three times in recent raids. Stores and valuable equipment had been destroyed by enemy bombs. Those who remained billeted there never knew what they might find on their return to HQ at the end of each day. On Sunday 26 April, Lieutenant Blackwell's anticipated day of rest was shattered by a morning raid directly on the barracks. Bombs rained down, demolishing the cook-house, ration store, shoemaker's shop and boiler house, and one block of the quarters on Msida bastion overlooking the creek. In the confusion which followed, all RE officers were engaged in checking the various buildings and ensuring the welfare of the men. Already on very short rations, the Engineers resorted to cooking in the open with field equipment, to keep up their strength and morale. On Monday Lintorn was hit again, with more bombs on Msida quarters, and on North Square. The sappers of Bomb Disposal heard that bombs had also landed near 24 Fortress Company's new camp at Bahar-ic-Ciaq, although luckily none of their comrades had been hurt. A move to Villa Fleri was beginning to look more attractive.

Floriana was being repeatedly subjected to heavy attacks. Opposite the barracks another hospital seemed to have been targeted – two unex-ploded bombs were reported in St Calcedonio Street, near the Central Civil Hospital. A squad was about to begin excavating one of the UXBs next morning, when enemy raiders swooped over and dropped bombs on Floriana's Parish Church of St Publius, with devastating results. The explo-sions sent shock waves across the area, causing the ground to tremble under their feet. Civilians could not escape the bombs and nine lost their lives in the district that day.

The shock of the attacks on hospitals, so soon after bombs had struck churches and civilian communities, left Malta's Governor and Commander in Chief in little doubt as to the determination of the enemy to destroy the island. He had already begun to fear the worst; in his bulletin to the War Office for the month to 20 April 1942, he described the perilous condition of the battered Island and its communities:

> … there were 227 alerts, 184 by day and 93 by night. These included 74 day raids and 58 night raids. 333 people were killed (139 men, 117 women and 77 children) …
>
> During the whole of this period the enemy has continued to deliver heavy bombing attacks two, three or four times a day. Only respite in all during two short periods of rough weather. Damage has been terrible in

Valletta, Floriana, Three Cities and Marsa but Luqa, Paola, Zabbar, Sliema, Hamrun and Mosta have also suffered heavily and most other places in the Island to a less[er] extent. In the first four places named, destruction is very widespread and almost every street in Valletta, Floriana and Three Cities is blocked with debris ...

Clearance of debris represents very heavy problem ... roads in the port area of the Grand Harbour have been cleared, stores are being cleaned of debris and a start has been made with the clearance of Valletta. So long as bombing continues all we can do is to keep essential roads clear, carry out such demolition work as is necessary to maintain essential services and make such preparations in the port area as are necessary for the reception of a convoy. In this last task, we are already ahead of schedule ...

Growing shortage of food is serious and the effect of the cut in the bread ration cannot yet be foreseen. Extreme shortage of fodder is also causing difficulties; I am confident however that we shall see our troubles through.

With all we have had to put up with both in bombing, in restriction and scarcity of food, the bearing and morale of the public has remained admirable. I cannot too highly praise the fortitude and endurance which they have shown under the most severe test to which they have been subjected. Without that spirit we could not have carried on.[8]

But as the month of April drew to a close, the number and volume of raids began slowly to reduce. On 29 April there were 220 enemy operational sorties against Malta; the next day there were just 68. Then on Thursday 30 April there were no new reports of unexploded bombs. The lull in enemy activity gave No. 128 BD Section the opportunity to settle in to Villa Fleri. It was reassuring for both sections to be up to strength and, as the remaining supplies of bomb disposal equipment finally arrived, they were better prepared to cope with the challenges ahead. And after ten long days of back-breaking work, the squad at Tigne revealed their buried bomb. It was a massive 1,800kg SC 'Satan' – the first recorded by RE Bomb Disposal in Malta. It had taken 24 feet of spade work to reach it. The impact fuze was a simpler matter, and within minutes it was harmless.

During April 1942, Malta's two RE Bomb Disposal sections had dealt with 269 HE bombs of 50kg and over, plus many anti-personnel bombs and incendiaries. In the first eleven days of the month, Lieutenant Blackwell and Lieutenant Carroll made safe nearly 60 large HE bombs between them, including thirteen 500kg and seven 1,000kg. With the help of the NCOs, 60 more high explosives were tackled in the ten days pending the arrival of Lieutenant Ashall. These sergeants, corporals and lance-corporals had taken on a far greater responsibility in Malta than could have been imagined when Royal Engineers Bomb Disposal was set up on the Home Front back in the summer of 1940.

Notes
1 An aggressive form of dysentery.
2 Cyril Thomas Meager, 2008.
3 Vella, P. (1985). *Malta: Blitzed But Not Beaten*. Malta: Progress Press.
4 Patrick Ashall, March 2008
5 From Nominal Rolls: the official weekly registers of officers and other ranks on the establishment and present in any Army unit.
6 Lieutenant G.D. Carroll, 2005
7 Ed. (1942) Situation Reports & Operational Messages Out. WO 106 The National Archives, London.
8 ibid.

CHAPTER 13

DIGGING FOR VICTORY

It was so sudden we didn't even have time to take cover, and perforce had to watch what was probably the fiercest and most concentrated aerial attack the world has ever known.[1]

Air Marshall Kesselring sensed victory. He despatched a message to inform German High Command that Malta had been neutralised, claiming 'There is nothing left to bomb'. There was one notable exception: according to rumour he had chosen to spare a beautiful headland palace to use as his future residence after the inevitable Axis victory. It seemed the Luftwaffe commander had his eye on Dragonara, where Lieutenant Carroll was now convalescing.

Just after breakfast on Saturday 2 May, the telephone rang at Villa Fleri. An unexploded bomb had been spotted not far from the Governor's Palace at San Anton: an A1 Priority. The messenger added the chilling news that there had been reports of several random explosions following the previous night's raids. The enemy had dropped another scattering of time bombs across the Island.

Lieutenant Ashall headed up the Valley Road towards Attard, expecting the worst. The bomb was in a field not far from the main road – a 250kg heavy-cased type. Moving closer, Ashall's eyes gradually focused on the number 17 – his first delayed-action fuze in Malta. He weighed up the situation carefully. The bomb was near a road which must be kept open at all costs. At least this type of bomb scattered its shrapnel less widely than the lighter SC version. Calculating the distance from the road, Ashall decided that if it was surrounded by sandbags, the bomb could be blown in situ. The job done, he joined his squad already working in nearby Notabile Road. They were clearing a batch of nine UXBs buried under rubble near the HQ of the Buffs Regiment at Villa Drusilla. It would take them three more days to clear all six 250kg and three 500kg bombs.

Meanwhile Ashall was on to his next UXB report, a few miles to the north at Gharghur. With no address and only a map reference to go on, he scoured the countryside for some time trying to find the bomb. He was about to give up when he spotted a cluster of farm buildings. Their owner came out to greet him enthusiastically and indicated a nearby field. As the officer looked around for the device, the farmer walked towards a low circle of stones and pointed downwards. Putting his hand on the farmer's arm to stop him from going any closer, Ashall walked on alone. Within the stones was a round hole, part of which was broken away: it was a well. Shining his torch down into the bottle-shaped cavity, he could just make out the curved flank of a bomb lying at the bottom; it looked like a 250kg. The farmer called out to him, gesticulating. He seemed to be saying that he had struck the bomb when trying to draw water that morning. Ashall stared at him, trying to look unmoved, but the man was lucky to be alive.

Ashall had to assume it was another delayed-action bomb – and it could have a second fuze, possibly anti-handling. It looked impractical to get down inside the well to blow the bomb – and the well would be lost anyway if he did so. Even if the bomb could be removed, any attempt might cause an explosion. He informed the owner that, regrettably, the bomb had to stay where it was for now. If it did not explode, he and his men would return in due course and get rid of it. Meanwhile the well could not be used and no-one could go within 100 yards of it. This was not good news for the farmer; water was a precious resource and his crops needed plenty before harvesting. Promising that the bomb would be got rid of as soon as possible, Ashall returned to Attard.

Harry Turner and his crew had a heavy day's work that day, with two massive bombs to shift from Tigne. The 1,000kg Esau at ground level was tricky enough, but then they had the job of retrieving the massive 1,800kg Satan from the bottom of its 24-foot shaft. It took a huge effort to haul up the lumbering nine-foot carcass and manoeuvre it onto the lorry, which crawled slowly away with its heavy burden.

That afternoon, Harry's wife Mary was at home in their apartment in Floriana. It would soon be time to try and conjure up from the meagre rations enough of an evening meal for them both. Just after 5pm came the familiar sound of the air raid alert. Mary resisted the temptation to stay where she was – there was no question of taking chances, now that she was expecting their first child. She hurried down to join her neighbours in the air raid shelter. They were just in time to hear the rumble of the raiders approaching, followed by the crash of bombs which seemed to fall directly over their heads: yet another strike on the already battered community of Floriana. It wasn't long before the 'All-clear' released them from their dusty underground chamber to the open air and Mary could go home to get on with Harry's dinner: he could be back at any moment.

She opened the door of the apartment and stepped inside, but something made her stop. Taking a step back she looked towards the bedroom. The door was slightly ajar and through the narrow opening the room seemed bathed in light. Mary was puzzled. She put out her hand and gingerly pushed back the door until she could see inside. She looked up and saw that light was flooding in from a massive hole in the ceiling – and she could even see the sky. Something made her look down and there, on the bed in front of her was the unmistakable, solid shape of a bomb. Thanks to Harry, Mary knew exactly what to do. Tiptoeing out, and then trying not to run, she went back downstairs and out into the street to get help.

As the Bomb Disposal lorry pulled back into Lintorn Barracks early that evening, Harry was met by a couple of the Sappers from his Section. They seemed to be telling him something about a bomb and his wife. The heavy bombing of Floriana had been heard across the Island all day, including where Harry was working. What had happened to Mary? It was alright they said, everything was fine – there had been an unexploded bomb but it was 'all sorted'. Still Harry couldn't get home fast enough, to see for himself. They might say it was all right, but there was the baby to think of.

He found Mary safe and sound, and she told him all about the bomb and how it had been taken away. Harry went to see for himself. The 50kg bomb had hit the roof at a shallow angle and passed straight through, piercing the ceiling of their apartment before hitting the bed. But how did it come to stop there? Then Harry understood. Mary kept a large suitcase packed with blankets and linen under the bed. It had absorbed the impact of the bomb and given it a soft resting place. If it had exploded he could have lost everything that was dear to him. It was a lucky escape - all they had to do now was find a new home.

On Sunday afternoon, a time when the Maltese liked to relax with their families, the *Regia Aeronautica* returned to the daylight skies over Malta. Five Cant 1007 aircraft crossed the north-east coast and scattered bombs in a south-westerly trail from Gharghur to Naxxar and on to Mosta. There were several casualties. Then reports started coming in to RE Bomb Disposal HQ: large containers had been found in a number of civilian areas. The Italians had been called in to support the Luftwaffe campaign, and they were dropping anti-personnel bombs again.

Just before 6pm, in another combined attack from both air forces, a formation of 28 bombers escorted by fighters tried to knock out the defensive gun position at Ta' San Pietru, before heading inland to bomb Luqa and Hal Far. Enemy reconnaissance pilots had spotted the extensive work around Safi to develop aircraft holding bays, and extend the capacity of the two airfields. This time there was no let-up in the bombing overnight, but still RAF ground crews and Army brigades worked on round the clock to repair the aerodromes and keep them operational.

It was clear something momentous was about to happen. Royal Engineers Bomb Disposal received top secret special orders that all outstanding unexploded bombs must be cleared from areas in and around Luqa and Safi with immediate effect. Lieutenant Blackwell led No.127 BD Section to the airfield first thing on Monday morning, taking with him all existing reports for the area. Small red flags dotted the airfield, each one placed by the RAF to indicate a suspected buried bomb. Blackwell toured the marked sites then set his men to work. The NCOs could cope with the straightforward UXBs up to 250kg, leaving him to concentrate on the rest. They had only just got started when the red flag went up to signal an air raid approaching. What seemed like seconds later, a formation of five Ju88 bombers attacked. The moment the raiders had passed, it was back to business.

The orders had stipulated that the area was to be kept free of UXBs at all times. As each new attack hit the airfields, unexploded bombs were plotted and cleared without delay. Delayed action bombs could not be allowed to remain in the way of aircraft or ground workers. Despite the risk to the bomb disposers they were defuzed at once, or exploded if necessary and the area repaired so that operations could go on. Blackwell stayed near at hand, so he could respond instantly to any UXB. Tom Meager sat in the car alongside his officer, on high ground overlooking Luqa airfield.

> watching the dive bombing ... [and the bombs] coming down, long strings of them. We'd see them all going off and then if one had gone in the ground with no explosion, he'd say 'I think we might have to go and deal with one there.' The most important ones to deal with were those that actually affected the runway for take-off and landing, or ones that had landed in the dispersal area, among the other planes.[2]

The enemy returned again and again through daylight hours. Everyone working on the airfields, including the bomb disposal section, carried on their duties under constant threat of attack. They had another near miss on Friday, about 30 minutes after they had resumed work at Luqa. Luftwaffe bombers and fighter-bombers attacked, aiming for the new aircraft dispersal areas. Three Ju87s peeled off to launch a deliberate strike on one of the gun positions defending the northern approach at Tal Handaq, leaving another three 250kg UXBs. At lunchtime, the enemy returned to raid Luqa and Ta' Qali, with repeated strikes on the dispersal pens. In all, the week's raids killed 16 servicemen and injured another 24.

By Friday afternoon, the section had cleared 29 UXBs from Luqa: 50kg SD, eleven 250kg SC, eight 250kg SD, two 500kg SC and three 500kg SD. Five of them held clockwork-controlled fuzes. The sappers had met their deadline and were told to pack up and get away from the area. They could take Saturday off.

While Lieutenant Blackwell was busy at Luqa, Lieutenant Ashall covered all the emergency calls for the rest of the Island. As he was heading back to the Mess in Floriana that evening, six Ju88 escorted by Messerschmitt fighters approached in a wide formation, aiming for Grand Harbour and the coastal forts. This time the Gunners had them in their sights soon enough to score a direct hit, bringing down one of the Ju88s on the edge of Fort San Rocco. The plane was still loaded with its bombs. The RA found themselves with a large number of primed and unexploded bombs in an unstable condition, still attached to the aircraft. A bomb disposal officer was needed right away. Ashall arrived to find two 250kg SC and six 50kg SD bombs at the scene – all intact. He was pleased to hear that the aircraft had already been checked and confirmed to be in a stable condition. He did not want the risk of fire or explosion while he worked. It was an even greater relief to discover, one by one, that all the bombs carried straightforward impact fuzes. Even so, night was falling before the last of them was carried away.

There was no break on Saturday 9 May for No. 128 Section, out working on buried bombs. One squad toiling away in the village of Siggiewi since early morning had a sight to cheer them while they worked. Hearing the unmistakable sound of Merlin engines, they looked up to see one, then another, then a steady stream of Spitfires approaching from the coast and coming in to land. Gradually it dawned on the sappers: surely this was a new delivery.

They were not the only ones to notice. Word quickly spread and it seemed as though everyone in Malta stood outdoors to witness the long-anticipated arrival of the new aircraft. Since March they had watched the agility of Spitfires in action, believing they offered the best chance of overcoming the determined enemy. But each time a batch of planes had reached the Island, hope had given way to disappointment when Luftwaffe bombers destroyed so many on the ground. Of the previous delivery on 20 April of nearly 50 Spitfires, only a handful survived. Now the sound and sight of these indomitable Allied fighters in the skies brought renewed hope. And it finally explained the intensive top secret work on the airfields.

This time 59 aircraft made it to Malta, arriving in three batches split between the Island's main airfields. No sooner had the earliest arrivals landed than they were back in the air, to provide defensive cover for batches two and three. At just after 1pm, 14 Ju88s and 10 Me109s attacking Hal Far and Ta' Qali were surprised by a counter-attack from 23 of the newly-arrived aircraft. The enemy retreated and sent in a reconnaissance flight to see what was going on. Their report prompted a heavy attack on the Safi strip by ME 109s followed by 15 Stukas. But the enemy's next attempt to destroy new Spitfires at Ta' Qali backfired; the target aircraft were not on the ground but in the air. Supported by Ack-Ack guns, they retaliated by destroying seven Luftwaffe planes, scoring eight more 'probables' (probably destroyed), and damaging another sixteen. After months of waiting, there were real signs that the Island could put up effective resistance to the continuous Luftwaffe onslaught. And while they were engaged in air battles, the enemy could drop fewer bombs.

Both bomb disposal sections could look forward to a rest on Sunday. Blackwell was due to take a day off, but he was apparently not one to take things easy. Early that morning, he called on Lieutenant Edward Woolley, the Rendering Mines Safe/Bomb and Mine Disposal Officer for the Royal Navy in Malta.

… why the hell these things always crop up on a Sunday I don't know, but on this particular day I was determined to have a bit of rest, but before I'd even had breakfast there was a violent blowing of horns below my window, and looking out, there was Blackwell, the Army bomb disposal officer, calling me down to say he had a job for me. Now Blackwell is a very nice chap, but he's got one big fault which is that he has no respect at all for the Red Flag, whereas I have, and many a time I've been out with him and he just ignores bombs and shrapnel. Well this time we got to the site alright, at Hamrun, in spite of plenty of activity overhead, and I found one of the most extraordinary cases of a 'G' mine I have ever seen. It had skidded along a road and through the open front door of a house, and had come to rest under a table. It all looked so silly to see a 2000-lb. mine lying inside a room with practically no damage around. It didn't prove to be particularly difficult except that the case was distorted and we had the very trying job of drilling all round the fuze to get it out.

Just as we left a most terrific barrage started right above us. It was so sudden we didn't even have time to take cover, and perforce had to watch what was probably the fiercest and most concentrated aerial attack the world has ever known. It so happened that during the night a single ship had run the gauntlet to Malta and was being unloaded at top speed. Jerry sent over about a hundred Stukas to get it. Only the day before we had received reinforcements of Spitfires and the Gunners were given unlimited fire and my God did they use it. The air was literally black with barrage, planes and bits of planes. The Spits got so excited they followed the Stukas right through the barrage and we lost a couple. Jerry lost about seventy the highest day's loss by a long way. The whole affair lasted about twenty minutes and we stood in the doorway to a house the whole time, never been so frightened in my life.[3]

The two officers were witnessing the Luftwaffe's attempted welcome party for the arrival in Grand Harbour of HMS *Welshman*. The ship was bringing desperately-needed supplies, including 84,000 rounds of Bofors ammunition. The mid-morning attack on the dockyard by 20 Stukas and eight Ju88s was thwarted by another new tactic: a smokescreen was used to mask the position of the *Welshman* and provide protection for the ship's unloading. Anti-aircraft batteries put up a formidable barrage to fight off aircraft approaching the ship's berth. At the same time, Spitfires launched a vigorous counter-attack. Lieutenant Woolley and Lieutenant Blackwell were not the only witnesses to the massive dog-fight. Many civilians and military personnel ventured out in the open to watch such a show of strength by the Island's defenders. During the three bombing attacks which followed, 21 enemy aircraft were destroyed, plus 20 more 'probables' and 20 damaged. The battle marked the climax of two days of intense fighting in the skies over Malta, in which the enemy suffered heavy losses. Next day, the Luftwaffe could only search the seas around the archipelago for survivors. The Spitfire reinforcements had assumed the leading role in the drama. Now that they had protected the unloading of the *Welshman's* precious cargo of ammunition, the Island's anti-aircraft guns were re-armed and could once again play their vital part in the defence of Malta.

Touched by the appreciation for their arrival, the Spitfire pilots were also full of admiration for the indomitable spirit they found on the Island.

> The tempo of life here is just indescribable. The morale of all is magnificent – pilots, ground crews and army, but it is certainly tough. The bombing is continuous on and off all day. One lives here only to destroy the Hun and hold him at bay; everything else, living conditions, sleep, food, and all the ordinary standards of life have gone by the board. It all makes the Battle of Britain and fighter sweeps seem like child's play in comparison, but it is certainly history in the making, and nowhere is there aerial warfare to compare with this.[4]

Air Marshall Kesselring was premature in claiming the demise of Malta's defences. But sadly his opponent who had led the Island through its trials so far would not witness the turn-around in fortunes. Lieutenant-General Dobbie had already left on the night of 7 May, to be replaced by General

Viscount Gort. Next day, his poignant farewell message was broadcast to the people of Malta. As a high-ranking member of the Royal Engineers Regiment, Dobbie would be especially missed by the Fortress Engineers in Malta.

The arrival of the Spitfires could not go unchallenged, and the Luftwaffe increased their efforts to wipe out the new threat to their supremacy in the air. Still smarting from Sunday's battle, on Monday they employed a new tactic, sending formations of fighters to protect bombers as they attacked. This time they concentrated on Hal Far which was closer to the coast and therefore easier to reach than the other airfields. For three days they pounded the area, occasionally venturing further inland to hit Luqa. Lieutenant Blackwell and his squad made daily visits to both airfields to keep them free of unexploded bombs so the Spitfires could continue to fly.

Late one afternoon, approaching a UXB lying perilously close to Hal Far's runway, Blackwell spotted two fuze pockets. He automatically looked at the forward pocket: a Type 17 fuze. They had to get it away quickly. Lance-Sergeant Parker was supervising the sappers:

> The clock had stopped but we used a clockstopper in case it would restart; we did not want to defuze it for fear of an anti-withdrawal device, which the Germans often used. We loaded it, plus clockstopper, onto a lorry, drove to the cliff, disconnected the clock stopper and rolled it over.[5]

The bomb disposal men dusted off their hands and moved on, not giving it another thought – until later that evening. Tom Meager was sitting in the mess with his comrades.

> We were having a meal, and all of a sudden there was one unearthly explosion and it turned out that bomb's ticker had started up again and it blew it up, along with the rest of the bombs. It brought down half the cliff, showered the farmer's grape field with seawater and so on. They grew grapes on the ground. It ruined his grape field and the government had to compensate him for his loss.[6]

The explosion broke many windows and rattled shutters miles away. It was a stark reminder that every stopped clock could easily restart.

When enemy aircraft did manage to escape the Island's defenders, they were more determined to strike swiftly and hard. On the second morning at Hal Far, a digging squad from No. 127 BD Section were forced to flee for shelter as an incoming formation of aircraft made a surprise attack, heading in from a new direction over the sea from the south, to avoid Spitfires sent up in defence. Several raid-free hours followed, allowing just enough time for the bomb to be unearthed, defuzed and removed. Then raiders attacked again – this time flying on towards Safi and Luqa. A squad from No. 128 BD Section working close to the Heavy Ack-Ack battery at Salina Bay had an even closer shave. Moments after they had exposed the bomb they had to sprint for cover as enemy fighters swooped and launched a direct hit on the gun position just yards away. Fresh reports of unexploded bombs were soon added to their list.

They joined a backlog of over 50 unexploded bombs still outstanding. Through the past four months, more and more UXBs not affecting the war effort or civilian populations had been cordoned off pending disposal – some lay for weeks in more remote or severely bombed areas. Now that the battle in the air was turning in favour of Malta's defenders, there was an opportunity to get rid of them. Reviewing all the UXB reports, the two bomb disposal officers devised a plan and briefed their sections. Working parties were assigned to each area with a high density of outstanding UXBs. NCOs leading excavation squads could continue to tackle straightforward HE bombs up to 250kg. The two BD officers revisited unburied bombs, and handled all the larger and complex cases. In the meantime they remained on call to respond to any new UXB reports, assign priorities and decide on the action required. The excavation of these bombs would be the most exhausting and dangerous task facing the squads. Many were deep in the ground, their fuzes not yet identified nor even their size confirmed. Every one was a potential time bomb. Any careless blow from a pick or shovel or a sapper's boot, could restart a dormant clock – or worse – trigger a booby-trap.

The clear-up operation started on Monday 11 May. While No. 127 BD Section concentrated on keeping Luqa and Hal Far open for business, Lieutenant Ashall's No. 128 Section was divided into squads to begin work on six sites at the Crown Works military depot in Floriana, and five more around the village of Siggiewi. Progress was good until Wednesday morning, when the NCO at Siggiewi called a halt to work on one of the shafts:

it contained a 250kg SD with a delayed-action fuze. By the time Ashall arrived on the scene to blow the bomb, the NCO had something else to report: two of the other bombs were a type he had not seen before. Their impact fuzes were easily rendered safe and the carcasses were taken back to the barracks to be identified. They were German 35kg 'concrete' bombs. Designed for anti-personnel use, their small casing was extra heavy to cause maximum damage on impact. The enemy had found another new weapon to try against the limestone of Malta.

Next day Ashall went northwards to the large military camp on the north-west coast, beside the beautiful bay of Ghajn Tuffieha. Unexploded bombs had been discovered spread across the hilly slopes overlooking the camp. As Ashall climbed the hill with his guide, he hesitated and put out a hand. They both stopped. The officer had spotted a hole in the ground a few feet away which looked very much like the point of entry of an unexploded bomb. Ashall looked around; the terrain was rough scrubland. With all the recent attacks there could be many more unexploded bombs here than the ones already reported. He would have to make a detailed search.

Reporting in later to the CO of the camp, the BD officer confirmed five bombs scattered over the hillside. Three were 250kg SC and two were 250kg SD – and every one had a DA fuze. These he planned to blow in situ. Now for the bad news: there were several more buried bombs, and he would need to bring a working party to locate and excavate them all. The work could take some time so, to save repeated journeys from their HQ, the CO agreed to provide temporary accommodation for a working party. Ashall started work on exploding the five unburied bombs but could only dispatch two before dusk fell. Next day, he was back with his team, overseeing their encampment and organizing his plan of action ready for an early start on Friday morning. His briefing included one bit of good news: his NCOs could give the men access to the refreshing waters of 'Golden Bay' during their rest periods. It would help them through the strenuous activity of sinking five shafts of 10–14 feet. All the bombs were 250kg SC with twin fuze pockets – and each held at least one clockwork fuze. It was Friday afternoon when the last of five explosions thundered around the once tranquil bay, and No.128 BD Section could pack up and head back to Villa Fleri. They had the weekend free and No.127 BD Section could join them, after unearthing six UXBs on the southern peninsula of Delimara. Only one bomb disposal officer worked on Saturday – and for the second time in a fortnight, Sunday 24 May was completely free of work.

The sappers needed their rest. Although 31 high explosive UXBs had been disposed of during the previous seven days, 72 more had been reported and 72 still remained outstanding. Back at Villa Fleri, Ashall was preparing for another major clearance operation, scheduled to begin on Monday morning. There were traces of nineteen unexploded bombs in the fields below Rabat. Another month of hard graft lay ahead of No. 128 BD Section, sinking one shaft after another, each up to fourteen feet in depth, to uncover the bombs. At the same time, No. 127 Section were digging for a dozen bombs around Luqa and Marsaskala, and burrowing beneath ruins in the streets of Zabbar.

All this heavy work was carried out by 30 sappers across both BD sections.[7] At the same time they were surviving on minimal rations, as it was still impossible for any significant supplies to arrive in Malta by sea. Since 6 May 1942, even bread had been strictly rationed. A typical daily military ration included just 12oz (340g) of bread, 1oz (28g) of margarine and ½oz (14g) jam or marmalade, with 1oz (28g) each of tea, tinned milk and sugar. Meals were small. On a Monday, for example, the lunch allowance consisted of ¾oz (21g) of tinned bacon and 1 oz (28g) of tinned cheese, dinner was 6oz (170g) of preserved meat, 1oz (28g) of onions, 8 oz (227g) of potatoes and of fresh vegetables plus 2oz (57g) of tinned fruit and 3½oz (99g) of flour. In a report for the three months to the end of June 1942, the chief of Malta's military Medical Services wrote

> It is agreed that the present ration is insufficient for men carrying out hard manual labour and training, as is the case with an appreciable number of troops. A supplemental ration scale is considered advisable and has been recommended. Arduous training and P.T. although not officially counter-manded on paper, is not being carried out in practice.[8]

The bomb disposal men had no such option. Arduous physical activity was an essential part of their job – and their sleep was frequently disrupted by increasing numbers of night air raids and alerts. The RAF recognised the cumulative impact of operational and living conditions on their pilots. Air command now considered conditions to be so acute that tours of duty were reduced from the six months to just three. The same did not apply to Army ground crew working on airfields – nor to RE Bomb Disposal. The demands proved so intense that Pioneer Sappers were drafted in from 24 Fortress Company to help with the digging.

Late in the afternoon of Tuesday 2 June 1942 two unexploded bombs were reported lying on the surface in the town of Naxxar. Ashall could take a detour to inspect them on his way to Rabat next morning. For once, an early start was made easier by an uninterrupted night's sleep and the officer and his NCO were soon on the scene with the help of a local guide. The two bombs had struck and partly destroyed a building but had failed to explode. Signalling to the guide to remain at a suitable distance, Ashall moved forward to inspect them.

Approaching the closer of the two, he could see it was a 500kg SC but something about the shape of carcass concerned him. He stepped carefully over the rubble – any stumble and he might fall, possibly onto the bomb. He could see that the bomb's casing had been ripped open, presumably as it hit the building and that the TNT filling had partly leaked out. The bomb had two fuze pockets. The fuze nearer the head of the bomb was partly exposed, with its base just visible. The other was hanging loose, barely attached to the bomb's carcass.

Two more light steps brought him close enough to see the fuze heads. The loose fuze was impact, the second was type 17. He stopped. Any fuze in a broken bomb was hazardous. A clockwork fuze in such a condition was doubly so. It would be almost impossible to avoid disturbing it and so possibly start the clock. Taking his weight on his hands, Ashall bent down to bring his ear as close as possible to the head of the fuze. No audible ticking yet. Given the state of the buildings and the condition of the bomb, he would prefer to explode it right away. But first he should take a look at the other one. He turned and picked out a route through the debris: another 500kg SC. It too was broken up, it had twin fuze pockets – and one fuze was a type 17.

There was no time to lose. Ashall checked with the local police to ensure a large enough area was evacuated, asking them to warn people in the locality of the impending explosions. By the time he returned to the bombs, his sergeant was ready with the detonator and primer. Although it was likely that the explosion of one bomb would set off the other, Ashall had to be sure that both exploded in a controlled way; any failure could mean return-ing to an even more volatile bomb. He connected the two bombs with instantaneous fuze wire, so that the electrical charge to one would transfer to the other within a split second. It was delicate and painstaking work attaching the charges to each of the broken bombs safely and in a way that ensured success. Eventually he was satisfied. Retreating to cover, he checked no-one was within the danger zone and gave the signal. In one swift move-ment, both bombs were destroyed.

Heavy rain on Friday 5 June made digging impossible; there was no alternative but to sit out the storm. The unplanned rest meant working on Saturday instead. That evening, good news spread among military forces throughout the Island: two dozen more Spitfires had arrived. In the air battle for Malta, there were real signs of a change of fortune, as the Spitfires repeated the tactics which had helped win the Battle of Britain. With the RAF taking greater command of the skies, the enemy retreated from day-light raids to concentrate on night attacks. The Island had endured 2,470 air raids from January to the end of May, with almost continuous attacks – for up to ten out of an average thirteen hours of daylight. Now massed daytime bombing had been brought to a halt.

The men of RE Bomb Disposal no longer operated under the constant menace of a raid exploding the very bombs they were trying to make safe. They could work undisturbed during the day, much as their counterparts had done during the London blitz – although they still suffered from the interrupted sleep caused by sirens and explosions at night. For the first time in nearly four weeks a day passed with no new UXB reports to HQ. Summarising their activity for the Weekly Bomb Disposal Report, the BD officers recorded that 33 new UXBs had been reported in the previ-ous seven days, and 52 awaited attention. With a reduction in the number of UXB reports they could begin to hope for a return to some kind of routine. And one bomb disposal officer had an extra cause for celebration. The *London Gazette* announced that Lieutenant Thomas Walter Townsend Blackwell was appointed MBE.

But the stormy weather had been followed by a false calm. The Luftwaffe were about to launch a new weapon in the air battle for Malta.

Notes

1 Extract from collection of documents written by Commander Edward Dutton Woolley, GM & Bar, RNVR, National War Museum Association, Malta. See also: Galea, F. (2008). *Mines Over Malta*. Malta: Wise Owl Publications.

2 Cyril Thomas Meager, 2008.

3 Extract from collection of documents written by Commander Edward Dutton Woolley, GM & Bar, RNVR, National War Museum Association, Malta.

4 Ministry of Information. (1944). *The Air Battle of Malta*. London: HMSO.

5 Letter from Major Reginald Parker GM dated 1 May 1980, National War Museum Archive, Malta.

6 Cyril Thomas Meager, 2008.

7 The Fortress Engineers War Diary for the week ending 15 May 1942 shows current total manpower of Lieutenant Blackwell's No.127 BD Section as 20 O.R. (NCOs and sappers) and Lieutenant Ashall's No.128 Section as 16.

8 Ed. (1942) *Medical Reports/Returns* .WO 216. National Archives, London.

CHAPTER 14

EXPLODING BUTTERFLIES

They were human after all, these men who were playing with death to save others from death …[1]

As the evening sky began to darken on Saturday 6 June, an ARP warden patrolling the elegant streets of Haz-Zebbug heard the drone of aircraft approaching from the direction of Luqa. Before he had time to reach shelter, two of the planes passed almost directly over his head. He could only watch as, in their wake, clusters of small winged objects spread across the sky and spiralled silently down between the rooftops. Then they began to explode. Stirring himself, the warden set off at a brisk pace towards his ARP centre. Everywhere he looked lay tiny, strangely-shaped bombs. The 'All Clear' was about to sound, bringing civilians out of the shelters and into great danger. They must be told to stay indoors until the bombs were attended to.

As one call after another reached RE Bomb Disposal HQ, the extent of the emergency became apparent. Hundreds of bombs had been showered along a flight path over Luqa, up to Ta' Qali and out towards the north-west coast. Both airfields; the lanes and fields around Dingli; and eleven streets in Haz-Zebbug were covered with the small bombs. The two civilian communities were the main focus for the Royal Engineers. One bomb disposal officer headed for Haz-Zebbug and the other for Dingli. They were about to be introduced to a volatile weapon: the German 'butterfly bomb'. Unexploded SD2 bombs had been discovered only a few times in England since 1940, but the two bomb disposal officers knew enough about them to realise the terrible danger now facing the Island's people. All affected areas must be sealed off immediately, and must stay that way until the bombs could be cleared.

The small and insignificant-looking SD2 was extremely hazardous. Although the bomb itself was just eight centimetres long, with its load of 225 grams of TNT and thick-walled construction it would kill anybody within 30 feet; it could injure people 300 feet away. It was a very effective anti-personnel bomb. The 'butterfly bomb' was so named because as it fell an outer shell hinged open to form 'wings'. The tiny 2kg bombs were packed into containers holding 24–100 each.[2] The container opened as it left the aircraft, releasing the winged bombs to float down like sycamore seeds. A spindle screwed into the fuze pocket of the bomb was attached by a steel cable to the winged section; as the bomb drifted slowly to the ground, the spindle rotated, arming the fuze. After it landed, the slightest disturbance of the bomb would set it off.

As more reports flooded in to Bomb Disposal HQ, it was evident this was an emergency on a scale similar to the dropping of Thermos bombs in November 1941. Butterfly bombs were designed to be difficult to spot, so that an unsuspecting passer-by could easily stumble into one, with fatal consequences. Like the Thermos they were potentially attractive to curious children – many of whom became their victims. Even Police Assistant Commissioner Edward Bonnici-Solar almost succumbed as he made a tour of inspection in one of the affected areas.

> The bomb disposal officer and I visited a garden dotted with a good number of them. Somehow I managed to touch one of them in a narrow passage, but no thanks to Mr Hitler it failed to explode. I may add that the B.D.O. had something to say about this! That very 'butterfly bomb' was later dismantled and despatched post-haste to London for the edification of other bomb-disposal men.[3]

Whole areas were being brought to a standstill. Unexploded butterfly bombs were marked and surrounded with sandbags; pedestrians and vehicles were kept well away. On Sunday morning, every available man from 24 Fortress Company with experience of bomb disposal was ordered to report for duty and trained to handle the SD2. They were left in no doubt as to the difficulty of the job facing them. Any unexploded butterfly bomb with its wings opened out had to be treated as armed and liable to explode if touched, or even disturbed by vibration. Once armed, the butterfly bomb could not be disarmed again. Defuzing was not a practical option; the only method of disposal was to demolish the bomb. This could be done by shooting at it, or by attaching a piece of string and retiring to cover, such as the far side of a stone wall, before giving the cord a jerk.

There was an added complication: as bombs in container loads fell close to each other, the detonation of one bomb could explode another concealed nearby, killing the bomb disposal personnel while they worked. It was therefore vital to locate every bomb in a batch before clearance work started. This was difficult as the small bombs were hard enough to see in the open, let alone among plants, rubble or buildings. Although they were usually painted green, a yellow colour was used in Malta and the Middle East – making the bomb all but invisible on sand, or among grain crops at harvest time. Knowing that Malta was desperately short of food, the Luftwaffe chose to scatter these bombs across the fields, to explode among precious crops or lie as deadly snares, ready to catch farmers and their livestock.

By Monday 8 June, butterfly bombs had been reported right across the Island. A general warning was issued to civilians and military personnel to look out for the devices, report any sightings to the authorities and, most important of all, not to approach or touch them.

BEWARE OF THE BUTTERFLY BOMB
Many people in Malta last Monday found in their fields, their gardens, courtyards and on their roofs, a queer yellow contrivance consisting of a small round box with metal wings attached. It was a 'present from Jerry'. A 'Yellow butterfly bomb', as this type of German anti-personnel bomb is called. To move it meant death.

A yellow butterfly bomb is a small round yellow box, shaped like the top of a flit gun and three inches in diameter. It is attached by about six inches of wire to four curved metal fins, two of them with red bars painted across them. The bomb is a delayed action one and may explode within 20 minutes of reaching the earth. If it does not explode then it will do if it is moved. ON NO ACCOUNT TOUCH IT. Report its presence to the police who will send for the bomb disposal officer to deal with it.

It is important to warn children about this anti-personnel bomb which the enemy scatter in the hope of killing a few more of us. Parents and teachers should describe the appearance of the bomb to the children.[4]

The open wings of butterfly bombs often caught on wires or branches, where any attempt at removal could trigger an explosion. Working with a squad clearing Valletta, Lance-Corporal Tom Meager found one especially hard to reach.

> it fell onto the ivy that was growing up the wall below the Barracca lift. There was a sheer drop down that wall, and one of them had got strung up there. We went on the bridge over the footpath into Valletta with rifles, firing at this thing trying to make it go off. We got rid of it eventually.[5]

In the first seven days, the two bomb disposal sections disposed of 350 butterfly bombs. At the same time there was no let-up in the Luftwaffe use of high explosives. 23 unexploded HE bombs were reported in the same period – and all but one of them had delayed-action fuzes. With their men occupied elsewhere, Lieutenants Ashall and Blackwell concentrated on the HE bombs they could manage alone. Without assistance, it was impossible to apply a clockstopper and remove a bomb for disposal. Every one was blown in situ.

The bomb disposal officers would soon have to spare some of their resources for another task. A convoy was expected and to avoid losing precious cargo to an enemy attack all available manpower and transport would be diverted to unloading and moving goods into store. For the Island's military forces all other non-essential work would cease as soon as the convoy arrived and until work was complete. RE Bomb Disposal were required to keep a BD squad on standby round the clock for any UXB which could hinder the convoy operation. They would also be deprived of their lorries while they were used for transporting supplies.

There was other bad news that morning for the CO of the Fortress Engineers. The Army medical authorities had decided that Lieutenant Carroll was to be repatriated for treatment in the UK. He had been convalescing with the family of the Marquis Scicluna since leaving hospital at the end of April. For him to make a complete recovery from a duodenal ulcer a special diet was required which could not be provided from the depleted rations available in Malta. Nor did Carroll want any kind of special treatment in the circumstances:

> The food situation had become desperate. When we started I was quite well fed and I was familiar with the Maltese workman's food of a loaf cut in half with fish and tomato. Even after I left hospital I was OK for a time – mainly thanks to the hospitality of the Scicluna family. But things had become increasingly difficult for the Maltese people and by the time I left they were down to severe rations – even of ordinary bread. They were given corned beef which I believe they hated.
>
> The situation of the Maltese people was desperate. People knew that the convoys had been sent carrying food, and they were being sunk. Not only were they eating little, they had little prospect of any more arriving. It's amazing really that they didn't protest about food.[6]

Lieutenant Carroll was ordered to report to Luqa aerodrome on the night of Saturday 13 June, where he joined a small group, including a Royal Navy captain and a RAF squadron leader, to be flown out to Gibraltar before daybreak on Sunday morning. Arriving at the airfield, Carroll was informed that only a few pounds of luggage per passenger could be carried on board: most of his kit would have to be forwarded later. Even so, the aircraft failed in its first attempt at take-off, hitting the limestone surround of a well at the end of the runway, and grinding to a halt. Everyone disembarked and transferred to another plane for a second attempt. Finally, they felt the aircraft gather speed as it rumbled along the runway and surged into the air.

Carroll had lived and worked through over 2,000 alerts during his time as bomb disposal officer in Malta, including months of constant air raids since January 1942. The experience had far outstripped his previous period of duty in London, when he endured eight weeks of raids without a break. Now his service on the Island was over and strong emotions welled up inside him. He was leaving behind unfinished business: his vital work had been interrupted while he knew the Maltese people were still struggling against impossible odds. As with so many others who served during the siege, the experience profoundly affected the young lieutenant and left him with vivid memories for the rest of his life.

Before 7am on Monday 15 June the order came to muster and report to Grand Harbour. The first ship of the convoy, HMS *Welshman*, had arrived. With all hands hard at work, by 10.30am the task of unloading the supplies was complete. More ships were on the way, and Spitfires and Beaufighters took off on sorties to protect the incoming vessels. That night a fierce air battle broke out over the convoy approaching Malta from the south west, as the Allied planes tried to fight off twelve Ju88s hell-bent on destroying the ships. At the same time, eight other enemy aircraft bombed the Island's three airfields in an attempt to prevent defenders from taking to the air. By first light on Tuesday, the remnants of the convoy had reached Grand Harbour and unloading began again, obscured from the enemy's view by a smokescreen. Some 2,300 men and 240 vehicles were deployed in the collection and dispersal of cargo to the Island's stores. After anticipation of the relief that a convoy might bring the outcome was disappointing. Seventeen Allied supply ships had embarked in two simultaneous convoys, from east and west; only two merchant vessels reached Malta. Their cargoes were nowhere near enough to replenish the Island's impoverished resources. The Lieutenant Governor, Sir Edward Jackson, had bad news to announce in his broadcast to the people of Malta. Until further provisions could reach the Island, rations would remain severely restricted.

Having disrupted the convoy the Axis seemed to sense that they were again within reach of subduing Malta. They struck hard, choosing the night of Sunday 21 June to launch one of the fiercest attacks for some time. 28 bombers raided the Island and scattered large numbers of anti-personnel and incendiary bombs across wide areas. Their main target was Luqa but Hal Far and Ta' Qali were also hit, along with Naxxar, Verdala Palace and Dingli en route. Precious fields of wheat around the Safi strip were set on fire. The attack was the first sign of a new enemy tactic: using flares to illuminate their targets.

At midday on Friday 26 June, five Italian Cant aircraft accompanied by twelve fighters swept over Marsamxett Harbour dropping anti-personnel bombs on the streets of Ta' Xbiex, Msida and Guardamangia, before being chased away by Spitfires as they headed for Luqa. A bomb disposal officer attended a Priority call-out from Ta' Xbiex to find a community rocked by tragedy. The raiders had showered bombs on civilians enjoying a picnic on the shore, killing twelve and injuring another twelve.

The enemy's use of anti-personnel and incendiary bombs was beginning to achieve its tactical purpose, disrupting the life of Malta's communities. Activities essential to survival and defence – farming and transport, operation of airfields and dockyards – had to be put on hold until an area was free of explosives. Although Malta's stone buildings were largely impervious to incendiaries, the weapons still presented a threat to life and property – and burned valuable crops in the fields. So many small missiles of various kinds were now strewn across the archipelago that everyone, civilian or military, was constantly at risk of accidental contact with an explosive. Casualty numbers were growing. Civilians were too often risking their lives by handling dangerous items in an attempt to try and identify them. The Governor's information office issued another strong warning not to touch any bombs or other unusual objects but to report them to the police at once, for referral to the RE Bomb Disposal officer.

The hands-on experience and initiative of the NCOs and sappers of RE Bomb Disposal was never more valuable than in meeting the challenge of small incendiary and anti-personnel bombs. In 24 days to the end of June 1942 they tackled at least a thousand butterfly bombs – with only a small fraction of the manpower available to cope with similar attacks on the Home Front. During the same period, German 1kg incendiaries and Italian 2kg anti-personnel bombs were also dropped very freely. The sappers handled so many small bombs that it was impossible to keep track of them all. At the same time, they dug shafts for 36 bombs, bringing the total of high explosive UXBs disposed of to 68. Of the HE bombs dealt with during the month, more than a third had clockwork fuzes. In the three months since April, thirteen per cent of unexploded HE bombs had contained at least one Type 17: it was twice the average of the Home Front.

They could expect many more. Despite having failed to subdue Malta's population with a shower of large and small bombs, Axis forces were not about to give up. Additional reinforcements of both Luftwaffe and *Regia Aeronautica* moved into Sicily as the enemy re-intensified their efforts. They had in their sights a new consignment of Allied aircraft, flying in from the aircraft carrier *Wasp* heading east from Gibraltar. After a night of violent and repeated explosions, air-raid alerts resumed at breakfast time on Wednesday

1 July, with three enemy air patrols before 10am. Frequent day raids had returned to Malta.

Unexploded HE bombs lay ominously among communities across the south of the Island. All were 250kg or 500kg: one in three of them was likely to have a DA fuze. While Lieutenant Blackwell was working on the bombs that morning, the enemy launched yet another attack. A formation of Italian Cant aircraft passed over the southern coastline and headed on to Luqa, dropping bombs as they went and leaving more UXBs for No. 127 Section in the fishing village of Marsaxlokk.

That day squads from No. 128 Section were taking their turn with hundreds more German and Italian anti-personnel bombs. Lieutenant Ashall was called out to a particularly difficult butterfly bomb. It lay among the ripening melons on the flat stone roof of a traditional Maltese farmhouse. There was no question of picking it up: the bomb could explode at the lightest touch. He decided the only chance was to loop a string over the bomb and pull it sharply: with luck he would have it away from the roof before it exploded. Now all he needed was somewhere to take shelter. Looking around, he saw his solution.

Moving as lightly as he could, he climbed onto the roof and inched towards his prey. Taking care not to disturb it, he deftly manoeuvred a noose of string over the bomb. He braced himself, but nothing happened. Playing out the string loosely as he went, he backed away slowly to the edge of the roof and, releasing it for a moment, lowered himself to the ground. He clambered through a window into a bedroom, feeding the string in behind him. He had spotted a wardrobe in the far corner of the room: he tucked himself inside and sheltered behind the door. He wound the string round his fist and, taking a deep breath, pulled sharply. The bomb flew off the roof, exploding over the open courtyard as it fell. Done.[7]

On Thursday night, two dozen aircraft flew over the Island again, scattering bombs as they went. By the time the bomb disposal officers reported for duty next morning several UXB reports were already in. Ashall was called out to Attard and Lija, where among large numbers of anti-personnel bombs there was evidence of four UXBs having penetrated the ground. According to the police in Attard, the raid that morning was unusual. Italian Cant aircraft did not make their normal descent to release their bombs but dropped them from an astonishing 23,000 feet. The story from the ARP warden at Lija was the same. Instead of the expected HE bombs, the squad was surprised to discover anti-personnel containers which had driven themselves deep into the ground after falling from such a great height.

The containers were among 55 UXBs reported on Friday 3 July 1942 – by far the highest daily total for some time. Seventeen of them were high explosive bombs, including nine around Luqa airfield. The BD officers again faced conflicting priorities. The men could not be asked to do more as they were already working six days out of seven. Even this was not enough to keep on top of the persistently high numbers of anti-personnel bombs: 321 during the following week alone. Yet there was still a backlog of dozens of buried HE bombs, the majority suspected to be the high-risk 250kg and 500kg.

All this would have been preying on Ashall's mind on Monday as he left Villa Fleri with his NCO, heading for the hilltop town of Rabat. In his pocket was a UXB report marked Priority. The Protection Office in College Street – the vital centre which looked after food distribution and other wartime matters for the local community – had been hit by a large bomb which had failed to explode. Directed to where the bomb lay, Ashall could see it was a 500kg SC and it had twin fuze pockets. He hardly needed to look at the front pocket to know its fuze would be marked 17. He turned to his NCO and nodded, frowning. He leaned his head close to the bomb and listened, but there was no ticking as yet. He looked at the second pocket: an impact fuze. This was small relief as the bomb could still detonate at any moment. The NCO had wasted no time and at Ashall's nod the magnetic clockstopper had already been unloaded. Within moments it was placed over the fuze and they could all heave a sigh of relief. However, they now had to decide what to do with the bomb. In some cases it had been possible to explode delayed-action bombs in situ, but this one was in the middle of a town. The bomb disposal officer would have to get the bomb away somehow.

Squads from No.128 BD Section were already digging elsewhere in Rabat. The NCO went to summon a team of sappers to assist. Approaching the policeman on duty to keep the public away, Ashall asked his help in finding the nearest open space to explode the device. The constable suggested fields at the bottom of the hill near the remains of the old Malta Railway. As he turned back towards the Protection Office, Ashall stopped.

Something was not quite right. He walked away from the building and towards a break in the ground; he looked again, confirming his suspicions. It was the entry hole of another unexploded bomb – fairly large, probably a 250kg. He went back to the policeman to break the bad news. However, as a buried bomb it would wait its turn – the site would be cordoned off until Ashall could spare the men.

Meanwhile the lorry had arrived bringing a squad to help shift the 500kg. It was not going to be easy hoisting and loading a bomb of such size with a heavy clockstopper attached. If the bomb fell even a few inches, there could be a massive explosion. The clockstopper was lashed securely in place. Next, ropes were tightly wound round each end of the bomb casing. The section's lorry was turned and reversed into place in the narrow street. Its crane was hooked up to the rope harness, then its pulley was cranked slowly until the rope was taught. It was vital to make sure the bomb was level as it rose: any angle could de-stabilise the load, causing it to slip out of the harness. Two sappers steadied the bomb while it was winched upwards. Once it was high enough, the crane was turned 180 degrees and the bomb lowered gently onto a bed of sandbags. One man had the task of driving the bomb away, followed separately by Ashall and the remainder of the team. Then the bomb was hoisted again and lowered to the ground. Finally, the magnetic clockstopper could be detached and the men retreated, leaving Ashall alone to place his charges. Joining them a few minutes later at the safe point, he blew the bomb.

The squad of sappers went back to their task on the other side of Rabat. They would work right through July in the town and in the grounds of the nearby hospital at Mtarfa, completing 13 more excavations between 10 and 18 feet in depth. It was hard going, especially without the hoped-for increase in rations. The back-breaking work was done under a blazing sun as the weather turned very hot, bringing large numbers of flies to add to their discomfort. And their much-needed sleep continued to be disturbed by night raids. Several times as they hacked away in deep shafts the sappers ran for cover from attacks on nearby Ta' Qali. Because of its position overlooking the airfield, bombs were still falling around Rabat almost daily, penetrating deep into the ground and adding to their workload. They had a break on Saturday 11 July – only to tackle more than 200 butterfly bombs scattered across the town in fresh attacks. Squads from No. 127 BD Section also had bombs to uncover – in Zabbar, Kirkop and Luqa – but with fewer bombs to dig for in the south of the Island, much of their time was taken up with hundreds of butterfly bombs.

All the same, they were getting on top of the backlog of HE bombs. With no reports of high explosives on Sunday 12 July, there was a rare chance for the officers and men of RE Bomb Disposal to take things easy. Still preferring to use his spare time exploring unusual incidents, Lieutenant Blackwell would use such an opportunity to call on Lieutenant Edward Woolley:

> Another affair I remember with Blackwell was when he dragged me out one Sunday evening, again during a blitz, to look at something at Senglea which he thought was a new type of mine. It certainly was a new one on me – rather like a mine, but not normal, and it was lying on the road on top of the bastion with the Dockyard about a hundred feet below. After a lot of messing about very cautiously, taking photographs, and making enquiries, I found it to be part of a torpedo off a Greek submarine! It had apparently been lying in the dockyard and had been blown up – over a hundred feet – by an explosion.[8]

After just one quiet day, attacks returned to normal. With the arrival of a fresh consignment of 31 Spitfires, the enemy launched another audacious daytime attack on Luqa and Safi, swooping down from 21,000 to 16,000 feet and showering the area with more HE and anti-personnel bombs. The presence of hundreds of small bombs on the airfields, made almost invisible by the uneven scrubland, created a sense of unease among military personnel trying to keep aircraft moving. Once more the RAF called on the Army for help. The Royal Engineers cleared 500 butterfly bombs from the airfields, bringing their total of SD2 bombs to 740 in seven days, double the rate of recent weeks. They were helped by a new technique for unexploded butterfly bombs. Tom Meager and his comrades had learned that not all of them were in a dangerous condition. Some landed before they were fully armed.

> If [the butterfly bomb] was dropped at low altitude, it wouldn't have time to [fully] unwind and arm itself before it hit the ground. You could tell by the number of threads – if there were five or more threads exposed you

would leave the bomb and deal with it where it lay but if it was four or less you could pick it up and move it around. As we were short of explosives, we could pile them up together and then blow them up in one go.[9]

The method made slightly shorter work of the airfields but it had a downside. In Lieutenant Ashall's case, proximity to so many explosions of butterfly and HE bombs ultimately damaged his hearing.[10]

In a determined effort to break up the runways and prevent aircraft from taking off the Luftwaffe had started using the heavier SD bombs again. The height at which aircraft were now releasing bombs, combined with the thicker walls of the *spreng dickenwand* construction, was proving more effective at penetrating the hard terrain. No. 127 BD Section had a tougher assignment than usual with two UXBs in open country at Ta' Kandja near Mqabba. Their picks and shovels made very show progress through the hard limestone. It was heavy going in the searing heat. They reached eight feet with no sign of a bomb. At least at that depth the diggers could have some shade for part of the day. Eventually they found the carcass ten feet deep, only to repeat the whole process hacking away another twelve foot shaft to find the second bomb.

As 28 more Spitfires were added to Malta's defensive force, their sheer strength in numbers began to deter the enemy. For the first time in months, more outstanding high explosive UXBs were disposed of in seven days than new ones reported. For one bomb disposal officer, it was the prelude to the end of his service in bomb disposal in Malta. In 1940, the War Office had stipulated that any BD officer who had served continuously for a period of six months could apply for a transfer to other duties. After his service in Portsmouth and the Middle East, followed by a strenuous three months in Malta, Ashall elected to take up this option. His request was granted and another new bomb disposal officer was needed for the Island. Lieutenant T. Whitworth (130878) was posted from the Middle East to take over command of No. 128 Bomb Disposal Section which currently had sixteen other ranks on the roll. Lieutenant Blackwell continued in charge of No. 127 BD Section, with nineteen other ranks.

Thomas Whitworth was born in 1917 and brought up in Oldham, where he achieved a scholarship to Manchester Grammar School. In 1937 he went up to Oriel College, Oxford, to read zoology. Following the onset of the

Second World War, he interrupted his studies to join the army as a cadet with the 11th Chemical Warfare Training Battalion, Royal Engineers, then based at Figsbury Camp near Salisbury. He was appointed 2nd Lieutenant in May 1940. In the spring of 1941 Lieutenant Whitworth married Joan Agarwala in Oxford, before being posted as a bomb disposal officer to the Middle East.

Reporting for duty on the morning of Monday 27 July, Whitworth was introduced to Lieutenants Blackwell and Ashall. After an explanation of RE Bomb Disposal operations on the Island, Ashall took his replacement on a tour of his northern area. Their journey took them inland to Zebbug and then northwards to Rabat, where Whitworth saw the extent of the digging the men in his new section had to do. From there they headed to another excavation on the coast at Ghain Tuffieha, then crossed the Island via Mosta and Naxxar to the north coast, before heading back to Villa Fleri.

It was a brief introduction to the Island. Next morning Whitworth was straight into action, leading squads working on anti-personnel bombs. Birkirkara had been in the line of fire for a raid centred on Ta' Qali late on Sunday evening. The village had become the most densely populated locality in Malta, housing many refugees who had fled from Grand Harbour. Now it had been showered with butterfly bombs. One fell in the yard of the home of seventeen-year-old John Mizzi and another in the garden of his neighbours, the Fenech-Adami family. John watched as a small squad of RE Bomb Disposal personnel worked their way up the main street, led by Whitworth. To him, the BD officer seemed:

a strapping lad of 21 [sic], with red face and unruly hair. He and the others were the coolest men on earth. They picked up the bombs as if they were loaves of bread and took them to a field and exploded them there. Father called them in and gave them drinks and our neighbours gave them fruit, grapes and figs.

They had been exploding bombs all day. The couple of NCOs went to where my brother was looking at some comics and picked up one each. 'Better than bombs,' grinned one, 'haven't seen any of these for ages.' They were human after all, these men who were playing with death to save others from death …[11]

Eight-year-old Edward Fenech Adami was sheltering with his family in their private underground shelter at the back of their garden, when they heard the All Clear. Luckily it was his mother who left the shelter first, before the children followed out to play. She noticed a bunch of grapes lying in the soil. Fortunately, she was smart enough not to pick it up – which would have been fatal. A bomb had pulled down the grapes before it hit the ground, embedding itself in the soil. It lay there concealed by the fruit. Edward Fenech-Adami would never forget his mother's quick thinking that day. Thanks to her he survived – and grew up to become the President of Malta.[12] John Mizzi wrote an account of the incident for *The War Illustrated* in London, which was published in October 1942.[13] Already writing regularly for the publication about life during the siege, John would achieve his ambition to be a journalist, later becoming editor of the *Times of Malta*. However, the following weekend the young Mizzi had a tragic coda to add to his report:

> Later in the week, on [Saturday] afternoon, the boys who lived in the street were playing hide and seek behind the rubble walls in the fields. At sunset when they returned home, one of them, 13-year-old Joe Galea, did not turn up. He was found later dead behind one of the walls; he had jumped on one of the butterfly bombs.[14]

The tragic loss of the young boy underlined the unpredictable nature of the butterfly bomb. Whitworth was able to pick one up without mishap because he could see that its spindle had not unwound enough times to arm the fuze. Yet only yards away, Joe Galea had the misfortune to land on another which was fully armed.

As part of his induction Whitworth was studying the records of previous Army bomb disposal work in Malta. Looking through the backlog of outstanding UXB reports for the northern area, one in particular caught his eye: a bomb in a well. He mentioned it to Lieutenant Ashall who remembered promising in May to return and tackle the bomb. He explained that it was a challenging case and they both decided to go to Gharghur with a squad to see what could be done. The landowner was pleased to see the bomb men arrive, expecting that his well was about to be freed of its unwelcome visitor. Ashall explained that it was unlikely things would be quite so simple. They did not yet know what kind of fuze they were facing. The BD officers walked over to the well and looked down. For once the Maltese weather had been kind. The summer heat had lowered the water level and the carcass of the bomb was now exposed. It was a 250kg SC – and it had twin fuze pockets.

There was a strong temptation to destroy it there and then. However, both BD officers were conscious of how important the well was to the farmer. They had to check if there was any chance of hauling the bomb out. That could only happen if it had two impact fuzes. If either one was a Type 17, there was no way of getting the bomb out with a clockstopper attached: the well's neck was too narrow. It was time to take a closer look. Someone had to get down into the well so that, with the help of a torch, they could see the head of each fuze pocket. Their discretion was well-founded: it had not one, but two delayed-action fuzes. The bomb would have to be exploded, despite the owner's wishes. Ashall gave instructions to his sergeant to make preparations for a controlled explosion. Then he went himself to explain to the unhappy owner and instruct him to keep his distance. Attaching the charges securely at the foot of the well was a tricky operation. With everything in place, Ashall gave the signal and pushed on the lever. He had destroyed his last unexploded bomb.

Friday 31 July was Lieutenant Ashall's final day with RE Bomb Disposal in Malta. All bomb disposal work was suspended for the day as he completed the handover of No. 128 BD Section to Lieutenant Whitworth. Then it was time for his farewell celebration. Although his service as a bomb disposal officer was over, Ashall was not leaving the Island. He was posted to join the roll of officers at Fortress Engineers HQ.

Lieutenant Blackwell missed the party. Late on Thursday night he was roused from his rest by an urgent call to Lintorn Barracks from the police at Birkirkara. An unexploded bomb lay in a ruined building in St Rocco Street and civilians were believed to be trapped in the rubble. Rushing to the scene, Blackwell was met by a policeman who took him to the house and pointed to where the bomb lay. Not hesitating for a moment, Blackwell clambered over the rubble with his torch – he had to know what he was dealing with. It was a 250kg bomb – and it had two clockwork fuzes. He pressed his ear to the carcass and found it was ticking. He had to think fast. Time was running out and lives were at stake; he must get the bomb away from the building. But it could explode at any moment. Normally he would have stopped the clock before doing anything else but there was no question of manoeuvring a magnetic clockstopper into position amid all the rubble. There was nothing for it; he must get the bomb away right now, despite the risk to his own safety. Turning to the duty police constable nearby, Blackwell explained what he was about to do. PC Baylis could see that the bomb disposal officer was alone and offered to help. The *London Gazette* described what happened.

Lieutenant Thomas Walter Townsend BLACKWELL M.B.E. 169308 Royal Engineers
At about 10 o'clock on the night of 30th July, 1942, a number of delayed action bombs were dropped in Birkirkara, Malta. One of these bombs partly demolished a house in a very built-up area, thereby burying a number of civilians. The bomb remained partially exposed. Lieutenant Blackwell on arrival at the site, discovered that the bomb contained two delayed action fuzes, the clocks of which were both working. He decided that the proper course was to remove the bomb as soon as possible to a less vulnerable area, so that efforts could be made to rescue entombed people. As no lifting tackle was available, he decided that the bomb must be towed away. It was necessary to first clear a passage for the bomb, and in this he was ably assisted by P.C. Baylis, a local Constable. Lieutenant Blackwell then tried to haul the bomb clear by means of a truck and a towing rope. The lay-out of the street permitted a towing rope of only 12 feet in length. The first attempt failed owing to the bomb becoming stuck in the debris. It was then obvious that two persons were required; one to drive the truck, the other to guide the bomb. P.C. Baylis volunteered to drive the truck, which he did, and with Lieutenant Blackwell guiding the bomb, the operation was completed. During the process of removing the bomb another bomb from the same stick exploded. The fact that the people buried under the debris of the house on which this bomb had fallen were, when extricated, found to be dead, does not detract from the gallantry of the action of Lieutenant Blackwell and P. C. Baylis.[15]

Blackwell was injured when the second bomb exploded and suffered concussion.[16] As well as missing the party, he was forced to take a proper rest for once. He later recorded his action for the Weekly Bomb Disposal Report as 'Hauled clear of house to permit rescue work to carry on. Left to self-detonate. D.A.' His words give little indication of the drama of that night, for which Lieutenant T.W.T. Blackwell was awarded the George Medal, and Police Constable Baylis the British Empire Medal.

Notes

1 John Mizzi, 2007
2 Former BD officer, Malta, Henry Lavington estimates approximately 50 per container in Malta. However, the Luftwaffe were known to have developed a plywood container which could carry up to 248 of the SD2.
3 'The Malta Police at War', Assistant Commissioner Edward J. Bonnici-Solar. Rixon, Frank, ed. (2005). *Malta Remembered*. Woodhouse Publishing.
4 Ed. (1942). *Times of Malta*. June.
5 Cyril Thomas Meager, 2008.
6 Lieutenant G.D. Carroll, 2005
7 Information from Patrick Ashall, 2008
8 Extract from collection of documents written by Commander Edward Dutton Woolley, GM & Bar, RNVR, National War Museum Association, Malta. See also: Galea, F. (2008). *Mines Over Malta*. Malta: Wise Owl Publications.
9 Cyril Thomas Meager, 2008.
10 Information from Patrick Ashall, 2008
11 John Mizzi, 2007
12 Edward Fenech-Adami: President of Malta April 2004–April 2009.
13 At the time of going to press John Mizzi is Editor of *Malta at War* magazine.
14 John Mizzi, 2007
15 Ed. (1942) *London Gazette*. 6 November.
16 Lieutenant Blackwell's Army Service Record shows that he suffered concussion from being 'blown up in Malta'. Evidence suggests that this was the occasion of his injuries.

CHAPTER 15

STING IN THE TAIL

The Germans introduced the unmarked fuze with a purpose: to kill any bomb disposer who might attempt to deal with it …

After only a week in Malta, Lieutenant Whitworth found himself in sole charge of Army Bomb Disposal for the Island. It was a relief to know he had the help of experienced NCOs who could handle straightforward HE bombs. Only ten remained, thanks to all the recent hard work. Whitworth could manage any urgent large UXBs which came up; the rest would be put on hold until Lieutenant Blackwell recovered. Before he could get started, some of his men had a commitment to fulfil. After the bombardment of July, the RAF Commander in Chief needed help with the building of more protective shelters on the airfields for the growing Spitfire strike force. On Saturday 1 August, sappers from RE Bomb Disposal were among a 2,000-strong workforce spending the weekend on the aerodromes. They were surprised at the lack of enemy action: only two Ju88s managed a single strike on Safi, on Sunday morning. Remarkably, it was the only daylight raid during the first week of August and there were just five bomb attacks by single enemy aircraft at night. The Island's defences seemed to be holding them off.

On Monday morning Whitworth got down to reducing the total of outstanding UXBs still further. He made his way north to Mellieha to defuze an 1,800kg Satan bomb which had been lying in a remote area above the

Bay since June. On his return, he inspected the traces of a suspected bomb at St Paul's Bay: a squad would be sent there next day to start digging. He had just one urgent call-out to an HE bomb – a 250kg SD near the runway at Hal Far. For one squad from No.128 BD Section, it was back to Birkirkara, to seek out and explode all manner of anti-personnel bombs. Despite the hazards, they might have been grateful. In the scorching August heat, the rest of their section sank four shafts in Zebbug and three more in Rabat. No.127 Section had its share of digging too: for one bomb at Tal Handaq and two in the rocky ground by the Island's southernmost fort at Benghisa. After so much strenuous activity, the sappers barely found the energy to cheer the announcement of a whole weekend off duty. Thanks to Malta's fighter aircraft Sunday passed free of bombing raids and not a single unexploded bomb was reported.

With only nine UXBs remaining, the officers, NCOs and sappers of RE Bomb Disposal felt on top of their task. The number of daytime air-raid alerts was still decreasing, from 128 in the month of July to 56 in August. Night-time enemy sorties reduced from 200 to just 73. Work could return to some semblance of a routine. Yet with 80 UXB reports in the first week of August and 65 in the second, demand for Army Bomb Disposal was still at or well above the average for the Home Front. And in Malta living conditions were far more challenging, with food and fuel still in desperately short supply. The hot August winds from North Africa, whipping up clouds of dust from the parched terrain and bomb-damaged buildings, made life even more uncomfortable.

The relative calm was shattered on Monday 10 August with a fierce attack on Ta' Qali by three JU88 bombers, escorted by 30 fighters. Another sharp raid followed that night, when a dozen aircraft bombed Luqa and the Sliema area. Blackwell was back in action in time to respond to nine UXB reports from Luqa, including one with a DA fuze. The reason for the activity soon emerged: a convoy was on its way to Malta. Despite determined attacks from enemy bombers and submarine torpedoes, three vessels – the *Rochester Castle*, *Melbourne Star* and *Port Chalmers* – entered Grand Harbour early in the evening of Thursday 13 August 1942. Word travelled fast and the ships were greeted by crowds lining the bastions on all sides of the harbour, cheering and saying prayers of thanks. On Friday, the ships were joined by the MV *Brisbane Star*, showing the scars of its violent passage through the Mediterranean. This time the cheers were somewhat subdued, as the spectators realised the ordeal endured by the convoy in its struggle to reach them. On Saturday, the throng massed again at every available vantage point of Valletta and the Three Cities; Lieutenant Ashall was among them. They watched with a mixture of horror and admiration as the US tanker *Ohio* was towed painfully slowly into Grand Harbour – barely afloat but still carrying her desperately-needed supplies of fuel. It was the Feast of the Assumption, known in Malta as Santa Marija – a name which became permanently linked with the convoy, and with the courage and perseverance of those who had brought it through.

RE Bomb Disposal work had been suspended since Friday morning so that the sappers could join the 3,000 men working night and day unloading the precious cargo. Another 1,500 army personnel helped on the aerodromes, servicing and refuelling the aircraft fighting off enemy attacks on the ships in harbour. On 22 August it was reported that a total of 32,000 tons of supplies had been retrieved from the merchant vessels and dispersed to stores across the Island. The news was not all good: the supplies were still not enough to allow for any major alterations in rations – only bread allowances could be slightly increased. The battle for survival in Malta was far from over.

For the bomb disposal officers there was other news. It was time to bid farewell to the commanding officer who had presided over Royal Engineers Bomb Disposal in Malta since 1940. Recently awarded the OBE, Lieutenant-Colonel G.R. McMeekan had completed his tour of duty and embarked for the Middle East on 25 August. The new CO of Fortress RE Malta was Lieutenant-Colonel R.R. Gillespie. Lieutenant Ashall was about to begin a new job too, but he was staying on the Island. His posting to CRE(N), the Royal Engineers Works Company covering Malta's northern sector, involved him in tunnelling and other construction projects, employment related to his career in civilian life.

After attacks on the convoy tailed off, air raids became few and far between and the last Sunday of August passed with none. The number of reported UXBs reduced to no more than a dozen on any one day; occasionally there was not a single one. But the bombs that were dropped had been released from a great height, often propelling them deep into the ground. The sappers faced three more weeks of heavy digging: another fourteen shafts up to fourteen feet into stony ground. Squads from No. 127 BD Section endured a gruelling week working in fields at the village of Qrendi, struggling to get at two large bombs. After seemingly endless shifting of rock and stone, one squad exposed a fuze pocket, unnerved to find that it held a DA fuze. Alerted by the news, the second team were not surprised to find another. In all, half the excavated bombs had clockwork fuzes. Thankfully the work was completed in relative peace while the Luftwaffe concentrated on night-time attacks.

By 11 September there were only four high explosive UXBs on the books. The hardy sappers could enjoy a whole fortnight free from back-breaking labour. Sunday 13 September provided a special reason for celebration as the Island was honoured with the formal presentation of the George Cross by His Excellency the Governor, on behalf of the King.

Despite a deserved sense of achievement, the men of bomb disposal could never afford to relax their guard even for a moment, without deadly consequences. On Tuesday 22 September Lieutenant Blackwell travelled down to Kirkop for his first UXB since Friday. It was a 500kg SC bomb with two fuze pockets. Routinely, he went towards the front one, anticipating a DA fuze, but there was no marking. The Luftwaffe could still be unpredictable: it was the first unmarked fuze he had come across in Malta for some time. He had to assume it was delayed-action since experience so far in bomb disposal made it almost certain. So what about the second fuze? Blackwell glanced at the rear pocket, but it had a dust cover, making it impossible to identify that fuze either. He assumed the worst: if the Luftwaffe had put an unmarked fuze in the front pocket, they might well have put a type 50 anti-handling fuze in the rear. He could not risk trying to take off the cap. One false move and the bomb could go off, clock or no clock. Taking care not to disturb the device, he placed his ear close to its flank and listened: no ticking. There was no time to lose. He collected his explosive charges, placing them gently but securely on the bomb, retired and gave the signal, at which the bomb was blown.

After a two-week respite, the sappers of No. 128 BD Section went back to the seemingly endless slog of clearing buried bombs. The weather may have cooled but there was plenty of hard graft ahead of them, one squad slogging across country daily to sink three 20-foot shafts at Mgarr, while their mates worked on another two of 12 and 14 feet near Rabat. By Friday 9 October they were making good progress and could hope to down tools for the weekend. But it was not to be. At 6am on Saturday they were roused by the wail of the alert. The enemy were heading in force towards Malta for the start of five attacks that day. Word soon spread that bombers had been spotted among the 132 aircraft approaching the Island – the first to appear in daylight for seven weeks. Although Spitfires quickly saw off the attackers, two Ju88s jettisoned their HE bombs over the Island of Gozo, causing over a dozen casualties. Three air raid alerts followed that night, and more bombs fell on Luqa and Dingli.

German command had evidently not yet given up on their objective of neutralising Malta. With the war in North Africa at a turning point, they had assembled another massive Luftwaffe force in Sicily. Saturday was merely a prelude to the main attacks. In a pattern more familiar in the spring of 1942, the Luftwaffe began their onslaught at breakfast time on Sunday morning. Nine Ju88s with a protective cover of 30 fighters bombed Benghisa and Hal Far, followed by even bigger formations mid-morning, then at lunchtime and at teatime, cutting a swathe across Birkirkara, Balzan, Lija, Ta' Qali and Mellieha Ridge. But the fiercest attack was yet to come. At just before six that evening, 30 bombers arrived unescorted, taking advantage of the failing light to attack Hal Far and Luqa, but also hitting the civilian communities of Tarxien and Qormi. At night, another 19 aircraft again bombed areas around Luqa and Birkirkara. Civilians were badly hit; the final total of casualties exceeded 30. Everyone in Malta – military and civilian – was reeling from the shock of this sudden return to blitzkrieg. By the end of Monday Axis aircraft had carried out 700 attacking sorties in 60 hours, in another all-out attempt to disable the Island's defences and put the airfields beyond repair. However, the high-risk strategy cost the enemy dearly. Out of 50 bombers and 225 fighters they lost 43 aircraft, with another 59 damaged.

It was thanks to a new tactic by the RAF: as soon as radar picked up an approaching attack their fighters were airborne, intercepting enemy raiders before they could even reach Malta's skies. Any who did make it to the coast ran the gauntlet of a heavy barrage from the Island's gun positions. The Luftwaffe responded with their own change in tactics; formations of aircraft began to approach from several directions simultaneously. Still the agile Spitfires intercepted them. Hundreds more sorties were launched day after day. And still the Island's defenders maintained their protective hold on the skies, reducing the number of bomb attacks successfully hitting target.

However, raiders under attack jettison more bombs. 137 UXB reports reached Bomb Disposal HQ during the first week of the new campaign and 55 in the second, all concentrated around the three airfields and the north-east coast. A third were for high explosives, the rest were anti-personnel bombs or incendiaries. This time the NCOs were kept busy with UXBs as the Luftwaffe resorted to the use of 50kg bombs again. More of them could be loaded onto each aircraft and, with fewer planes reaching target, a single successful bomber could drop a greater number of bombs in one attempt.

The Luftwaffe were using a wide variety of fuzes in their bombs – keeping the bomb disposal services at a disadvantage when facing every UXB. As he started to receive Weekly Bomb Disposal Reports, Lieutenant-Colonel Gillespie asked for details to be added of the fuzes in each HE bomb. The reports reveal the variation in types and combinations found during just one fourteen-day period:

BOMB	NO	FUZE POCKET(S)	FUZE(S)
50kg SD	1	Single	15 (impact)
50kg SC	6	Single	25A* (impact)
50kg SC	5	Single	25B (impact)
50kg SD	6	Single	55 (impact)
50kg SD	3	Single	unseen
German 250kg SC	1	Single	17 (DA)
German 250kg SC	2	Twin	17A (DA) and 25A (impact)
German 250kg SC	1	Twin	17A and 17A (DA)
German 250kg SC	1	Single	unseen
German 250kg SC	3	Twin	17 A (DA) and unseen
German 250kg SC	2	Single	unmarked (DA)
German 250kg SD	1	Single	35 (impact)
German 250kg SD	2	Twin	55 (impact)[1]

As one squad was getting stuck into the all too familiar job of locating unexploded butterfly bombs, their NCO heard a strangled shout from one of his men. When the sapper had bent to check the number of exposed turns to the spindle, he saw something to send a shiver down his spine. Instead of the normal number 41, the fuze was marked 67. Picking his way carefully to the spot, the NCO took one look and doubtless muttered an oath. He knew about the Type 67 from his training. It was a delayed-action fuze. It could be set to blow the bomb at any time from 5 to 30 minutes after it fell. Although that time had passed, like any clockwork mechanism, if this one had merely jammed any movement could restart the clock. And then there was no way of knowing how long it had left to run. This butterfly bomb could not be moved an inch. The NCO gave the order to clear the area and with a single rifle shot the bomb was blown to pieces.

From that moment, butterfly bombs could no longer be considered relatively harmless if left undisturbed. Any number of them might explode at random, triggering others within range. With hundreds more butterfly bombs strewn across houses, streets and fields, the Type 67 fuze brought even more fear and disruption for civilian and military alike. It was well known in bomb disposal that butterfly bombs with different types of fuze were often mixed in the same container. Who could guess how many would now have these clockwork fuzes? It made the job much more time-consuming. Every one of the 380 tackled by RE Bomb Disposal in the last two weeks of October had to be treated as a possible time bomb, until its fuze had been identified.

Civilian and military populations struggled to bear up under the renewed onslaught, little knowing the effect that continued heavy losses were having on their enemies. After just one week, the Luftwaffe were reduced to sending only a few bombers on each raid. And despite continued protection by their own fighters they were often prevented from reaching their target. None of Malta's airfields was put out of action for more than 30 minutes. Axis commanders began to realise that their latest all-out effort to subdue the Island was having little impact, and at a very high cost. Reluctantly accepting that this round of the battle for supremacy in the skies had gone to the Allies, they retreated. The Luftwaffe force committed to attacks on Malta was scaled down; even with support from the *Regia Aeronautica* raids were fewer and less effective. The numbers of UXB reports fell back again, to just twenty in the final week of October 1942. The last major excavations for buried bombs were completed, including two of over 20 feet near Rabat. By the end of the month only seventeen unexploded HE and a handful of butterfly bombs remained. The sections finally had their work under control.

Despite a growing sense of optimism after the Luftwaffe retreat, one challenge remained for all those living and serving in Malta: the Island was facing starvation – of food and essential supplies. Despite the successful shipments, rations continued to be reduced in an attempt to eke out the remaining meagre stocks. The Governor and his superiors in London were facing a crisis: unless Malta could be re-supplied by the beginning of December, the Island's situation would be untenable. With Allied dominance in the skies there was an opportunity to run in further convoys. On 11 November, the fast minelayer *Manxman* made it into Grand Harbour with a cargo of dried milk and concentrated foodstuffs. Within days another four ships berthed intact, bringing more essential military and civilian supplies. As crowds returned to the bastions to cheer the approaching vessels, there was renewed hope.

Thankfully, the workload for bomb disposal in November was less strenuous: only sixteen HE bombs during the month, plus 274 butterfly bombs and many German 1kg incendiaries. At the start of December, only eight HE UXBs remained and for several days no new ones were reported. A working party from RE Bomb Disposal was off to Gozo to clear all outstanding unexploded bombs from the sister island. Almost all turned out to be anti-personnel bombs and were easily disposed of. Back on the main island, traces of three possible bombs came to light on 11 December around the southern bay of Birzebbuga. Out came the picks and shovels again, as shafts of six to ten feet needed to be sunk to reach them. All three were 250kg SD with impact fuzes; they soon went over the western cliffs.

Lieutenant Blackwell was approaching the end of a year's service in Malta and it was time for him to leave. By 19 November Bomb Disposal Headquarters in the Middle East had identified his replacement and told him to stand by for imminent posting to Malta. However, the anniversary of Blackwell's arrival came and went, and he was still on the Island. Instead, at 11pm on 18 December, the relative peace was broken by the sound of the air-raid alert. 40 enemy planes, mainly Ju88 bombers, waged a concentrated attack on Luqa and the Safi dispersal area, destroying seven aircraft. Two civilians, one officer and two other ranks were killed in the raid and there were several casualties. Although sudden and harsh, the action proved to be a one-off.

But there was a sting in its tail for RE Bomb Disposal. The raiders dropped large numbers of butterfly bombs and sappers were back on their least favourite job. After their experiences in October, they approached every single bomb wary of finding a clockwork fuze. Suddenly a shout went up to stop. Every man was ordered to back off carefully. One butterfly bomb had been spotted carrying the most lethal fuze of all – the 70B. It was an extremely sensitive anti-handling fuze, designed to go off as soon as the bomb was even slightly disturbed. It was no longer safe to approach any butterfly bomb to check the fuze. Even if one had a simple fuze, another with a booby-trap could be lying inches away, hidden in rubble or undergrowth. The lightest step was fraught with danger until the fuze was identified. This time the enemy's selection of bombs made a toxic mixture: out of 150 tackled, 132 were booby-trapped.

Somehow another convoy of four cargo ships got through to deliver 55,000 tons of supplies to the Island and Lord Gort could start to ease restrictions. Malta was better equipped for a sustained offensive against the Axis in the Mediterranean. Not only could the sappers look forward to better rations, there was to be no more digging for a while. Having dropped 12,300 tons of bombs on Malta during 1942, the enemy were now on the retreat. There had been just 35 air raid alerts in December 1942 compared to 169 in the same month the year before. The General Staff War Diary could afford a note of optimism: 'This month was remarkable as the turning point in the fortunes of Malta.'2

On 24 December, worshippers filled the Island's churches, looking forward to Christmas. The siege of Malta had been lifted: the time for celebration had come at last.

Notes

1 Ed. (1942). War Diary Fortress Engineers, Malta. WO 169 National Archives, London.
2 Ed. (1942). War Diary General Staff, Malta. WO 169 National Archives, London.

CHAPTER 16

SLEEPING MENACE

Suddenly from round the corner came a Maltese soldier with his hand blown off, and blood pouring everywhere.[1]

The officers and men of Royal Engineers Bomb Disposal had come through the siege unscathed. In their battle to keep the Islands free from unexploded bombs, they had overcome one challenge after another, as the enemy tried every bomb and fuze in their arsenal, in an effort to destroy Malta's infrastructure and its people. With exceptional levels of responsibility for a lieutenant, the RE Bomb Disposal officers had coped with an extraordinary workload, despite minimal manpower and largely insufficient equipment. NCOs had also taken on duties normally beyond their rank, and a handful of sappers on meagre rations had dug endless shafts into rocky terrain, and shifted tons of rubble and stones, to reach buried bombs. Yet despite extreme pressures, coupled with the strain of sleepless nights and constant bombing raids – even while they worked – no RE Bomb Disposal officer, NCO or sapper had lost his life.

Now the need for bomb disposal reduced to a minimum. There were only three 250kg and a sprinkling of anti-personnel bombs in the first six weeks of 1943. After nearly fourteen months on the Island, Lieutenant (now Acting Captain) T.W.T. Blackwell was leaving. He completed his last duty on Friday 12 February, and embarked for the Middle East the following day. His replacement was already in Malta. Lieutenant H. Lavington had arrived on Wednesday and reported in to Lintorn Barracks as 'relief for Lieutenant Blackwell GM MBE.'[2]

Born in Southampton in 1914, Henry Lavington was already married and working as a municipal engineer when the war began. In February 1940, shortly after becoming a father, he was commissioned as a 2nd Lieutenant in No. 662 General Construction Company, Royal Engineers. After a period building aerodromes in northern France, Lieutenant Lavington and the men of 662 Company joined the thousands evacuated from Dunkirk. Lavington was soon posted overseas again, to an Artisan Works Company in Palestine, where his unit was deployed to build anti-tank pyramids in Trans-Jordan. Apart from the unpleasantness of a daily afternoon sandstorm, there was not enough to challenge the young officer and he decided to volunteer for bomb disposal. After a training course in Egypt, Lavington joined 18 Bomb Disposal Company RE in January 1942 and dealt with his first unexploded bomb on 8 March, at Sidi Hamish in the Western Desert: a 250kg with a 25(A) impact fuze. Like Lieutenant Ashall, Henry Lavington spent much of his time in the Middle East getting rid of bomb dumps. Then, as Rommel's forces advanced in the Western Desert, Lavington's BD section was moved back to Alexandria, where there was little to do until they came across a new type of UXB:

> … the Germans were pressing home their advantage by dropping anti-personnel bombs … these bombs which were about the size of a round tin of 50 Players [cigarettes] and painted desert yellow, armed themselves on the way down from the aircraft.[3]

It was an encounter with tragic consequences. One of his lance-corporals was killed tackling his first butterfly bomb – a tragedy which shook Lavington. His BD section disposed of 400 butterfly bombs in the month of July 1942. It was good preparation for the BD officer, who was pleased at news of his posting to Malta, only to be frustrated by a three-month wait for his transfer. As Lavington disembarked with his fellow passengers in Grand Harbour on 10 February, the enemy attacked the convoy, forcing them to sprint to the shelters beneath the bastions. It was too risky to return to the ship for his kit so he went on to Lintorn Barracks without it. Lieutenant Blackwell gave him a more friendly welcome to Malta and his new duties.

I took over from a chap who had a George Medal. He also wore wings. He left and I took over the same troop of men – about 20 of them. There were two lots [in bomb disposal] – for the north and the south of the Island.[4]

Blackwell took his replacement over to Villa Fleri to meet Lieutenant Whitworth and No. 128 Bomb Disposal Section. The two BD officers then toured the Island; the effects of the intensive bombing of 1942 were plain to see. Writing in his diary, Lavington summed up his initial impressions of Malta in few words: 'It looks all right but hellish smashed [up]'.[5] Then it was over to the dockyard, where he was introduced to the Royal Navy team, including Bomb Safety Officer Lieutenant Cyril Rowlands, GM, RNVR. The two officers became good friends, taking to 'comparing notes' on bomb disposal work and often accompanying each other as they worked on unexploded bombs.

My naval opposite number was … a school teacher from N Wales, and he was one of the very few service people who managed to get married abroad … the Rowlands were a very friendly couple who had a furnished flat in Sliema and I often used to visit them and stay the night.[6]

Though Lieutenant Lavington felt busy compared to his experience in the Middle East, air raids on Malta had halted for the time being: there were none in the first three months of 1943. Soon after his arrival, he was appointed mess secretary, a key role in supporting the comfort and sustenance of his fellow Royal Engineer officers. As one of the few with access to a car, the bomb disposal officer took advantage of his mobility to supplement the rations for the mess.

The Maltese farmers were always reporting to their local police station odd bombs from previous raids, which were non priority; [dealing with them] gave me a wonderful opportunity to buy eggs for the Mess; the going price was one shilling each … it doesn't seem much these days, but then they seemed very expensive.

Life in Malta was spartan as food was, even for the army, in short supply … To augment our army rations, we were issued with an ascorbic acid tablet daily, which is concentrated Vitamin C, also a bar of chocolate per week. The civilian population at that time were thin and hungry and we used to give our chocolate to the children ... These poor kids' arms and legs were covered with what looked like bruises, the result of malnutrition.[7]

With rations still at a minimum, thankfully there was little hard physical work for the bomb disposal sections to do. All 70 UXB reports in the three months to 31 March 1943 were for anti-personnel bombs. But plenty more HE bombs would come to light before the archipelago could be free of its sleeping menaces. UXBs were sure to lurk beneath the rubble of demolished buildings or lie undiscovered in the undergrowth, in some remote and rarely-visited corner of the Island.

Five-year-old Francis Borg had spent most of his short life in the village of Siggiewi either cooped up indoors or down in the air-raid shelter. Now at last he was allowed out to play in the sunshine, under the watchful eye of his older brother Emmanuel. Enjoying his new-found freedom, little Frances made straight for the rubble lining the narrow lane, looking for interesting souvenirs. Something shiny caught his eye. He picked it up and called to his brother, holding out his new-found treasure. An explosion burst like a lightning strike between the houses, bringing their terrified occupants running to the scene, to find the brothers and two other children lying dead, and seven people injured.[8] It was a terrible reminder of the continuing threat. The tragedy prompted a repeat of warnings to the public – and especially children – to beware of UXBs which were still spread across the Island, and not to touch anything resembling a bomb. Yet even the military could be caught off guard:

One morning, after breakfast, we were all leaving the mess to go our separate ways, and I was with an RAF Doctor who messed with us, when there was a terrific bang nearby. It was strange, as there was no air raid warning; but suddenly from round the corner came a Maltese soldier with his hand blown off, and blood pouring everywhere.

Doc Parry put on a tourniquet and sent me off to 'phone for an ambulance. By the time I had it arranged, three other dead Maltese soldiers had been discovered in one of the workshops attached to the barracks.

It turned out that a [Maltese] Sgt … had picked up an Italian Thermos bomb. Now these anti-personnel bombs were extremely dangerous, and although we used to pick up German AP bombs if they were not fully armed, we never, repeat never, touched Thermos bombs … It appeared that the Sgt wanted to open up the mysterious object he had found, with disastrous results.

I was sent for by our Lt Col and we both went to the workshops – what a mess! The three soldiers had been standing round a bench and had the bomb in a vice; the explosion was so severe that the jaws of the vice were shattered and you can imagine the state of the bodies. We just had to find pieces of the bomb for the court of inquiry, and so hunted for pieces of metal which we could be certain came from a Thermos bomb.[9]

As bomb disposal officer, Lavington was called upon to attend a military court of inquiry into the incident on the following Monday morning, 19 April 1943. He would use the experience of Saturday's accident to underline the dangers of explosives to army personnel he was helping to train for a forthcoming Allied invasion of Sicily. The invasion force was due to assemble in Malta. Minefields which had been laid to prevent a seaborne enemy invasion of the Island needed to be lifted and selected ones re-laid. Like their counterparts in Britain, Malta's two RE Bomb Disposal sections were chosen for the perilous task of clearing Allied mines from around the coastline.

We were employed in lifting the British anti-personnel mines from the beaches and rocky inlets where invasion barges would be disembarking their troops. Not only were there mines but concrete pyramids with bits of angle iron sticking out to impede an enemy invasion. Over the years, these obstacles had sunk in the sand… we had to blow them up. Luckily, there is very little tide in the Med, so we could work at all hours …

The British anti-personnel mines were a different matter. They were all fitted with trip wires, which zig-zagged up the narrow rocky gorge where they were laid. The only way to remove them safely was to insert a nail as a safety pin. Although we had the mine laying diagram roughly showing where they were, and also the total number laid, it was essential to account for the exact number laid, but some had been set off by sea birds perching on the trip wires, and we produced bits of casing to prove it.[10]

The following Sunday, a sapper from 24 Fortress Company RE out at Bahar ic-Caghaq spotted a mysterious object floating in the water near the shoreline of the cove below the camp and reported it to his superiors. Deciding to investigate, Captain William Watson and Lieutenant John Johnson clambered down the rocks to examine the object. It exploded, killing one of them outright; the other died later that day from his injuries. Captain Watson had joined 24 Fortress Company only three days before. Once again Lavington had the solemn duty of investigating the accident for an official enquiry.

> the Germans had lain mine fields ... to prevent, or at least hold up, mine sweeping operations, they laid anti-sweep devices which consisted of floating canisters tethered to the sea bed, on the boundaries of the [mine] field so that when the mine sweeper dragging its hawser first touches a canister, it duly explodes and cuts the sweep. Now these anti-sweep devices occasionally broke loose and several were washed ashore.[11]

One of them had killed the two RE officers. Only days later Lavington was called across to Gozo to inspect an object which had been handed in to the police station. It was another anti-sweep device. With memories of the tragedy still fresh in his mind, he handled it very cautiously and blew it up on the beach.

News of Sunday's accident was passed on to the sappers and NCOs of 24 Fortress Company working in Bomb Disposal, with a reminder to take extra care while on mine clearances. In spite of their increased vigilance, a threat to their safety came from an unexpected source. They were camped out at Mellieha, where they were shifting Allied mines and barriers from around the bay. Even with an officer and men on site round the clock, an intruder attempted to steal some of the explosive. The would-be thief accidentally blew himself up, injuring four of the Royal Engineers at the same time. After three years of bomb disposal under the most trying circumstances, the first casualties among Malta's Royal Engineers from unexploded bombs had all been tragic accidents, and not brought about by any official action on a bomb.[11]

By the end of May 1943, the main job on Allied mines was finished, ready for the anticipated arrival of the Allied invasion forces. With only the occasional short, sharp enemy air attack there was a mere handful of butterfly bombs for Army Bomb Disposal each week, and only two reported high explosive UXBs, both 50kg. But as the Island's farmers began their harvest they were met with the menace of anti-personnel bombs hidden under the crops. Dozens of fresh calls came through for the help of the BD men. After recent events, Lavington was doubly alert to the possible consequences.

One day I was following a farmer and a policeman across a field; the farmer was showing us the bomb he had found. We arrived at a cactus [prickly pear] hedge, quite common in Malta, when much to my horror, the stupid farmer picked up an anti-personnel bomb from the cactus leaf and dropped it at my feet! Just to teach him a lesson, I told him I would blow it up where it lay, and made him lie down behind a dry stone wall about 20ft away. I made an extra heavy charge and blew it, with the result that part of the wall was blown over on top of the farmer! He did not touch any more bombs and I hope he told all his friends not to touch butterfly bombs.[12]

It seemed the public still needed reminding of the continuing danger of unexploded bombs and other missiles, and their potential to kill or maim. Malta's civil defence chiefs decided to mount an exhibition of all types of unexploded bombs and shells, Axis and Allied, to tour every police station in Malta. Lavington was asked to provide the examples for the display and had to approach the RAF and Royal Navy in order to gather everything he needed. The exhibition opened in Qrendi on 24 June and toured 24 main town and village centres across the Island, ending in Mellieha on 15 August.

While the macabre display was still being organised, Malta's people gathered to enjoy a much happier occasion. King George VI honoured the Island with a personal visit. Crowds lined the bastions as bells rang out to greet His Majesty's arrival in Grand Harbour on the forward deck of HMS *Aurora*. Lieutenants Lavington and Whitworth joined their fellow officers of the Royal Engineers standing to attention outside the symbolic ruins of the Opera House in the centre of Valletta. The two bomb disposal officers could afford to relax a little. They had ticked off every single unexploded bomb on their list.

Then at the end of June Lavington was sorting through paperwork preparing for the quarterly Composite Summary of Bomb Disposal when some UXB reports caught his eye. They dated back to Christmas 1941 – and they all concerned high explosives – but there was no sign they had been dealt with. If not, the bombs threatened not only their surroundings, but anyone who might subsequently try to tackle them. It was generally recognised that an impact fuze lost its electrical charge and was ineffective after a maximum of one year.[13] However, there was picric acid in the pellets between the gaine and the fuze mechanism, which could gradually deteriorate. Over time it might become so unstable as to ignite if any attempt was made to withdraw the fuze. Clockwork fuzes could be even more volatile. If the mechanism had corroded, the slightest disturbance could cause a clock to run down very quickly, detonating the bomb almost instantly.

The two officers shared the task of checking every one of the reports. Lieutenant Lavington decided to invite Lieutenant Rowlands and his fellow RN bomb safety officers to join him as he investigated two in Ghaxaq. Enlisting their help, he made safe one 250kg SC and one 50kg SD, as well as three anti-personnel bombs. His diary reads: 'Fairly shook the Navy. I made them work hard.'[14] The other outstanding reports brought Lavington face to face with the largest UXBs of his bomb disposal career. After defuzing two 500kg SC bombs at the Command Hall in Valletta in one morning, he made for Naxxar, where he recognised the shape of a 1,000kg SD Esau. As he finished defuzing the bomb, he turned his mind to the job of removing it, thinking: 'That will give the boys something to do.'[15] All nine long-standing reports were signed off without incident. There were no UXBs waiting for disposal, at least for the time being. Yet they could never afford to relax their guard.

On Sunday 18 July 1943 enemy aircraft launched their first strike in response to the invasion of Sicily a week before. A series of sharp raids brought a vivid reminder of the threat still hanging over Malta. After midnight on Tuesday, enemy aircraft bombed Sliema, Floriana and Valletta, killing six people and seriously injuring seventeen. Soon afterwards, UXB reports came in from a military rest camp at St Paul's Bay and from Rabat: the Germans had been dropping anti-personnel bombs which were reported to be 'unusual'. Lavington decided to inspect them himself. To his surprise, the small bombs held fuzes marked 73A – a new type, as far as he knew.[16] On Monday he took Lance-Corporal Tom Meager with him to Rabat, where they packed a few examples among sandbags in the boot of the car, to take back to barracks for forwarding to the Middle East.

With the renewed enemy attacks, the Island braced itself for a replay of the previous October's onslaught, unaware that they had already experienced the last heavy raid of the Second World War. On Wednesday 8 September came the announcement that the Islanders had been longing for: Italy had surrendered. Sicily was no longer available to the Luftwaffe as an air base and a final end to the bombing was in sight. With the battle for Malta won, the services of 24 Fortress Company Royal Engineers were needed elsewhere. They were off join the British North Africa Force. There was some dismay among the NCOs and sappers. Despite the immense challenges they had faced, they would miss the comradeship and relative freedom they had enjoyed. But with so few unexploded bombs, and little prospect of many to come, it was decided that Army Bomb Disposal on the Island could be managed by just one BD officer and section. No. 127 BD Section was to be disbanded. Two of its members could return to the UK in recognition of their long service overseas. A few experienced hands, including Sapper Harry Turner, stayed behind and were absorbed into No. 128 BD Section, now consisting of one officer, four NCOs and ten sappers/drivers, four of them Maltese. Lavington was the bomb disposal officer to leave. After overseeing the transfer of all remaining men and equipment to Villa Fleri, he handed over to Lieutenant Whitworth and sailed from Malta on 31 October 1943, bound for Egypt. His bomb disposal duties were over.

As the process of stripping away the debris of more than three years of war got underway, inevitably more unexploded bombs came to light, undermining the security of communities anxious to rebuild their lives. Almost every week a handful of anti-personnel bombs, or even a high explosive, were reported to Bomb Disposal HQ. On 4 November, he travelled west to Dingli to find a 250kg SC with a DA fuze lying a few hundred yards inland from the radar station. There was no need to explode the bomb: with the coast so close by, it was easier to strap on the clockstopper and drive it to the nearest steep cliffs for dumping.

It was three weeks into 1944 before the bomb disposal sections saw their next high explosive UXB. For the first time in months the sappers had some digging to do, for a 50kg SD six feet underground at Qrendi air strip.

For the last time Harry Turner transported the bomb to the western cliffs of Malta. After more than four years on the Island he left on 20 February 1944.

Work on Malta's shattered buildings was bringing more UXBs to light. Three 1,000kg devices had to be cleared from ruins in the Three Cities. At the beginning of March, work was scheduled to start on the wrecked fish market in Valletta – but there was a problem. A large unexploded bomb had demolished the building in February 1942 and was still covered by layers of stones and ironwork. Now the structure was being stabilised and the debris removed, RE Bomb Disposal were called on to recover it. The task was a difficult and hazardous one for the sappers, picking through the masonry and beams. Pieces of tail fin indicated they were looking for a 1,800kg 'Satan'. Several days and twenty feet of rubble later, the massive bomb was exposed. It took the entire BD section to hoist the two-metre long carcass out of the ruins and transfer it to a lorry to be driven away.

Call-outs for Lieutenant Whitworth could still bring the occasional surprise. In June 1944 he took a squad to Gozo, to investigate a two-year-old report of a suspected UXB in the village of Nadur. As the excavation progressed, an unfamiliar collection of fragments was assembled. The bomb disposal officer had a mysterious missile to report to his superiors

Dimensions: 2´ 6´´ diameter; circular cross section 5´. Fins running whole length of body at Cardinal points. Apparently nose fuze, armed by 3 bladed propeller. Possibly a rocket projectile.[17]

On 21 July he defuzed his last high explosive in Malta – a 500kg SD near the Union Club in Tigne Street, Sliema – only a few streets away from the Island's first UXB in June 1940. At 8.43pm on 28 August 1944, the sirens sounded their final air raid alert of the Second World War, followed by the final 'All Clear' at 9pm. A month later Whitworth was admitted to hospital and command of his squad, with its new standard title of 'No.128 Bomb Disposal Platoon', passed to the Adjutant of the Fortress Engineers, Captain J. Osmaston. Under his command the platoon disposed of three unexploded HE bombs, including a 50kg SC discovered by workmen shifting debris from the upper storey of Messrs Richard Ellis, well-known photographer and retailer, in Kingsway, Valletta.[18] After leaving hospital in late November 1944, Lieutenant Whitworth was posted to R.E.T.D. Central Mediterranean

Force. The last Royal Engineers bomb disposal officer of the Second World War had left the Island.

Notes

1 Henry Lavington: *A Family History*, 1990
2 Ed. (1943). War Diary Fortress Engineers, Malta. WO 169. National Archives, London
3 Henry Lavington, April 2008
4 Henry Lavington, diary 1943. The wings signify Blackwell's former career as a Fleet Air Arm pilot in the Royal Navy.
5 Henry Lavington: *A Family History*, 1990
6 ibid.
7 Galea, M. (1992). *Malta Diary of a War 1940–1945*. Malta: Publishers Enterprises Group.
8 Henry Lavington: *A Family History*, 1990
9 ibid.
10 ibid.
11 The Maltese servicemen killed in this accident on 17 April 1943 have been named as Lance-sergeant Carmel Galea (30101) of Paola, Corporal John Calleja (30392) of Birkirkara, and Sapper Anthony Troisi (91005). They were buried in Pieta Military Cemetery.
12 Henry Lavington: *A Family History*, 1990
13 Post-war bomb disposal estimated that the ECR fuze was useless after 1000 hours.
14 Henry Lavington, diary 1943
15 ibid.
16 The bombs were possibly German SD1 anti-personnel, which carried 73A fuzes.
17 Ed. (1943). War Diary Fortress Engineers, Malta. WO 169. National Archives, London
18 Galea, M. (1992). *Malta Diary of a War 1940–1945*. Malta: Publishers Enterprises Group.

EPILOGUE

Of the 17,000 tons of bombs dropped on Malta between 1940 and 1943, more than fifteen per cent did not explode and were referred to the bomb disposal officers of the three armed services. In just two years between December 1940 and December 1942, Malta's RE Bomb Disposal Section(s) made safe over 7,300 unexploded bombs: 5,500 anti-personnel bombs and incendiaries, and more than 1,800 high explosive bombs of 50kg or more. Yet for half that time there was only a single RE Bomb Disposal officer with one section of 20 men. In the month of April 1942 alone the two bomb disposal sections between them dealt with 267 HE bombs of 50kg or over. The workload was at least ten times the average for a bomb disposal section across all theatres of war.

Operating at the heart of Malta's communities, the officers were ever conscious of their role in protecting the civilian population. They developed a feeling of solidarity with the Island's people, sharing many of their deprivations and sense of isolation throughout the siege. Close co-operation with the volunteers and professionals of Malta's civil defence organisations was essential to the success of Army bomb disposal on the Island. Working relationships formed during the war developed into friendships remembered long afterwards.

The Royal Engineers remained in Malta until the British Army garrison left the Island at the end of March 1979. Their responsibility for clearing unexploded bombs from across the Archipelago had continued uninterrupted since the war. Around the time of their departure, 24 Fortress Company, Royal Engineers, Malta, wrote in their commemorative folder:

> The menace of the UXB still hangs over Malta. During the period 1955–70 the RE BD team was called 760 times. In the last 10 years, 1,155 items of unexploded ordnance were made safe, 29 of which were bombs of 100lbs [50kg] or larger.[1]

Notes

1 Royal Engineers commemorative portfolio, National War Museum Association, Malta

APPENDIX 1

PERSONNEL IN ROYAL ENGINEERS BOMB DISPOSAL MALTA 1940–1944

Bomb Disposal Officers

	November 1940 –April 1941	April 1941 –December 1941	December 1941 –April 1942	April 1942 –July 1942	August 1942 –February 1943	February 1943 –October 1943	November 1943 –September 1944
Lt E.E. Talbot 10 November 1940 –9 May 1941	▓						
Lt G.D. Carroll 21 April 1941 –13 June 1942		▓	▓				
Lt T.W.T. Blackwell 18 December 1941 –12 February 1943			▓	▓	▓		
Lt F.W. Ashall 23 April –31 July 1942				▓			
Lt T. Whitworth 27 July 1942 –November 1944					▓	▓	▓
Lt H. Lavington 12 February –27 October 1943						▓	

LIEUTENANT FREDERICK WILLIAM ASHALL (166504)

Lieutenant Ashall was awarded the MBE in February 1943. Promoted to captain, he remained in Malta until the end of the war in Europe. In 1945 he was sent to Ripon in Yorkshire for a training course. Rejecting an offer of the rank of major if he returned to Malta, Ashall chose to resume his former civilian career and eventually became the Chief Quantity Surveyor for the County of Cheshire. Leaving to become a consultant chartered surveyor, he found himself working alongside one of his former fellow Royal Engineer officers from CRE(N), Malta. Frederick Ashall died in Warrington in January 2004.

LIEUTENANT THOMAS WALTER TOWNSEND BLACKWELL (169308)

After a short period of leave, Lieutenant Blackwell was posted to the Royal Engineers Works Pool of Military Personnel in the Middle East and from there was appointed an instructor at the RE Training Depot. Promoted to the rank of captain, he remained in the Middle East for another two and a half years before finally returning to the UK and civilian life, at the end of September 1945. Walter Blackwell later returned to life at sea, piloting his yacht on several intercontinental voyages. He died in South Africa in 1980.

LIEUTENANT GEORGE DANIEL CARROLL (132085)

Lieutenant Carroll returned to service as a bomb disposal officer in London but spent several periods in hospital in the UK before being diagnosed with amoebic dysentery – a disease contracted in Egypt in 1941 which had precipitated his duodenal ulcer. Invalided out of the Army in 1944, he realised an early ambition to become a professional actor, achieving success in repertory and then on the London stage. The father of his would-be bride insisted on a more secure occupation and he changed career, becoming head of science in a large and pioneering secondary school in Kent in 1957. George Carroll died in 2012.

LIEUTENANT HENRY LAVINGTON (119689)

Within two weeks of arriving in Egypt Lieutenant Lavington sailed for the UK; he was reunited with his wife and son on 14 December 1943. With the end of the war in sight, he applied for a transfer to service more related to his civilian career, joining RE Works Services, where he was promoted to captain. Captain Lavington left the Army in 1946, returning briefly to Civil Engineering, before making a career in the oil industry. The job took him back to the Middle East but finally he settled in Gillingham, Kent just three miles from Lieutenant G.D. Carroll. Despite Carroll having taught Lavington's daughter, each remained unaware of the other until research for this book in 2008. Henry Lavington died in June 2009.

LIEUTENANT ELLIS EDWARD ARTHUR CHETWYND TALBOT *(100411)*

Lieutenant Talbot was killed while a passenger on board one of two Blenheim aircraft from 107 Squadron RAF which collided during a shipping sweep off Cape Alessio, Sicily on 9 October 1941. He was buried in Catania War Cemetery, Sicily.

LIEUTENANT THOMAS WHITWORTH *(130878)*

Lieutenant Whitworth returned to Oxford after the Second World War and obtained a first in geology in 1947, followed by a D.Phil in 1950. He served as university demonstrator in geology at Oxford and lecturer at Oriel College from 1949 to 1956. Dr Whitworth was then appointed Master of Hatfield College, University of Durham where he was a keen promoter of rugby, in addition to his academic interests. He died in office in 1979.

Other Ranks

Members of 24 Fortress Company, RE believed to have served in Malta's bomb disposal sections during the Second World War.[1]

NON-COMMISSIONED OFFICERS

Sergeant John Holland
Sergeant Thomas Piggott (1863676)
Lance-Sergeant George Henry King (1864077)
Lance-Sergeant John Henry Lockett (1873317)
Lance-Sergeant (later Sergeant) Reginald Charles Parker (1871236)
Corporal (later Lance-Sergeant) Cecil Arthur Brewer (1866450)

Corporal (later Lance-Sergeant) Robert Ralph Cushen (1867240)

Lance-Corporal Rowland Hilliar (1873804)

Lance-Corporal George Jackson (1873958)

Lance-Corporal Cyril Thomas Meager (1872626)[2]

Lance-Corporal Claude Elliot Reeves

SAPPERS

Sapper Joseph Birchenall (1872550)

Sapper George Codling

Sapper Rex Garvin

Sapper Thomas Hammond 1872638

Sapper James Lee Leonard 858620

Sapper Lockyer

Sapper Duncan MacDonald 1871171

Sapper Daniel 'Jack' McCarthy (1875751)

Sapper Laurence 'Bing' Miller (1875725)

Sapper Rattenbury

Sapper Henry James Reeves (1877565)

Sapper William Douglas 'Scotty' Scott (1871172)

Sapper Harry Turner (1875560)

Sapper Robert Henry Walter (1873669)

Notes

1 There are no official records giving the names of other ranks; the list is compiled from available information and may be incomplete or inaccurate in some cases.

2 Served as Sapper in bomb disposal from 1940, promoted January 1942.

APPENDIX 2

UXBs DEALT WITH BY RE BOMB DISPOSAL SECTIONS MALTA 1940–1944

(see Table overleaf:)

Ack-Ack and Bofors shells etc are not included

+ Total incomplete as reports for AP/incendiaries not fully recorded during this period

* December 1940 only

AP: anti-personnel

e: estimated figures based on serial numbers of UXB reports as no Weekly Bomb Disposal Reports were produced from 21 February to 27 March 1942.

L: large number

Q: quarter

S: several

A: Lt. Ashall B: Lt. Blackwell C: Lt. Carroll Lv: Lt. Lavington T: Lt. Talbot W: Lt. Whitworth

	1940* Q4	1941 Q1	1941 Q2	1941 Q3	1941 Q4	1942 Q1	1942 Q2	1942 Q3	1942 Q4	1943 Q1	1943 Q2	1943 Q3	1943 Q4	1944 Q1	1944 Q2	1944 Q3	1944 Q4
Code	T	T	C	C	C	B / C	B / C/A	B / A/W	B / W	B / W	Lv / W	Lv / W	W	W	W	W	W
BD Officers																	
Total UXB Reports	13	177	415	178	621	474 +	1187	801	339	65	87	91	71	388			
HE BOMBS																	
German																	
50kg GP/SC		31	176	3	19e	39e	35	6	24	1			1			1	1
50kg SD					37e	94e	141	23	17		3	4		1		1	
250kg GP/SC		18	24	2	15e	91e	133	77	15	2	1	1	2			1	1
250kg AP/SD		2			33e	72e	110	55	10	1	1	1	2				
500kg GP/SC		3	12	3	17e	32e	40	42			1	3				1	
500kg AP/SD		29	3		9e	24e	42	7	2								
'Rocket' SD						1	1								1		
1000kg GP/SC		3			1e	12e	29	1		1				1	1	1	1
1000kg AP/SD		5			3e		5							1			
1800kg SC							1	1						1			
35kg concrete							5	6	10	1			9				
Italian																	
15kg SAP			20	21	2e	2e	2										
50kg		1	1	6	5e		7										
130lb	3			1	2e												
250lb (100kg)				8	4e		33		1								
300lb (150kg)				2	1e												
500lb (250kg)			1	3	3e												
Total HE	3	92	237	49	146e	370e	584	218	81	6	6	9	14	4	2	5	3

	1940*	1941	1942	1942	1942	1942	1942	1943	1943	1943	1944	1944	1944	1944	1944
AP BOMBS															
German															
2kg butterfly					783	2145	854	49	92	84	27+	5	30	17	26
1kg										14	9				
Italian															
'Thermos'			6+	454	45	41+	4	1	2		19				1
2kg 'Spezzoni'		3		1	31+	107	38	8	70	83	72	5	7	1	10
AP container					33		1								
12kg		1			5										1
Total AP		4	6+	455	897	2293	897	58	164	181	127	10	37	18	38
INCENDIARY															
German															
1 or 2kg				21+		S		L			1				
Italian															
2kg	2	173		1+	21	58	87								29
43lb	5						3								
70kg	1	2		1+			3								
Total Incendiary	8	175		23+	21	58+	93	L			1				29

APPENDIX 3

GERMAN FUZES IN HE BOMBS ENCOUNTERED BY RE BOMB DISPOSAL SECTIONS MALTA 1942

(See Table opposite:)

There is no recorded incident of a DA fuze before January 1942.

+ Total incomplete as no Weekly Bomb Disposal Reports were produced from 21 February to 27 March 1942.

I: impact fuzes: 93 per cent were series 5; the remainder were 28 or 38.

D: delayed-action

U: unidentified

s: single fuze pocket

t: twin fuze pocket

	Q1			Q2			Q3			Q4			Total	Total	%
	I	D	U	I	D	U	I	D	U	I	D	U	All	D	D
50kg GP/SC	29+			22	4	9	6			22		2	94	4	4
50kg AP/SD	61+		2+	130		11	23			14	1	3	234		
250kg GP/SC (s)	3+	1+		57		16	43		2	2	1		125	26	21
250kg SC (t)	5+	7+		33	27		14	18		1	11		116	59	51
250kg SAP/AP/SD	45+	3+		96	5	9	47		8	8		2	223	8	4
500kg GP/SC (s)	22+		3+	13		10	3		1				52	3	6
500kg SC (t)	7+			11	6		14	24					62	30	48
500kg SAP/AP/SD	24+		1+	37		5	2		5	2			76		
Rocket SD	49BIII			49BIII									2		
1000kg GP/SC	4+		2+	5		24	1		2	1			37	2	5
1000kg SAP/AP/SD	1+			4		1							6	1	17
1800kg SC				1			1						2		
Total													1029	133	

APPENDIX 4

OFFICIAL REPORT OF CLEARANCE OF THERMOS BOMBS FROM THE OPERA HOUSE, DECEMBER 1941

APPX F: THERMOS BOMBS IN THE ROYAL OPERA HOUSE

On 1st Nov 1941 the police of Valletta unwittingly risking their lives, stored 19 complete Thermos bombs, and 15 fuzes from same (complete with detonators) in a lower basement room of the Royal Opera House. Removal of the complete bombs was inconvenient at the time owing to demands of more bombs lying in the open. The basement was heavily sandbagged, and research and experiment commenced to devise a means of removing the bombs when opportunity presented itself. The detonators were unscrewed and removed.

The Thermos bomb is designed to explode under movement induced by vibration or handling, after impact. Falling on hard ground, the mechanism of the fuze may become so distorted as to act progressively on handling, and not instantaneously. This was the state of the bombs in the Opera House.

After much experimenting, a self closing grab was devised, which could be slid over the bomb without disturbing it. This grab was suspended from a cord, passing over pulleys on a curtain railway, leading to outside the room. Pulling on this cord caused the grab to close round the bomb and lift it in a horizontal position.

By means of a second cord the suspended bomb was caused to travel along the curtain railway, until it was opposite to the basement window. In this position a further cord was affixed which passed outside the window, over pulleys, and was operated from cover by a party in a shelter across the street. By balancing the tensions of the two cords, one suspending it and the other pulling out of the window, the bomb was manoeuvred over a tray carrying sand, resting in the bottom of the window bay, and lowered into it.

Lying in the sand, the grab was slid clear of the bomb and the tray hauled to street level by means of a third tackle, operated by the outside party. When clear of the building this lifting tackle was allowed to run out from the face of the Opera House, lifting the tray with it, until the latter was free to be lowered into a sandbag emplacement built in the roadway. By means of a spilling loop the bomb was then thrown into the emplacement onto 2′ of sand therein. Steel plates lined the emplacement to economise in sandbags and the bombs were blown up in it singly.

The 19 bombs were taken out on two successive days. The bombs were in two shelves. The afternoon of the first day was spent shifting the curtain railway. The system did not work perfectly, for two bombs which were in most remote positions fell out of the grab, due to indirect and uneven lifting. They did not explode and were picked up again by the grab.

The Lieut. Governor wrote thanking us for this successful operation.[1]

Notes
1 Ed. (1941). War Diary Fortress Engineers, Malta. WO 169. National Archives, London

APPENDIX 5

REPORT ON GERMAN ROCKET BOMB DROPPED IN MALTA, JANUARY 1942

(Advisory Council of Scientific Research and Technical Development, Research and Development Sub-Committee and Unexploded Bomb Committee)[1]

INTELLIGENCE BULLETIN NO 17
German Rocket bomb – P.C. 500 R.S.

1. <u>GENERAL</u>

Details have been received of a German Rocket Bomb dropped on MALTA. The P.C. 500 R.S. is a 500kg armour piercing bomb with a rocket attachment for greater penetration effect. It is intended that these bombs shall be used against fortifications and warships.

The rockets last while the bomb travels from a height of 2,000 metres (6,500 ft.) and are said to increase the speed up to a maximum of 1,000 k.p.h. They leave behind a flame 50 metres long. P.C. 1000 R.S. has also been referred to in captured German documents and there is a rumour of a 1800kg rocket bomb.

2. <u>DESCRIPTION</u>

(a) The complete bomb consists of a 500 or 1000kg. armour piercing bomb with an electrical impact fuze screwed into the base, and the rocket assembly, including a distance piece with a fuze head in its side, which is threaded to the bomb case. A tail made of light alloy metal is fitted to the end cap of the rocket container.

(b) The bomb is fitted with a normal type suspension band, 5½ inches wide, and carrying lug. The diameter of the base plate is 13¼ inches and it has a hole in its centre threaded to take the fuze container. Right up in the nose of the bomb recovered in MALTA, there was a dome shaped aluminium sheet container, 6½ inches high and 8 inches in diameter at the base, which held pure T.N.T. The main filling was surrounded by a cardboard material, and consisted of layers of about 3 inches of good quality T.N.T. being spaced alternately with layers of poor quality.

The fuze, stamped [49]B.III on its side, (see para 3 below) with its gaine, 4¼ inches long and ¾ inch diameter, is held in the fuze container, which is of heavy construction, by a locking ring. The gaine is not screwed to the bottom of the fuze.

(c) The rocket container is attached to the bomb by a cylindrical distance piece, which is threaded internally at both ends. In the side of the distance piece is fitted an electric fuze head marked [49]B.I with charging plungers which connect to fuzes [49]B.III and [49]B.II. (The fuze head and fuze [49]B.II were missing from the bomb recovered in MALTA). Fuze [49]B.II serves to ignite the rockets.

Six rockets are held in position in the rocket container by means of spacers. Fitted centrally to the end cap of the rocket container is a heavily constructed adjustable relief valve. Around this fitting are spaced six venturi tubes, in between which there are six supporting lugs for the tail.

3. <u>FUZING SYSTEM</u>

The fuzes [49]B.II and [49]B.III are connected to the fuze head, marked [49]B.I which is fitted in the side of the distance piece of the rocket container. Fuze [49]B.III is an electrical impact fuze, giving a fractional delay action of the bomb after striking the ground. It differs from the standard Rheinmetall type in that: –

(a) The top has no collar, locating pin or plungers. There is an insulated wire projecting from the centre, which connects to the fuzing head [49]B.I.

(b) The bottom of the fuze is slightly dome shaped.

(c) The tremblers take the form of a ball bearing mounted on a piece of wire. The wire, as found in the fuze recovered in MALTA, had no spring effects whatever; the ball bearings would, in fact, remain in any position to which they were displaced. Fuze [49]B.II, a pyrotechnic fuze with a delay of 3 seconds, is used for igniting the rockets. It may be assumed that it is similar in construction to the flare fuze No.[59]A.

4. DISPOSAL

The detail of the fuzes is not known; but it can be assumed that the [49]B.II, which ignites the rocket, is safe when found in UXBs.

If access to the base fuze [49]B.III can be obtained, it should be susceptible to discharge by the steam jet method as described in T.I.No.129.

If steam is not available, it is possible that discharge can be effected either by the use of the Plug Discharger applied to fuze head [49]B.I.; or, if the insulating lead joining the fuze head [49]B.I. to the base fuze [49]B.III can be reached, by exposing the wire and making contact with the [49]B.II or the bomb casing.

These methods are, however, untried.

G.H.Q. Capt G.S. for Brigadier Home Forces Inspector of Fortifications & Director of Bomb Disposal
24 Feb. 42

Notes
1 WO 195/1766, National Archives, London

APPENDIX 6

UXB IN MOSTA ROTUNDA
9 APRIL 1942

The 'miracle of Mosta' is one of the best known of the many stories which recall the ordeal of Malta during the Second World War. The bomb carcass now displayed within the Rotunda has become a symbol of the many unexploded bombs dealt with during the Siege. Former military personnel and their families visiting the Island are understandably drawn to the story of Mosta, as a focus for memories of wartime service and achievements. Because of the exceptional circumstances surrounding this unexploded bomb, there has been much speculation on who was responsible for its disposal. However, there is no official or reliable evidence to identify those who actually worked on the bomb, except that they were Royal Engineers.

• From December 1940 onwards, all unexploded bombs in Malta and Gozo, outside of Royal Navy or RAF premises, were the responsibility of the Royal Engineers Bomb Disposal Sections.
• The only known official document recording the action taken to deal with the bomb in the church at Mosta on 9 April 1942 is the Weekly Bomb Disposal Report for 4 to 11 April 1942.[1] The Report lists all HE bombs dealt with by both Nos. 127 and 128 RE Bomb Disposal Sections in Malta during that period.
• The document includes UXB report no 2075/2075a, which is for two bombs reported at Mosta on 9 April and dealt with on that day. Four other UXB reports listed for Mosta on 9 April (Nos. 2079, and 2081–3) were

reported later and also dealt with the same day – all were for 50kg SD bombs.

Serial No	Location	Date reported	Nationality	Type	Depth	Remarks
2075	Musta	9/4/42	´´ (German)	500kg.S.C.	4´	Defuzed & removed 9/4. Priority.
2075a	Musta	9/4/42	´´	50kg.S.D.	Surface	´´ 9/4.

• The 500kg SC dealt with in the Church on 9 April 1942 is recorded on the Weekly Bomb Disposal Report as lying four feet below the surface. This would normally indicate that the bomb broke through the floor and remained at some depth – differing from previous accounts of the bomb 'skidding the whole length of the Church'.[2]

• The UXB Report No. 2075 is marked Priority. It was policy in RE Bomb Disposal at the time for all Priority UXBs to be dealt with by a bomb disposal officer, because he alone had the authority to weigh up the importance of a sensitive location against the risks to personnel, and then to determine the action to be taken.

• There were two RE Bomb Disposal officers on duty on Thursday 9 April 1942: Lieutenant T.W.T. Blackwell and Lieutenant G.D. Carroll. There is no evidence in the official documentation to identify which of them attended the Priority incident at Mosta that day.

• The photograph on display at Mosta is of Lieutenant E.E. Talbot and No.1 Bomb Disposal Section and was probably taken in January 1941. Lieutenant Talbot was killed in October 1941. The bomb in the photograph is believed to be a 1,000kg 'Hermann'.

• Under Bomb Disposal regulations, no-one who was not essential to the action of defuzing the bomb would be allowed to remain in the Church.

• From May 1941 it was standard procedure for all carcasses of neutralised unexploded bombs (except for samples of new bombs required for experimental purposes) to be taken to the western cliffs and dropped into the sea.

• Speaking to the author in November 2006, Don Salv Magro said 'We didn't ask for the bomb to come back to be displayed in the Church [straight away]. We'd had enough of bombs.'

Those who served in Nos. 127 and 128 Bomb Disposal Sections in Malta have every reason to identify closely with the bomb in the Mosta Rotunda. Some have provided stories of the events of 9 April and names for those involved, for histories such as Major A. Hogben's book *Designed to Kill*, published in 1987[3] and 'Il-Hbit mill-Ajru fuq ir-Rotunda tal-Mosta'[4] researched in the early 1990s by the late Anthony Camilleri.

However, thorough examination of these recollections alongside hard evidence has only cast doubt on much of their information, including the names put forward of those who were actually present or dealt with the bomb. Collected over 40 years after the event, and long after the bomb was displayed in the Church at Mosta, it is not surprising that such recollections are inaccurate and conflicting – especially given the sheer volume and extent of work carried out by these men in April 1942.

In the circumstances, the author believes it preferable for the credit for dealing with the UXB in the Mosta Rotunda on 9 April 1942 to be shared among all those serving in RE Bomb Disposal in Malta at that time, rather than to single out any individuals in the absence of reliable evidence.

Notes

1 Ed. (1942). *War Diary Fortress Engineers, Malta*. WO 169. National Archives, London
2 Rev Salvatore (Don Salv) Magro, interviewed by NWMA, Malta (1975). Vella, P. (1985). *Malta: Blitzed But Not Beaten*. Malta: Progress Press.
3 Hogben, Maj A (1987). *Designed to Kill*. Wellingborough: Stephens.
4 Camilleri, A. (1992). *Il-Hbit mill-Ajru fuq ir-Rotunda tal-Mosta*. Pubblikazzjoni tal-Gazetta il-Mosta.

BIBLIOGRAPHY AND SOURCES

Attard, J. (1980) *The Battle of Malta*. London: Kimber.

Bartimeus (pseud) et al. (1993) *The Epic of Malta*. Malta:Valletta Publishing.

Birchall, Peter. (1997) *The Longest Walk – The World of Bomb Disposal*. Arms and Armour Press.

Boffa, C. (1995) *Illustrious Blitz: Malta in Wartime 1940–41*. Malta: Progress Press.

Boffa, C. (1992) *Second Great Siege: Malta 1940–43*. Malta: Progress Press.

Boffa, C. (2000) *Malta's Grand Harbour and its Environs in War and Peace*. Malta: Progress Press.

Bonner, R.A. (1992) *The Ardwick Boys Went to Malta*. Fleur de Lys Publications.

Bradford, E. (2003) *Siege Malta 1940–1943*. Barnsley: Pen & Sword.

Cameron, I. (1959) *Red Duster, White Ensign*. Fredk Muller.

Camilleri, A. (1992) *Il-Hbit mill-Ajru fuq ir-Rotunda tal-Mosta*. Pubblikazzjoni tal-Gazetta il-Mosta.

Dobbie, Sybil. (1943) *Grace Under Malta*. London: Lindsay Drummond.

Forty, G. (2003) *The Battle for Malta*. London: Ian Allan.

Frayn Turner, J. (1961) *Highly Explosive*. London: Harrap & Co.

Galea, F. (2008) *Mines Over Malta*. Malta: Wise Owl Publications.

Galea, M. (1992) *Malta Diary of a War 1940–1945*. Malta: Publishers Enterprises Group.

Gerard, F. (1943) *Malta Magnificent*. London: Cassell.

Gilchrist, Maj R.T. (1945) *Malta Strikes Back: Story of the 231 Infantry Brigade.* Aldershot: Gale & Polden.

Hartley, Major A B. (1958) *Unexploded Bomb.* London: Cassell.

Hay, I. (1943) *The Unconquered Isle: The Story of Malta GC.* London: Hodder & Stoughton.

Hogan, G. (1978) *Malta, The Triumphant Years 1940-43.* London: Hale.

Hogben, Maj. A (1987) *Designed to Kill.* Wellingborough: Stephens.

Holland, J. (2004) *Fortress Malta.* London: Phoenix.

Jellison, C.A. (1984) *Besieged: the World War II Ordeal of Malta.* Hanover, NH, USA: University Press of New England.

Kemp, P. (1988) *Malta Convoys 1940-43.* Arms & Armour, No 14 Warships Illustrated Series.

Lucas, L. *Malta, The Thorn in Rommel's Side: Six Months that Turned the War.* London: S.Paul.

Luke, H. (1949) *Malta, An Account and an Appreciation.* London: George C. Harrap.

Micallef, J. (1981) *When Malta Stood Alone (1940–1943)* Micallef, Malta.

Monsarrat, N. (1973) *Kapillan of Malta.* London: Cassell

Moorehead, A. (1965) *The Desert War.* London: Hamish Hamilton.

Oliver, R.L. (1942) *Malta at Bay.* London: Hutchinson.

Oliver, R.L. (1944) *Malta Besieged.* London: Hutchinson.

Pankenham–Walsh, Maj. Gen. (1957) *History of the Corps of Royal Engineers, Vol VIII: 1938-48.* Chatham: Institute of Royal Engineers.

Perowne, S. (1970) *The Siege Within the Walls: Malta 1940-43.* London: Hodder & Stoughton

Rixon, Frank, ed. (2005) *Malta Remembered.* Woodhouse Publishing

Shankland, P. and Hunter, A. (1961) *Malta Convoy.* London: Collins.

Thomas, D.A. (1999) *Malta Convoys 1940-42 The Struggle at Sea.* Barnsley: Leo Cooper Ltd.

Tonna, E.S. (1969) *Floriana in Wartime.* Malta: Progress Press.

Vella, P. (1985) *Malta: Blitzed But Not Beaten.* Malta: Progress Press.

Wakeling, E. (1998) *The Lonely War.* BD Publishing.

Weldon, Lieutenant Col. H.E.C. (1946) *Drama in Malta.* BAOR

Wragg, D. *Malta The Last Great Siege 1940-1943.* Barnsley: Leo Cooper (Pen & Sword Books)

PERIODICALS

Ed. (1941) (1942) *Times of Malta.*

Ed. (1941) (1942) *Sunday Times of Malta.*

Ed. (1941) (1942) *London Gazette.*

Ed. (2001) *Malta at War.* Vol. 2 Issue 6.

Ed. (2001) *Malta at War.* Vol. 4 Issue 10.

WEBSITES

Lacey, J. *Diary of Jim Lacey*. http://www2.army.mod.uk/royalengineers/ assocations/reabd/diaries/jimlacey. Last accessed August 2008.

Ministry of Information. (1944) *The Air Battle of Malta.* London: HMSO. ww2airfronts.org. Last accessed June 2008.

Editor. (2008) *Luftwaffe Bombs of World War II.* Available: www.warbirdsre-sourcegroup.org. Last accessed June 2008.

RE Bomb Disposal Officers Club. *History of RE Bomb Disposal.* www. bombdisposalclub.org.uk/BD_history.htm. Last accessed June 2006.

PRIMARY SOURCES

Ed. (1940/41/42/43/44) *War Diary Fortress Engineers, Malta.* WO 169. National Archives, London

Ed. (1940/41/42/43/44) *War Diary General Staff, Malta.* WO 169. National Archives, London.

Ed. (1941/42) *War Diary 18 BD Company* (Middle East) WO 169. National Archives, London.

Ed. (1940/41) *War Diary No 24 B. D. Company* (London) WO 166. National Archives, London.

Ed. (1941) *War Diary 16 BD Company* (Oxfordshire/Wales) WO 166. National Archives, London.

Ed. (1941/42) *Situation Reports & Operational Messages Out.* WO 106. National Archives, London.

Ed. (1941/42) *Lt Gen W.G.S. Dobbie, Governor & Commander in Chief Malta. Demi-official Correspondence.* WO 216. National Archives, London.

Ed. (1941) *Headquarters Papers.* WO 201. National Archives, London.

Ed. (1941/42) *Orders of Battle.* WO 212. National Archives, London.

Ed. (1942) *Medical Reports/Returns .*WO 216. National Archives, London.

Ed. (1942) *Manual of Bomb Disposal.* WO 287. National Archives, London.

Reports & Correspondence, ARP Malta. National Archives of Malta.

Correspondence, Chief Secretary & Lieutenant Governor's Office, National Archives of Malta

Date/author unknown. *Historical account of 24 Fortress Company, Royal Engineers in Malta.* Royal Engineers Library.

Major R.C.M. Parker GM. (1980) *Account of defuzing of a radio-controlled bomb recovered from Vittoriosa or Cospicua in January 1941.* National War Museum Association, Malta.

Spr. R. Walter. Date unknown. *Manuscript: The First Bomb I Dug Out.* Royal Engineers Library.

Spr. R. Walters. Date unknown. *Memoir: Story of Events Leading up to the First German Plane I Shot Down in Malta in 1942.* Royal Engineers Library.

PRIVATE DOCUMENTS

Army Service Record, Lt G.D. Carroll. Army Records Office.

Army Service Record, Lt T.W.T. Blackwell. Army Records Office.

Personal papers Lt F.W. Ashall. Mrs Mary Ashall and Mr Patrick Ashall.

Private diaries and family history. Lt Henry Lavington.

Personal papers Sapper Harry Turner. Maurice Turner.

Camilleri, A. Collection of documents relating to UXB at Mosta on 9 April 1942.

Mifsud Bonnici, Ing Maurice. Personal account of hoax bomb St Aloysius School.

INTERVIEWS

Mrs Mary Ashall and Mr Patrick Ashall

George D. Carroll

Henry Lavington

Rev Salvatore (Don Salv) Magro

Cyril Thomas Meager and Maria Meager

Maurice Turner

INDEX